baseball

PRENTICE-HALL, INC., *Englewood Cliffs, New Jersey*

Jack Coombs

baseball 4 *th ed.*

Revised by *Danny Litwhiler*

**Head Baseball Coach
Michigan State University**

PRENTICE-HALL INTERNATIONAL, INC., London
PRENTICE-HALL OF AUSTRALIA, PTY. LTD., Sydney
PRENTICE-HALL OF CANADA, LTD., Toronto
PRENTICE-HALL OF INDIA (PRIVATE) LTD., New Delhi
PRENTICE-HALL OF JAPAN, INC., Tokyo

LIBRARY OF CONGRESS CATALOG CARD NO.: 66-27590

Printed in the United States of America   C-05625

Current printing (last digit):
10   9   8   7   6

The Jack Coombs book, *Baseball,* has been the leader of baseball books since its first printing in 1938. My purpose in revising this great book is to keep it in circulation. Baseball terminology has changed somewhat and methods of play, in some phases of the game, have in my estimation improved. There was a time when there was only one accepted way to complete certain fundamentals of the game. Today there are several accepted ways to work the same fundamental. I have attempted to give readers the benefit of my thirty years of experience as a major and minor league player, major league coach, minor league manager, and college coach, in addition to the methods prescribed by the Old Master, Jack Coombs.

I am indebted to my Assistant Coach, Frank Pellerin, for his research on the "Rules of Scoring." Final decisions on the more complicated interpretations were clarified by Mr. Allen Lewis of the *Philadelphia Inquirer* Sports Staff, who served in 1965 as Chairman of the Major Leagues Scoring Rules Committee. Credit must also be given to Coach Ernie Lanford, who assisted me at Florida State University; to our Freshman Coach, Tom Smith; and to the members of the Michigan State University Varsity Baseball Team, who helped proofread the manuscript. I am equally indebted to Coach L. C. "Cap" Timm of Iowa State University for compiling the material in the chapter, "Construction and Maintenance of Baseball Fields." In my estimation, he is the only person qualified to write this chapter. He has devoted many years of study and research to this important phase of the game. For the section, "Training of Players," a special thanks goes to Don Fauls, Head Trainer of Florida State University. To help explain certain fundamentals, I thought it would be best to use a sequence camera. Thanks must be given to Jack Griffith, editor of *Athletic Journal,* for taking pictures, and for permission to use some photographs that have appeared in past articles.

Some of the illustrations and drills used in the following chapters have been taken from my book, *Baseball Coach's Guide to Drills and Skills,* published by Prentice-Hall, Inc. I would recommend it for supplementary reading and study.—D.W.L.

preface

ONE
the defensive game

the pitching game 1

the catching game 2

the infielder's game 3

playing first base 4

contents

THREE

a mythical ball game

FOUR

official scorers

FIVE

practical problems

baseball

ONE

the

defensive game

the pitcher himself

Mere physical size does not make the pitcher. Men of widely varying stature have become great professional pitchers. However, most successful pitchers have been large men, tall and rangy. It takes a good constitution, good physical condition, muscular strength, reserve energy, an alert mind, and much courage to make a great pitcher. The bigger and stronger the man, the better are his chances of becoming a great pitcher.

The pitcher has the most difficult position in the game, a position which calls not only for great physical exertion but also for a mind alert to each defensive and offensive situation. The master pitcher must be aware of every situation in which any member of his team may find himself. This alone means that pitching is a man's job.

A good pitcher must have free arm movement—especially in the wrist and elbow of the pitching arm—and be able to put some speed on the ball. The proper use of arms, body, and feet can be learned from older and more experienced men—provided the player has sufficient natural ability.

the position of the ball in the pitching hand

The ball is gripped in about the same way for every kind of pitch. It is held so that three contacts are made between the thumb, first, and second

the pitching game 1

fingers and the three seams. For every ball pitched, the space between the flesh and the ball is nearly the same. The following are common mistakes made by inexperienced pitchers:

1. Holding the ball across the seams near the tips of the fingers for a fast ball, but forcing it deep into the flesh between the thumb and forefinger, or holding it with the seams, for a curve ball.

2. Holding the first and second fingers close together for a fast ball, but spreading them for a curve ball, or vice versa.

3. Forcing the ball into the heel of the hand, with all the fingers showing, for a slow ball.

Obviously, a good hitter can easily detect such variations of position and tell immediately what kind of ball the pitcher is about to deliver.

figure 1

Until it is actually pitched, the ball should be kept covered by the glove. For a wind-up pitch, the gloved hand is brought straight up in front of the face. As the glove comes up, it catches the other hand so that the ball is pushed up between the thumb and forefinger of the glove, and both palms touch at the outer edges. The position of the hand and wrist in the glove is the same for all pitches. When no wind-up is intended, the ball is kept covered in the glove (see Figure 1).

the proper stance upon the pitching rubber

When getting ready for the wind-up stance, the pivot foot should be on the front of the rubber and about perpendicular to it. The front half of the foot should be extended over the rubber toward home plate. The back foot is free: it can be upon the back edge of the plate, directly behind it, or touching the side of the rubber. The weight of the body may be distributed in any manner that is comfortable for the pitcher, but preferably it should be on his back foot (see Figure 2).

After taking his stance, the pitcher may not raise either foot from the pitching rubber except in the act of pitching the ball or throwing to a base to catch a runner. He may, however, remove his pivot foot from the rubber in a backward step, providing he does not make any motion which might look like the start of a wind-up or pitch. A very common mistake of inexperienced pitchers is to raise the pivot foot from the rubber and then step on the rubber again just before beginning the wind-up. This movement of the pivot foot is illegal; the umpire will justly call the pitch an unfairly delivered ball. The pivot foot, then, may rotate on the rubber, but it must not leave the rubber until the ball is delivered.

With a runner on first base only. The pitcher should not take a wind-up in this defensive situation. He stands with the back foot parallel with or upon the rubber so that the front spike of the shoe is just over the edge of the plate. Most of the weight of the body is upon this foot. The front foot is placed far enough in front of the rubber to maintain perfect balance, and a little to the first base side of home plate. The pitcher's elbows rest upon his hips and his hands are held belt-high directly in front of the body. The ball is covered by the glove (see Figure 3).

figure **2**

With a runner on second base only. The pitcher never takes a wind-up in this defensive situation. He stands with the whole of his back foot resting on the front edge of the pitching rubber, shoulders in nearly direct line with the home plate and second base, elbows resting on hips, hands belt-high, the ball covered by the glove, and most of his weight resting upon the back foot. An occasion may arise for a quick throw to second base in an attempt to catch the runner. For such a throw the left-handed pitcher turns clockwise, the right-hander counter-clockwise. For the young player, it is sometimes advisable to spin forward in the opposite direction in order not to lose sight of the base and fielder. This helps prevent overthrows, and still keeps the baserunner close to second base.

figure **3**

With a runner on third base. A wind-up—if it does not allow a runner to steal from first to second—should be taken. A possible squeeze play might best be stopped by using a set stance as with a runner on first base only, or by taking a short, quick wind-up. Left-handed and right-handed pitchers spin clockwise to throw to third base.

proper delivery

The pitcher assumes the same position after every ball delivered to the batter. His body and shoulders rotate in unison with his feet. The shoulder farthest from the batter before delivery is the front shoulder after the ball has left the pitching hand. The feet hit the ground in such a manner that perfect balance is maintained. As soon as the ball has left the hand, the body is positioned with the back parallel to the pitching rubber. This terminating position enables the pitcher to protect himself from a hard hit ball, and to go to either side of the diamond to field grounders or swinging bunts (see Figures 4 and 5).

The pitcher should stand in the terminating position until he receives the ball from the catcher. He then returns to the pitching rubber, takes the sign from the catcher, and comes into his pitching position. The pitcher should never leave the terminating position and wander around the diamond: to do so is a needless waste of energy, especially on hot days. It is always advisable to take the sign on the rubber.

figure **4**

Proper stance, proper body motion, and a natural pitching swing of the arm are essential physical requirements for a successful pitcher. A natural throwing swing of the arm, whether sidearm, underhand, or overhand, should not, under ordinary conditions, be changed. The pitcher should become proficient in pitching from one angle only. It is a great mistake, for example, to pitch a fast sinker ball with a sidearm or underarm motion and a curve ball overhand. If the pitcher unconsciously forms the habit of pitching fast balls sidearm and curve balls overhand, a batter will easily detect the variations in delivery. Changing positions of delivery often affects the control of the ball.

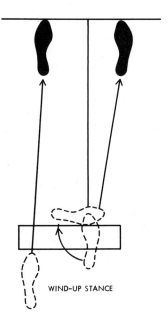

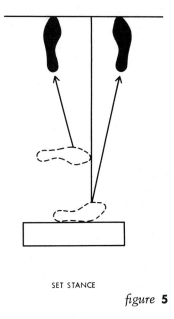

WIND-UP STANCE   SET STANCE

figure **5**

The curve ball. The pitcher should not try to deliver a curve ball with a big crook in the arm at the elbow. The arm should be bent, but still almost as fully extended as in pitching a fast ball. The ball is gripped more tightly with the middle finger, regardless of the pressure placed upon it by the forefinger. It is the twist or spin given the ball by the thumb and middle finger that makes it curve. The ball can go over the index finger or the index finger can be held off to the side. The more the wrist and arm are bent, the greater and slower the curve.

Proficiency and perfect control of a curve ball can be obtained only by conscientious practice in pitching from one position or angle. A three-quarter or an overhand position is very satisfactory. A curve ball pitched from this angle has a downward spin, which causes it to drop as it comes toward the batter. The sidearm curve has no variation in height, and it comes to the batter parallel to his stroke. Even if he is completely fooled by such a curve, he is more apt to hit it than a downward curve.

In warming up, it is very important that the pitcher take a position parallel to the position he will take on the diamond. The pitcher will notice that even a slight wind blowing toward him will increase the width of his curve ball, whereas a wind blowing from behind him will decrease the width of his curve ball.

The slow ball or change of pace. The ball is held in the natural position, but slightly closer to the palm than is a fast ball or a curve ball. As the slow ball is about to leave the hand, it is relieved from the pressure of first and second fingers, but is gripped tightly by the thumb. The two fingers released should, as the ball leaves the hand, point directly at the batter in a natural way, so that only the thumb and index finger are visible to the pitcher. The ball is held in position against the upper part of the palm by the pressure of the thumb. If, in leaving the hand, the ball touches the tip of the finger, the resulting spin makes it curve. A slow ball of this type is not as effective as a change of pace that floats with little or no rotation. The slow ball is always pitched so that the catcher receives it below the batter's knees.

A slow ball or change of pace must never be pitched to a weak-hitting batter: a weak batter does not have the same *timing swing* as a strong batter and is more likely to hit a slow pitched ball.

A slow ball should never be thrown with a good runner on first base, as it would make it easier for the runner to steal second. Never throw a slow ball to a left-handed hitter with a runner on first base. In this case, the first baseman is holding the runner on base, and a big hole is left for the hitter.

freak deliveries

The fork ball. The fork ball is another type of slow ball or change of pace. It is delivered with more speed than the slow ball. It can be used more often and with less caution when bases are occupied by runners. However, some thought should be given before delivering this ball with first base occupied by a runner. Because it is caught low, the catcher must make more of an effort to assume the correct throwing position.

The ball is held firmly between the second joints of the first and second fingers, which are spread wide apart. The thumb holds the ball in position with some pressure. The tips of the fingers are bent a little toward the palm of the hand. With the swing down movement of the set stance— when the bases are occupied by runners—the ball is placed in the correct position. The ball leaves the hand without any spin or rotation. Contact with the air on its way toward the hitter causes it, as ball players say, to "float." The pitcher must be very careful not to let the batter see how he sets the ball between his fingers.

We do not recommend the use of this pitch by the average young ball player.

The screw or fadeaway ball. The screw ball, which has made a number of professional pitchers famous in the baseball world, should never be taught to a young man before he has mastered the fundamentals of pitching. It is doubtful whether it should ever be taught to a young man, as it calls for muscle movements in the wrist, forearm, and elbow that are contrary to the laws of nature.

A roll must be given to the arm and the wrist so that the ball, in leaving the hand, passes over the tip of the second finger, the back of the hand being the only part visible to the batter after delivery. In other words, the ball leaves the hand between the second and third fingers. The ball is pushed over the second finger by the thumb. The ball is held very loosely near the tips of the fingers. A tightly held ball cannot be given the proper spin. For this pitch it is best to have the arm swing at about a forty-five degree angle to the body.

The ball has a downward trend caused by the spin given to it. Pitchers will find it rather effective against opposite-handed batters. The ball is caught by the catcher below the batter's knees when it is thrown properly.

The knuckle ball. This pitch is very similar to the fork ball after it has left the pitching hand. It is delivered with the thumb and either the third or the little finger pressing against the sides of the ball, and with the other fingers bent at the first joint and resting on top of the ball. The ball is held tightly in the hand and is thrown from the natural pitching position. This and the following fingernail ball are not recommended for the young pitcher.

The fingernail ball. This is another type of slow ball that is thrown in much the same way as the knuckle ball. The difference is that the fingers are not bent at the first joint on top of the ball: the tips of the fingernails rest there instead. The ball is gripped as tightly as possible. The delivery is more of a push from the fingers than a snap of the wrist.

The slider. This pitch, although very popular in the major leagues, must be included in freak pitches for the young player. It is a difficult pitch to master and frequently winds up a home run ball, a pitch that "didn't break." It is better to master the fast ball, curve, and change of pace before working on any freak delivery.

The slider is a fast breaking ball that breaks or curves closer to home plate than a curve ball. It is a nickel curve ball that looks like a fast ball when delivered. The ball is held slightly off center, and the index finger is released first with more pressure being exerted by the middle finger than the index finger. The arm is fully extended as in the fast ball delivery. The wrist is thrust downward to make the ball spin like a football or a corkscrew.

pitching strategy

The pitcher makes every possible effort to pitch his first ball for a strike. The first pitch need not always be a fast one. Fast balls, in fact, should be mixed with curves and slow balls. If the pitcher can get one strike and no balls on a batter, the latter is then on the defense, and the pitcher can make him swing at balls pitched to his weakness.

The heady, alert, smart pitcher tries to make the batter swing at balls going over a corner of the plate. Any batter should be able to hit perfect strikes, but balls delivered across the corners of the plate, high, low, inside, or outside, will be hit with much less force than the perfect strike. The pitcher should never deliberately waste a pitch unless such a ball is called for by the catcher, or the count is no balls and two strikes on the batter. To pitch a ball so far from the plate that the batter makes no attempt to swing at it is a waste of energy. Every pitcher should have a definite idea with regard to pitching: *Every pitch must count!* Random pitching eventually results in a ball being pitched over the middle of the plate, where any batter ought to be able to hit it.

Successful pitchers try at all times to catch the batter off balance. The batter should never be allowed to get set for the pitch. A great number of variations in the speed of pitches does not give the batter much opportunity, as he tries to protect himself at the point of his weakness, to get set for a change of pace. He will swing either too soon or too late.

control

Control is the greatest of all pitching assets. To obtain full control of oneself and of the ball requires constant practice—even after proper stance and body motions are mastered. The position of the ball in the hand, the stance, and the delivery should at all times follow the suggestions governing the practice for control. The pitcher should be able to hit a very small target at the pitching distance, sixty feet and six inches. There are times when a pitched ball must be over the plate, and a pitcher must be able to put it there.

A change in the position of the pivot foot will often help a pitcher achieve control. If a right-handed pitcher's fast ball breaks to the outside for a left-handed batter and to the inside for the right-handed batter, a change of position on the rubber toward first base may bring the ball nearer the center of home plate. If the ball shoots to the inside corner of the plate for a left-handed batter and to the outside for a right-handed batter, the pitcher should shift his pivot foot on the rubber toward third base. If this doesn't work, he should try moving the opposite way.

A change of position will also help the left-handed pitcher. If his ball is shooting to the outside for a right-handed batter, a change of the pivot foot toward third base will cause the ball to go over the plate. If the ball goes to the inside corner of the plate, a shift of the pivot foot toward first base will bring the desired result.

Here is a suggestion: Practice pitching a fast, straight ball directly over the plate, belt-high. When this can be done satisfactorily, practice pitching directly over the plate, high or low. When the pitcher is satisfied with this part of his control, it is time to practice inside and outside pitch-

figure **6**

BEHAN—

ing. The pitcher should bear in mind that a fast ball properly controlled is far more effective than the random pitching of either fast or curve balls. *Control is absolutely essential to efficient pitching!*

We have found from personal experience that it is better to throw the ball at some particular part of the catcher's body or glove, rather than at a mental object quite apart from the catcher. If a batter is a successful high ball hitter, the pitcher should not pitch the ball across the shoulders of this batter. Instead the pitcher should keep his eyes on the catcher's knees, making sure that the ball is received in the position hardest for the batter to hit. If the batter is weak on high pitched balls, the pitcher should keep his eyes on the shoulders of his catcher and pitch accordingly. If the batter is weak on inside balls, the pitcher throws to the catcher's shoulder that is nearest the batter. If the batter is weak on outside balls, the pitcher should pitch to the shoulder farthest from the batter. In the case of the high ball hitter, the pitcher would throw for the catcher's knees inside and outside according to the hitter's weakness (see Figure 6).

the use of the eyes and ears

There are many things which the average pitcher does not see or hear. The best way to learn baseball is by observation and by listening to what an older and more experienced person has to say. The young pitcher should learn to keep his eyes and ears open. Before the pitcher steps upon the rubber to assume his pitching position, he should turn around to see how his fielders are playing the man at bat. If the defense is playing the batter as a right-field hitter, the pitcher should be careful not to pitch so that the batter can possibly hit the ball to left field. (A right-handed batter will probably hit an inside ball to left field; a left handed batter will probably hit an outside ball into that territory.) If the pitcher sees his fellow players playing the batter as a left-field hitter, he should never give that batter an opportunity to hit the ball to right field.

The pitcher should watch closely the base runners of the opposing team and study intently the man at bat. The good pitcher has a strong memory for faces and position of feet in the batter's box. The following points should be emphasized:

If the batter's front foot pulls away from a straight line toward the pitcher, pitch low and to the outside. A batter who has this fault will, at the time the bat meets the ball, be far away from the line of flight of the oncoming pitch and will not be able to apply full power to the ball.

If the batter's rear shoulder drops, pitch high since the dropping of the rear shoulder will naturally cause the bat to swing with an upward motion and all balls will be hit in the air as flies.

If the batter takes too long a stride, pitch high. The ball will look like a strike as it comes toward the batter, but it will be above his shoulders after he takes his stride. There is only one place a high pitched ball can possibly be hit by such a batter, and that is into the air. A slow ball or a slow curve is also effective against the batter who takes too long a step.

If the batter takes too short a stride, pitch low. Such a stride does not give the batter sufficient arm movement to reach and meet such a pitch squarely.

If the batter appears anxious, take plenty of time.

With a man on base in scoring position, pitch curve balls, low. A low curve ball is hard to hit into the air for a long fly. Have some particular pitch in reserve for this situation.

Watch every base runner closely. Many times stolen bases should be black marks against the pitcher's record. When an opposing player steals a base, the pitcher is often to blame rather than the catcher. The good base runner watches the pitcher's knee and arm movements. The motion of the pitcher's knee joints tells the base runner exactly what the pitcher is going to do. Similarity of the knee motion for throws to first base and home plate is a very important factor in the effectiveness of the pitcher's position.

It is important to time each pitched ball to the batter, especially with the bases occupied. It is a mistake to take the same length of time between deliveries. The time from the second the pitcher takes his pitching position on the rubber until he makes his delivery should vary with every throw; otherwise, the base runner or runners are invited to steal bases. I would advise all pitchers to accustom themselves to a variation in time by counting between pitches. After the proper stance has been taken, count two and pitch, count four or five and pitch, count three and pitch, and so on. Be sure to mix up the time between each delivery.

A pitcher is allowed a limited amount of time between each pitch: he should check the rules of the league in which he is playing.

Make no false moves. After the stance is taken, any movement of the arms or body without delivering the ball, either to a base or to home plate, constitutes a balk. All the necessary pitching motions are these:

With the feet in proper position and the elbows resting on the hips, the hands are brought up in front of the body belt-high. The ball is covered by the glove, and the weight is on the pivot foot. With the body pivoting, the pitching arm drops vertically to the lowest point of the arm swing, then ascends to the highest point assumed in order to obtain the natural delivery. The pitcher's hands should remain stationary until the pivot movement of the body starts.

If the pitcher wants to step off the rubber after he has taken his stance, he must keep the ball in his glove and step backward from the rubber with his pivot foot. If he steps otherwise, he has made a balk.

Defensive situation for a bunt. With a runner on first base only, pitch hard and high. Low balls are much easier to bunt on the ground. The batter shows by dropping his bat that he is going to bunt, and this is the signal for the pitcher to rush straight from his pitching position toward the plate as soon as he delivers the ball. This is the pitcher's part in the defense for this particular play. A hard-bunted ball often gives an opportunity for a forced play at second base. Listen to the catcher for instructions. He has the play in front of him.

Situations prompting a bunt. The batter is quite likely to bunt when there are runners on first and second bases. In such a case, watch the runner on second for he is the one on whom a forced play can be made at third base. In any case, when a bunt is expected, pitch the ball to the outside for a left-handed batter and to the inside for a right-handed batter. When the ball is delivered, rush to the third-base line, the only place to which a properly pitched ball can be bunted. The idea behind this defensive maneuver is to allow the third baseman to cover his base and force the lead runner at third base. The ball must be fielded quickly. Listen to the catcher for instructions as to which base the ball must be thrown. Some coaches like the third baseman to call this play.

When there is a runner on second and a base hit is made to the outfield, get into direct line with the outfielder who is to make the throw and behind the catcher approximately twenty feet or more. Back up all throws.

All balls not accurately thrown toward the plate by a fielder should be cut off by the cut-off man without any instructions whatever from his catcher. An accurately thrown ball is the only one on which a play can be made on the runner who occupied second base.

the pitcher as a fielder

The baseball club with a good fielding pitcher has a distinct advantage over the club with a weak fielding pitcher. The pitcher who is active on his feet and able to field bunts, to back up throws from the outfielders, and to put himself in a correct position on the diamond at the right time, is a big percentage winner. On ground balls hit to him, the pitcher always waits for the first baseman to reach the base and then throws the ball to him. He crow-hops on his pivot foot and steps toward first, throwing the ball firmly. Many a game has been lost by a pitcher who *tossed* the ball over his first baseman's head. A fairly hard thrown ball gives the baseman time to recover it if he fumbles for the putout. The pitcher always tries to keep the opposing runner or batter from getting into a scoring position —that is, to second or third base. He cannot possibly succeed in such a situation with slow-hit balls. Hard-hit balls give him an opportunity to make forced plays, but slow-hit balls never do so. Make this your rule in fielding with the bases occupied: *"Never will I throw a slow-hit ball to any base but first, unless ordered to do otherwise by my catcher."* Many a game is lost because an unthinking fielding pitcher has not firmly established in his mind the difference between a hard-hit and slow-hit ball when attempting a forced play.

One of the most difficult fielding plays to judge correctly is known as the swinging bunt. The batter swings hard at the pitched ball and hits it, not squarely, but in such a manner that it rolls slowly, close to the base lines. The difficulty for the pitcher is to decide whether to let the ball roll, hoping that it will go into foul territory, or to pick up the ball for a play at first base. This is one of the plays in which he should listen to the shouted instructions of his catcher.

When a ball is hit by a batter to the pitcher and a runner stops running between bases, apparently uncertain which base to approach, the pitcher should rush toward him and make him commit himself. Try starting the runner back toward the base which he left, throw the ball to the baseman covering that base and fade from the picture. This play often comes up when third base is occupied by an opposing base runner. The runner, seeing that he is a sure putout at the plate, stops and tries to get into a run-down play so that the batter can get into a scoring position. The pitcher should rush toward him and try to make the putout at third base, always starting the play by going between the runner and the plate.

With a runner on first base, on a base hit to the outfield, back up your third baseman at least twenty feet or more in direct line with the throws.

With a runner on second base, back up home plate on every base hit. Most coaches and many authorities on our great national game insist that the first baseman be in line for the throw upon a base hit to right field and the third baseman in line upon a base hit to left field. However, the pitcher, of high school age and younger, might be the logical player to line up for this play because of the insufficient strength of the average outfielder, and because of the large open spaces not inclosed by fences or walls now used for playing fields. Also, the pitcher may be your best ball-player. Should this situation arise, the second baseman goes out toward right field on a hit to that field for the possible relay throw; the first base-man covers first base and the shortstop covers second base. The shortstop goes toward left field on a hit to that field for a possible relay throw; the first baseman covers first base, the second baseman covers second base. In both cases if the pitcher, on the advice of the catcher, catches the ball which is being thrown toward the plate by the outfielder, or catches an inaccurately thrown ball, both first and second bases are properly protected. Either of these plays might result in a putout—that is, pitcher to second to first—provided the player who hit the ball makes an effort to reach second base on the throw to the plate. If the player who made the base hit overruns first base, there is an opportunity to retire him—pitcher to first. This last play could not be executed if the first baseman acted as the cut-off man within the diamond. The most important defensive tactics would be to keep the runner from scoring. Next in importance would be to keep the runner who hit the ball from reaching second base, a scoring position. Each base should be protected for these run-down plays.

With a runner on third base, if a fly ball is hit to the outfield, back up home plate by at least twenty feet or more in line with the throw.

With a runner on second base, if a fly ball is hit to the outfield, back up third.

With no runners on base, if a sharp base hit is made to right field, the pitcher backs up first base for a possible throw to that base by the rightfielder, who attempts to catch the batter rounding first base too far.

Always be one base ahead of the leading base runner in order to protect that base if he attempts to reach it.

waste balls or pitch outs

By a waste pitch is meant a ball pitched so far away from the plate that it cannot be hit by the batter. An intended waste ball should be a quick pitch. When a waste ball is called for by the catcher, every player on the field should be able to leave his position. *The waste pitch must not be hit!* The waste pitch allows the fielders to back up any possible play. For instance, if a runner is on third base and a play is to be made to catch him off base, the left fielder and shortstop can safely leave their positions to back up the attempted play. The same is true of an attempt to make a play at any base.

signs from the catcher

While the pitcher is obtaining the catcher's signals, every player on the defensive team, except the first baseman, also looks for them. At this point of the game, the pitcher should not throw to bases. All eyes are on the catcher, and all eyes shift to the pitcher when he takes his position on the pitching rubber. It must be said that normally only the shortstop and second baseman can see the signs, which they may relay to the other fielders.

breaking up squeeze plays

In a squeeze play, the batter signals to the runner on third that he is going to bunt the next ball, on which the runner must attempt to score. A big mistake many runners make on this play is, after having seen the squeeze signal, to break from third too quickly, trying to score on the play before the ball has left the pitcher's hand.

The only way to break up a squeeze play, with a right-handed batter at the plate, the base runner making a break for the plate as the pitcher starts his wind-up pitch, is to pitch the ball inside far enough so that the batter is made to hit the dirt. Always remember the rulings given to us by the major leagues, who are the mentors and directors of the national game. A ball cannot lawfully be pitched directly at a batter's head. (We refer to what is commonly termed the "bean ball.") With a left-handed batter, if the base runner makes a break for the plate as the pitcher starts his wind-up pitch, the pitcher should pitch the ball outside of the plate, thus giving the catcher a chance to get the ball and fall upon the runner as he tries to score. Remember this pitch must not be bunted when a squeeze play is in progress. (It is impossible to break up the bunt-and-run squeeze as discussed under *Squeeze Play*, page 118.)

In a squeeze play, if the catcher has signaled for a fast ball before assuming his natural catching position, pitch the ball that we have just described. If, however, the signal has been given for a curve ball, the curve ball must be pitched away from the batter. In other words, the ball signed for by the catcher must be delivered, because the catcher expects that particular ball and would be completely fooled or "crossed" by any other. The result, without doubt, would be a wild pitch.[1]

balls hit to left of pitcher

Every time the ball is hit between the pitcher and first base, the pitcher starts for that bag in order to take the throw from the player who fields the ball, either the first or the second baseman. If, however, the first baseman goes to the bag and does not field the ball, the pitcher stays where he is and saves his energy. This break to first is a must and should be practiced diligently by all pitchers.

first or second baseman fielding the ball

The pitcher runs in an arc toward first base (running parallel to the baseline) and should receive the ball at least two steps from the base so that he has ample time to touch the bag. The right-handed pitcher hits the bag with his right foot; the left-handed pitcher also hits it with his right foot. The left-handed pitcher pivots into his throwing position by stepping back with his right foot pivoting clockwise, his left or pivot foot firmly on the ground. As he steps back, he throws his right foot in the direction of the base to which he might throw. The right-handed pitcher pivots counter-clockwise on his left foot to set his weight on his right foot for the throw. In any case a well-balanced throwing position is essential, for a runner may try to score from second base or move to third base on this play at first. Feet and body must remain on fair territory to avoid a collision with the oncoming base runner. Hit the bag with the right foot then quickly pivot into a throwing position. If there are no runners on base, the pitcher, after he has tagged the bag with his right foot, continues running down the line toward fair territory.

pop flies

Any ball hit high enough into the air should be caught by an infielder. The infielder has had more practice than the pitcher in handling such fly balls and is better able to do so. There are some very low pop flies which only the pitcher can catch. He should do so calling for it loud and often.

[1] This has been debated. Some catchers prefer a medium speed straight ball on all squeeze plays.

infield strategy

It is the infielder's duty to keep the runner as close to the base as possible. The pitcher should not pitch to the batter when an infielder is away from his correct position on the diamond.

When the offensive team has runners on first and third bases and a double steal is anticipated, the catcher gives the sign for a waste ball. The pitcher goes to first base as soon as the ball leaves his hand to protect that position. The first baseman follows the runner toward second. Another player then comes to first base, and the pitcher fades out of the picture.

When runners are on first and third and a waste ball is not signed for by the catcher, the pitcher has on his hands a situation inviting stolen bases. The first ball should be pitched for a strike. He can then waste three balls, if necessary, to get the runner trying to start a double steal.

When a runner is caught in a run-down by any defensive player, the pitcher protects the base from which the play started until some other player takes the position.

Should the pitcher fumble a fairly hit ball with men on bases, he can make only one play—a throw to first base.

If, with runners on first and second and less than two outs, the batter drives a hard bounding ball to the pitcher, the situation calls for a double play, second base to first base. The play may not be successful, but even so, it leaves an opportunity for another similar play by the pitcher or the infielders. A fumbled ball in this situation calls for a play to first. A slow-hit ball always means a play to first, unless the pitcher is otherwise instructed by the catcher.

In attempting to catch a runner off his base, the pitcher throws so that the baseman receiving the ball catches it about knee high and on the side of the base into which the runner is making his slide.

When a forced play on a runner is made, it should be so managed that the baseman catching the ball receives it about shoulder high and can make his throw for a possible double play with no waste motion. The throw is made to the bag, not to the fielder. The fielder's job is to get to the ball. A throw made to the fielder will end up behind him as he moves to the bag.

picking a runner off second base

A strong defensive play, if properly executed, is to catch the runner by throwing to the protectors of the keystone base. If the play fails, it at least keeps the runner close to the bag for fear he may be put out. There should be no hesitation about making such a play, for if it is not made, the man on second may score a very important run.

In throwing to second base, the pitcher whirls around on his pivot foot, his body describing more than a half circle. The right-handed pitcher whirls around from the natural pitching position by the way of first base. His right shoulder points toward right field after the ball has left the hand. The left-handed pitcher whirls in the opposite direction. His left shoulder points toward left field after the ball has left the hand.

To catch a runner on second, throw so that the infielder covering the bag can catch the ball on the run and immediately place it on the runner with his glove. This is a very hard play to make correctly; only constant practice will perfect it.

The shortstop and the second baseman must work perfectly with the pitcher in order to make a success of this play. Both infielders watch the lead of the runner very closely. If either of them thinks that there is a chance of getting the runner, the play should be made. In this case, some simple sign should be given to the pitcher while he is in pitching position but looking at the runner (see *Pick-Off Plays*, page 78).

Quiz on pitching

1. Describe fully the correct position of the ball in the pitching hand.
2. Describe the proper stance for a wind-up pitch; the proper stance with a runner on first base, and the proper stance with a runner on second base.
3. Describe what a coach can do to teach his pitcher similarity of body movements when runners are on base.
4. What movements of the pitcher's body, arms, legs, and feet are important to him when second or first base is occupied by a runner?
5. If the pitcher, after taking his stance, finds it necessary to step from the rubber, how should he do it?
6. Is it necessary to time each delivery?
7. If a pitcher's control is imperfect, what advice would you give him?
8. Describe some of the weaknesses which batters have. How should a pitcher pitch to any one of these weaknesses when he discovers it?
9. How would you teach a young man to throw a curve ball?
10. Describe one of the freak deliveries.
11. How should you advise your pitcher to break up a squeeze play?
12. What is a waste ball and how is it pitched?
13. When should a pitcher cover first after he has pitched a waste ball?
14. What is probably the hardest fielding play for a pitcher to make? Why?
15. What is the rule relating to a ball which is hit hard or slow to the pitcher?
16. Describe fully the duty of a pitcher on all balls hit to his left.
17. Why is it advisable for a pitcher to hit the first base bag with his right foot and stop, after taking a throw from the first baseman?

18. If the batter hits a ground ball back at the pitcher and a base runner with a big lead from his base decides to stop between bases, what should the pitcher do? Why?

19. How can a pitcher use his eyes and ears advantageously?

20. What plays should bring the pitcher back of third base? What plays should bring him in back of his catcher? What play should bring him back of first base?

21. With a runner on third base, a ball is hit to the third baseman. The runner, seeing that he is to be tagged out on the throw, stops and goes back toward third base. What should the pitcher do in this situation?

22. When the offensive team has runners on second and first bases, how can a pitcher pitch to a right-handed batter and what should he do the moment the ball leaves his hand if the play is a sacrifice bunt? How should he pitch to the left-handed batter.

23. With one man out, where would the pitcher attempt his first put-out under the same conditions as in question 22, if the situation did not prompt a bunt and the batter hit a sharp ground ball to him?

24. What should a pitcher do when a runner is on first base and the situation prompts a bunt?

25. Where should the pitcher be in a defensive situation with runners on second and first bases and a base hit to the outfield? Where does he go if a fly ball is hit to the outfield?

26. How should a pitcher pitch to a batter with a runner in a scoring position?

27. Explain how the pitcher attempts to catch a runner off second base.

28. As a coach, whom would you term a heady alert pitcher?

29. From the chapter studied, discuss a successful pitcher.

30. If you were a coach and a large number of men reported to you for a baseball team, how would you go about selecting your pitchers and what would be the final deciding factor in your selection? State fully.

31. What infield flies should a pitcher attempt to catch? Why is it best for him not to go for the others?

the catcher himself

The catcher is one of the most important parts of defensive baseball. Any man who wants to be a successful catcher must constantly bear this fact in mind: he is one player who sees all the action and directs a large part of defensive infield play. The catcher is the busiest player in the game, and his service to the team as a director of plays and an inspirer of confidence is far greater than that of any other player.

Physical requirements. A good physique is obviously an important asset to a catcher, but there is some argument as to whether a catcher should be tall or short. The argument in favor of the tall catcher lies principally in his greater ability to reach high, wild deliveries by the pitcher. The shorter catcher is better able to defend low, where he is most vulnerable, and to give a good, low target for the pitcher. But, a tall catcher may be perfectly able to defend well low, and a short catcher may be excellent at handling wild pitches, so size is less important for the catcher than for any other infielder, with the possible exception of the pitcher.

Three physical requirements essential to every good catcher are a good strong arm, rather large hands, and fast reflexes. A catcher who can get the ball to a base quickly and accurately is extremely valuable to his team. The catcher must be properly coached in the coordinated use of his feet, arms, and body, and he must be strong enough and quick enough to handle any situation that will come his way.

the catching game

Ability to catch. The ability to catch all thrown and batted balls calls for great agility, and it is a constant test of a catcher's efficiency in making proper use of his hands and feet. It is not only ability to catch that makes a man a great catcher, but also the "head work" he uses behind the bat. He must use sound judgment in signaling for every pitch, and in directing all plays properly. A good catcher constantly studies the batter, his style, his stance, and his swing in order to discover any strength or weakness.

Throwing ability. A catcher must be able to throw quickly and accurately to any base where a play has to be made. Catchers who have difficulty in throwing accurately will find that the fault rests in their feet and in their balance. The basic position for any type of throwing, especially where speed and accuracy are prime requisites, is with the balance resting on the back foot (in this case the right foot) and with the left foot used as a guide. The catcher should get in the habit of throwing off the right foot, and when returning the ball to the pitcher, should throw it as close as possible to the pitcher's shoulder. This practice will prepare the catcher for the throw to second base, which is simply a harder version of the throw to the pitcher.

The mechanics of throwing include proper grip of the ball, coordinated arm and body movements, and complete follow-through. The ball should be gripped across the seams so that it will rotate directly backwards, four seams biting into the air. Any other rotation could easily cause the ball to sail or fade. The fingertips should be held on the seams, fingers slightly spread for better control of the ball, while the inside edge of the thumb supports the ball. The full fingerprint of the thumb does not touch the ball (see Figure 7).

As the pitch is received, the right hand moves over the ball and the fingers feel for the seams. The mitt and ball move back toward the right shoulder as the catcher shifts his weight to his right foot. The ball is taken from the mitt before it reaches the shoulder, and is cocked at the ear as the hips and shoulders rotate 90°.

The throw is started when the catcher shifts weight from his right to his left foot, in the direction of the target. The left arm drops across

figure **7**

the chest, pulling the hips and shoulders around, as the right arm comes through with the throw. The entire weight is now on the left foot as the right foot drives into its follow-through, much like a pitcher's, and lands ahead of the left foot.

When the ball is released, the wrist snaps straight downward. So that the ball will spin straight backward, it should be thrown with the arm moving straight down, perpendicular to the ground. The elbow leads at the start of the throw, pointing toward the intended target. The forearm moves in a downward arc and the wrist snaps to release the ball at the same time as the arm is straightened out. The forefinger is the last finger to leave the ball. This, plus a slight bend in the back as the weight shifts forward, helps to impart the proper spin to the ball.

Footwork. Footwork can be taught to a catcher and is not, therefore, the most important consideration in the selection of a player. But a catcher must realize that footwork is a vital part of receiving and throwing. Catchers have a tendency to slow up in their running game. They, therefore, should practice sprinting. Footwork may be practiced by assuming a catcher's position, moving the left foot to the right and stepping to the side with the right. It should be practiced to the left by moving the right foot to the left and stepping to the side with the left foot. It is a simple step, but it should be practiced daily until it is done by habit. It will then be turned into almost a jumping or hop step, both feet moving almost simultaneously.

Mental alertness. The catcher should keep his pitchers informed as to the position of the runners and the number of outs. A lapse of thought on the part of the pitcher for a fraction of a second may mean a stolen base, or a rather precarious position for the defensive team. "Watch that runner" should cause any pitcher to become alert. The catcher also reminds the pitcher to cover first base on all balls hit to the right side of the infield. In anticipating any play, the catcher should constantly keep in mind the game situation, the score, the inning, the number of outs, the strength of the hitters, the strengths and alertness of the pitcher, the wind direction and velocity, the sun, and the condition of the base paths. He must never neglect to keep his fellow players informed as to the proper play to make.

signals

Signaling for the various pitches is usually done in the squatting position, with the fingers or different hand positions. For example, one finger may mean a fast ball, two fingers a curve, three could mean an off-speed pitch, and the thumb or a fist might mean a pitch out. Additionally, wagging the finger might call for a side arm delivery, the type of pitch determined by the number of fingers wiggled. Hand positions or "flaps" are generally used more for night ball because visibility is better. The hand against the thigh could mean a fast ball, when flipped out it would be a curve. Again, a change up would be signaled by wiggling the fingers or by flapping the hand back and forth.

When preparing to give a sign, the catcher should go into his crouch with his feet parallel and pointed straight ahead, or toed in slightly. The spread of his feet should be no wider than his shoulders to prevent a spread-legged effect. It is also well to cover up the signs with the mitt by letting it hang off the left knee, curled in slightly. The signaling hand itself is placed deep between the legs in the crotch, and clapsed against the right inside thigh. The right arm and elbow are held against the body so they will not move while signals are given. The catcher should be careful to conceal his right hand when he flashes signs, because it is very easy for the on deck hitter, the base coaches, or the batter himself to steal them.

It is advisable that the battery use a series of three signs whenever signaling, regardless of whether there are men on base or not. This will make sign-stealing more difficult. Also, when there is a runner on second base and series signaling is a must, the pitcher will be used to seeing all three signs before he starts his wind-up. A failure on the part of the pitcher to wait until all three signs are flashed, when, for example, the live sign is one of the first two, would increase the chance of sign-stealing and, equally important, may find the catcher unprepared to receive the pitch. Naturally, the order of the live sign can be switched according to an odd or even count on the hitter, the number of outs, or the inning.

When a catcher signals for a certain pitch he can usually expect the pitch to do one specific thing. Curve balls, for instance, are usually wild low and fast balls are usually wild high. Also, he knows which way the curve will break or how the fast ball tails or sinks. Some forethought can save a wild pitch and an advance by a runner.

A catcher should never fall into the habit of developing a call pattern for succeeding batters: he should mix his calls. The catcher, as well as the pitcher, should constantly study the hitter and stay ahead of him with strikes if possible, but never at the expense of always throwing a fast ball or a slow curve on the first pitch, or always following one pitch with another certain call. It is very easy for the other team to pick up a pattern and be prepared for a certain pitch. The catcher must know the strengths and weaknesses of his pitcher, and in a tight situation he must call for his hurler's best pitch—even if the hitter is a good fast ball hitter and your pitcher's best pitch is a fast ball. In a jam, you must match strength against strength. Again, the score, the number of outs, and the inning must be considered in determining the call.

It is important that the catcher warm-up the starting pitcher. It is not advisable for the catcher to catch the whole warming up practice of his pitcher, but just the latter part of it. This gives the catcher an opportunity to judge for himself how effective his hurler's pitches may be on that particular day. Knowing what your pitcher can do before the game starts will be a great help to the catcher throughout the game. It is also advisable to make sure the signs are straight before the game in order to save time and avoid mix-ups.

the catching position

The catcher assumes many positions as he signals, readies himself, and receives the pitch. After the batter takes his place in the box, the catcher stations himself in a crouch near enough to the plate to reach out and just miss the hitter's back elbow with his mitt. As the hitter moves forward when he swings, the catcher is in little danger of getting hit with the bat, even though he is sitting close.

With nobody on base the catcher assumes a low, relaxed position. He may wish to move his feet wider apart as he crouches to receive the pitch, or even to drop to one knee. In this position the catcher must be alert for a bunt or a topped ball, for which he is now more vulnerable. In assuming this kneeling position, the toe of the right foot must be dug into the dirt in the same way as a sprinter digs in to get a good start.

The target is set up by extending the arms, slightly flexed at the elbows, with the palm of the mitt facing the pitcher, thumb up. The "meat hand" should be held in a semi-closed, relaxed position, with the index finger covering the tip of the thumb, and the backs of the fingers facing the pitcher (see Figure 8). As the ball is received the right hand, still clenched, should move toward the mitt pocket, traveling in a slight counterclockwise rotation and opening only as it cups over the ball. If a foul tip

figure **8**   *figure* **9**

does hit the hand, it will merely slap the relaxed fingers, as the joints bend naturally upon impact. Most injuries occur when the hand is held rigidly, or when the fingers are pointed into the flight of the ball. To give the pitcher a low target, the catcher merely turns his glove and hand with the fingers pointing downward and the palm facing the pitcher. This eliminates a crouch which is too low and cramped for the catcher (see Figure 9).

With runners on base the catcher must sit higher to be in better position to throw. His feet are also spread more and they assume a "heel and toe" alignment: the left foot placed in front of the right by about six inches so the heel of the left foot is opposite the toes of the right foot. The right foot should also be pointed outward slightly toward first base, to facilitate shifting and throwing.

To compensate for sitting higher, the catcher now turns his mitt and hand over, palms still facing the pitcher, but with the thumbs pointed down. This lower target is also held by slightly flexed arms, and will help the pitcher keep the ball low for a better chance of a double play. The catcher must remember to move into receiving position in the same rhythm —not to jump into readiness when he calls a fast ball, or lumber into position for a breaking or off-speed pitch. To prevent the opposition from reading him, he should always make the same movements.

Nearly anyone can catch thrown balls, but it takes a great deal of ability and practice to receive pitches so they appear to be strikes. All pitches should be received as close to the plate as possible, by extending the arms. The low pitch, especially the curve, must be caught "up." The catcher reaches out to meet the ball, and as he catches it, turns his wrist upward so his mitt is nearly parallel to the ground, pocket facing up. The high pitch should be caught "down" in a similar manner. As the ball is caught the mitt drops about 90° so that the pocket faces the ground.

The pitch off the catcher's left shoulder on the corner of the plate is likewise caught with a wrist flip. The mitt is positioned to receive the ball with its face toward the pitcher and the thumb pointed to the left. On contact with the ball, the mitt is turned in 90° so the thumb now faces the pitcher. The pitch off the right corner of the plate is caught with a twist of the mitt, rather than a "flip," since the latter would require a clumsy backhand position. As the ball is caught, the mitt is twisted gently in a clockwise manner, allowing the pocket to move inward about three inches.

The receiving mechanics described above enable the catcher to very subtly influence the position of the pitch. The more obvious "jerk" of the mitt is easily noticed by umpire and fans alike. Feeling he is being cheated by the "jerk," the umpire will consistently call those "close ones" balls. The less movement there is to the catcher's arm and mitt, the greater the probability of receiving strikes on close pitches.

balls in the dirt

Many pitches will bounce in the dirt before they get to the catcher. Such pitches are hard to handle, but the task can be more easily accomplished if the catcher will block the ball, instead of trying to field it cleanly. The ball that bounces straight into the catcher should be blocked by dropping to both knees. The mitt and the right hand, held wide open, are thrust between the legs, and are tilted slightly forward, as is the upper trunk. If the catcher does not lean forward and tilt his mitt and bare hand down, the ball is likely to glance over him and roll, instead of bouncing straight out in front of him (see Figure 10).

The ball in the dirt to the catcher's left is blocked by stepping out with his left leg and dropping to his right knee. He must be careful that his shin guard faces away from the pitcher, exposing his calf and the inside of his leg. This will reduce the possibility of the ball striking the hard guard and bouncing farther than advantageous. The upper trunk and glove should again be tilted slightly, and if possible, the catcher should twist his upper trunk very slightly to the right to keep the bouncing ball as close to the plate as possible.

On dirt balls to the right, the same procedure is used. The catcher steps out with his right foot, shin guard facing away from the ball, and drops to his left knee. The position of the glove, arms and upper trunk are the same as above (see Figure 11).

This phase of the catching game needs much practice. Put the catcher against a fence in his full gear, including a boxing glove on his right hand, and forearm guards on both arms. Stand approximately thirty feet in front of him, throw balls in the dirt to his left, his right, and straight at him. He should attempt to block the ball and keep it in front of him, then, scrambling after it,

figures **10,** **11,** *and* **12**

gain control by sweeping it up in his mitt and boxing glove (see Figure 12).

It can be seen so far that the feet, knees, hands and elbows are used in the proper receiving of all pitches. The catcher, with his legs spread properly, will normally lean left or right to receive an inside or an outside pitch, instead of actually stepping with his feet. This allows the umpire to remain in his position to call the pitch; the catcher who acts like a jack-in-a-box loses strikes for his pitcher.

The arms are not held rigid in receiving the pitch, but flex at the elbows. The concussion of the pitch is not absorbed by "giving," or letting the ball push the mitt back, but by keeping the mitt as motionless as possible and simply twisting or flipping it on contact. The slight flex at the elbow will absorb most of the shock. Quickness and agility of mitt mechanics can be improved by strapping a one pound weight to the catcher's wrist, or better yet, by using a loaded mitt, and having him catch batting practice or warm up pitchers. Ankle weights and a ten-pound weighted vest will also improve shifting ability and quickness of the feet.

the waste ball or pitchout

The pitchout is used in various situations: to foil an attempted steal, a hit and run, or a squeeze play. It may also be used to pick a runner off base, or merely to find out what the opposition may do—whether they intend to bunt, for instance. The intentional pass is used, of course, to walk a hitter. In receiving pitchouts, the catcher should not give away his intentions by sitting higher than normal, or by leaning to one side.

The catcher must also use the proper footwork. It should be noted that the footwork here is different from normal catching procedure. If there is a right-handed batter at the plate, the pitchout would be to the catcher's right. He would assume his normal catching position, and as the ball approaches, step out with his right foot to receive the pitch, then swing his left foot around into throwing position. On a pitchout to a left-handed batter, the catcher steps out with his left foot, brings his right foot behind it, and steps again with his left as he throws. The quicker the catcher moves and positions his feet, the quicker he can throw the ball.

The procedure for the intentional pass is nearly the same, except the catcher now assumes a relaxed, standing position with his feet inside the catcher's box on the side of the box to which the pitch is to be thrown. To move outside the box before the pitch is delivered would be a balk on the catcher's part. He may also give an arm length target with his mitt or his right hand to aid the pitcher's control. It is a good idea for the catcher to remind the pitcher to check his runners; carelessness can easily result in a stolen base or a balk. As soon as the ball leaves the pitcher's hand, the catcher steps out of the box to receive the ball.

defensive throwing strategy

Footwork, as mentioned earlier, is very important to a catcher, especially when throwing. With a right-handed batter, the catcher has only to take a short step, or crow hop, with his right foot, and swing his left foot around to throw, regardless of whether the pitch is inside or outside. The inside pitch can be caught with a sweeping motion as the first step is taken; the outside pitch is met as the step is taken.

With a left-handed batter, the situation is more difficult. With a runner on first base, it is advisable for the catcher to move back a foot or two in order to have a better look at the runner. Now if the pitch is inside, the catcher takes the same steps as with the right-hander, waiting a fraction of a second longer so as not to tip the hitter's bat. An outside pitch is usually received by taking a jab step with the left foot, crow hopping to the right foot, and making the throw.

With a runner on first base. The catcher watches the runner and the sign-giving base coach, anticipating a steal. He brings his feet, arms, and body into the proper throwing position after receiving every pitch, but keeps his body in the same vertical plane so as not to interfere with the umpire's view of the pitch. The runner may attempt a clean steal or a delayed steal, but in any case the catcher is ready. The throw back to the pitcher is made only after it is clear that the runner is not stealing. This throw should be varied as to the steps and movements made in returning the ball to the pitcher—further preventing the possibility of a delayed steal. This return throw should be firm, never a lob, and should be thrown to the pitcher's chest, where he can catch it with least effort.

With a runner on second base. The greatest care must be exercised in making a throw to second. The catcher should never indulge in random throwing to second base when attempting to pick off a runner. To do so is a dangerous play, except when the runner loafs, or when he drops his head every time the ball is returned to the pitcher. When, on a bunt attempt, the runner gets hung up, a throw to second could enable him to advance to third. The catcher might fake a throw, and then run straight at the runner with the ball cocked in throwing position, until he commits himself. Should a runner on second base attempt to steal third while a right-handed batter is at the plate, the catcher must remember to step and throw to the inside of the diamond in front of the hitter. *Never throw over or behind a batter.*

With a runner on third base. The catcher will rarely pick a runner off third base. If he does attempt this difficult throw, he must make sure to get the ball about two to three feet on the inside of the diamond. The third baseman, breaking toward the bag, cannot handle any other throw.

The throw should also be about knee high to further facilitate an easy catch by the moving fielder.

With runners on first and second bases. The catcher seldom tries to catch the runner off first base, unless his team's lead permits a gamble or both runners are loafing. A bad throw would allow the runner on second to move up a base, or even to score. Often when a double steal occurs, the man on first breaks only after he is sure the runner ahead of him is going. If the runner on second gets a good jump from a big lead, especially with a right-handed batter at the plate, the catcher may have a better chance of throwing out the runner advancing from first, since he usually starts late and does not run at full speed. The catcher should be sure, however, that the middle infielders are awake: a throwing mishap could easily mean one run.

With runners on first and third bases in an attempted double steal. The catcher throws toward second base, making a head fake—a quick look at the runner on third—in the middle of his throwing movements. The throw should be high enough so that the second baseman, who may be charging in or playing on the infield grass about half way between the pitcher and second, can either catch it or let it go to the shortstop covering the bag. If the batter is a weak hitter and an important run is on third, the catcher should bluff a full throwing motion toward second base, but right himself, and snap the ball to third for an attempted putout there. This bluff throw should be made with the feet, body, and arm motions as near to the natural position of the catcher as possible, but should not include the head fake toward third. The arm movement must be a complete follow-through as in throwing the ball to second base. Omitting the head fake usually makes the runner on third about three steps braver. If the plan of the defense is to throw the ball back to the pitcher on this double steal, the throw to the pitcher must be firm and above the pitcher's head so as to look like a throw to second base. The pitcher's motion upon catching the ball is a pivot toward third base to catch that runner off base. If he is not off far enough, continue the pivot to second base for a play there.

The catcher should watch for a delayed steal by the runner on first base. Every ball delivered should be caught with the intention of throwing the base runner out if he attempts a steal. This thought, if acted upon, should make it impossible for the runner on first base to attempt a delayed steal, as he will see that the catcher is always ready.

With bases full. In this situation the catcher must decide where the ball should go in the event of a ground ball to the infield (Does the score warrant letting the shortstop and second baseman try for a double play, second to first, or should all balls be played at the plate first?), and set the infield accordingly in advance.

The catcher should stand in front of the plate, with his right foot touching it, to receive the ball from an infielder. As he catches the ball, he should crow hop onto the infield and complete the double play to first base. The catcher must make this throw well inside the first base line. The crow hop onto the infield enables him to get out of the way of the runner coming in from third, and also gives the first baseman—who should give an inside target—a good look at the ball and a fair chance to catch it.

With runners trying to score. One great mistake made by many catchers when runners are trying to score is to play the man and then the ball instead of the ball and then the man. The catcher should never try to tag a runner before the ball is firmly in his mitt. He should brace himself firmly to withstand any collision with the runner. On this play the catcher can usually get the runner to slide away from him rather than at him if he lets the runner see part of the plate. The catcher should stand blocking half the plate, blocking off the rest only when he has received the ball. He should never take the throw in back of the plate because the runner can slide under the tag and be safe. He should not move forward to meet the ball, but wait for it, to reach the plate.

The tag itself is made with a sweeping motion, with the ball held firmly in the right hand and the mitt clasped over it. When the catcher has secured the ball properly, he will drop to his left knee to block off the plate from the sliding runner, who will usually try to touch the back half of the plate. As the catcher drops to his knee, he times his tag, applies it firmly, and then draws it away from the runner, so he will not have a chance to kick the ball away.

If the catcher ever has to make the tag up the line from home plate, he should sidestep the runner as he tags him. This will prevent a collision and possible injury. Sometimes the catcher receives the throw up the line and does not have time to sidestep the runner. In this case, where a collision is unavoidable, the catcher should take a firm grasp on the ball and then get his body as low as he can by taking a wide stance. The tag is made on impact, of course, but it is made with the arms drawn up, much like a forearm maneuver in football. Also on impact, the catcher should lift with his upper trunk. The combination of the low position, the forearm tag, and the lift, applied in very rapid succession, should send the runner over the catcher with little harm to the latter.

A perfect throw from an outfielder attempting to catch a runner at the plate is never, as a general rule, cut off by the catcher. He never rushes into the diamond to catch a perfectly thrown ball when there is a possibility of making the putout at the plate. However, if he sees that the runner will be safe, he can move out to meet the ball and make a throw to another base for a possible play there.

When a runner attempts to score, but stops before reaching the plate. The catcher gets the ball, and chases the runner at full speed toward third with the ball in throwing position, cocked at the ear. With an easy, accurate throw to the third baseman, the putout should be obtained. The catcher, when he is only fifteen feet from third, must never think he is a pitcher and throw the ball too hard for his fielder to hold. If, however, the runner is not tagged out after the throw to the third baseman and starts again for the plate, the catcher, after throwing the ball, goes to the bag at third, passing both the runner and baseman on the inside of the diamond. Home is covered by either the pitcher or the first baseman (see page 51). Should the catcher or any defensive player run into or interfere with the base runner, the base runner will be safe and will be awarded one base in advance of the last base he legally held.

With runners in scoring position. The catcher never leaves his post to back up throws to the bases when a runner is in scoring position. (An exception to this rule is explained in the next paragraph.) Otherwise, the catcher backs up first base on all throws from second, short, and third; all throws from the first baseman to the pitcher, when the latter is covering first; and all attempts for double plays with a runner on first base only.

With a runner on first base only. The catcher goes forward for all bunted balls, remembering that he must direct the play. If the ball is fielded by the third baseman, the catcher continues to third and protects that position for a possible play on the runner who was sacrificed to second base. In other words, the runner who was on first when the play began may make an attempt to advance from first to third on this bunt, and if he does so the catcher is the logical man to be at third base. The catcher will also cover third base when the shortstop and second baseman go out on short pop flies and the third baseman covers second base.

instructions to other players

In the course of a game, fielding plays arise in which the catcher must give instructions to the pitcher and to the first or third baseman. These men have their backs to any play which can be made on a bunted ball. The cut-off man has his back to the play when a runner on second base attempts to score on a base hit to the outfield. The pitcher has his back to the play when first base is occupied and a slow or hard hit ball is driven to him by the batter. The first or third baseman has his back to the play when a runner on third base is attempting to score on a fly ball to the outfield. The catcher must give instructions in a very loud voice, making sure that he can be understood. Good words to use are "Let it ride," or "Let it go," since they have a distinct sound. If the cut-off man hears nothing, he will automatically cut the throw off. To use the words "cut it" or "take it" is sometimes confusing. The opposing team's players or player on deck can yell "cut it" and have the cut-off man intercept an apparently good throw. If the defensive team never uses verbal cut-off signals, they are less likely to be confused.

The catcher must also assist his infielders who are catching pop flies near the fence, dugout, or pitcher's mound. He can easily do this by yelling "Okay," or "Room." The catcher, when possible, should get near the fielder making the play, so that he can be heard clearly and can inspire confidence.

important fielding plays

Fly balls. The catcher lets the infielders catch all fly balls when it is possible for them to do so. When a foul fly is to be caught by the catcher, he tries to get under the flight of the ball so that it appears that it will hit him on the head as it comes down. This position gives him an opportunity to step either back or forward to catch the ball squarely in his mitt.

Catching foul flies calls for speedy movements. A slight wind can blow the ball a good distance toward or away from the diamond. The direction of the wind is always an important factor in catching foul fly balls, and the catcher must make allowances for it. After much practice behind the bat in full gear, the catcher will be able to tell, by using his eyes and by listening to the sound, whether the ball swung at by the batter is a high foul fly or a slight tip, and in which direction it is going.

When the mask is removed from the catcher's face, it should be grasped firmly and quickly by the bare hand and thrown aside so that it cannot obscure the catcher's view of the ball, or hinder his footing. The mask is thrown in the opposite direction to that in which the catcher moves for the ball, and only when he knows exactly where the ball will fall.

Many catchers cannot tell, at the moment a ball is fouled, where it is going—whether to their right or left. The catcher then finds himself going around in a circle after a foul because he did not whirl in the right direction at once. If the ball delivered to a right-handed batter comes to the inside corner of the plate, and the sound of the ball against the bat denotes a foul fly, the catcher should whirl to the left, and as his body is turning, pull the mask from his face and look up. The ball is then easy to find. If the ball is delivered to the outside corner of the plate, the catcher turns to the right, pulls off his mask, and looks up for the ball. It is practically impossible for an inside pitch to a right-handed batter to be fouled over the catcher's right shoulder, and it is also practically impossible for an outside pitch to be fouled over his left shoulder, unless the catcher is in a most awkward position.

The same rule is reversed with a left-handed man at bat. The inside pitch is fouled over the catcher's right shoulder, the outside pitch over his left shoulder. All balls popped *directly up in the air* tend to come down in an arc toward the infield. This ball should be fielded in front of the body if the catcher's back is toward the infield. If his face is toward the field, the ball should be caught as if it were going to land on his head. In either case, the catcher should keep his weight on his toes and his knees flexed. If the ball is in the sun, the eyes are shaded by the bare hand, held with fingers spread and palm down ready to clap over the ball when caught.

Bunts. The catcher should be ready to go forward from his catching position whenever the batter drops his bat to bunt, or a swinging bunt is made. Many bunts can and should be fielded by the catcher. A bunt should never be fielded with one hand when both the mitt and the bare hand can be used. The mitt is placed in front of a rolling, twisting bunt to stop it; the ball is then picked up from the ground with both hands. If the bunted ball has stopped, practically the same procedure is used except that the mitt is placed in front of and beyond the ball, which is then picked up with the aid of the bare hand in a clapping motion. The eyes should never be taken from the ball until it is firmly held in the mitt and hand.

It is essential that the catcher assume his correct throwing position as soon as he has fielded a bunt. On bunted balls down the third base line, the catcher charges slightly to his left, moving into the ball and toward the base where the throw is to be made. On bunts along the first base line, the catcher must field the ball, and then shift into the infield to avoid hitting the baserunner with the throw to first base. Throws to second and third base are made from the spot where the ball is fielded, with only a crow hop used to gain power and direction.

Quiz on Catching

1. What is the correct position of a catcher in giving signals to his pitcher? What should a catcher use for signals? How many signals should he have?
2. What position should a catcher assume to catch high pitched balls? Low balls? Balls that hit the ground?
3. State the arguments for and against tall and short catchers.
4. State every situation in which a catcher may at times make dangerous throws to bases occupied by runners.
5. What common mistakes do catchers make with regard to runners trying to score when the ball is thrown to them for the putout?
6. Name four plays in which the catcher must give instructions to his fellow players.
7. Describe the foot action of a catcher when he has signaled for a waste ball to be pitched.
8. When should a catcher back up first base?
9. When should the catcher be in a position to take a throw at third base?

10. How can a catcher advise his pitcher to pitch to batters when he knows their hitting ability?
11. How can a catcher instill confidence in his team?
12. How can a catcher break up a double steal with runners on first and third bases?
13. When a run-down play is being made between third base and home plate, what must the catcher, who ran after the baserunner, do as soon as he throws the ball to the player covering third? Why?
14. How should a catcher catch the ball at the plate for an attempted double play, the first out being made at the plate? How should he make his throw to first base? Why?
15. What should be the thought of the catcher at all times when there is a runner on first base?
16. Explain how to catch a foul fly.
17. How should the catcher field a bunted ball?

the qualifications of an infielder

An infielder must first of all be able to field ground balls. Sometimes he has to go back from his position into the outfield to catch a fly ball over his shoulder, but his ability to do that is not so important as his ability to handle grounders. The infielder must have the right kind of wrists, and the way he uses his wrists constitutes a big factor in the defensive success of his team. A man with rigid wrists can never become a great infielder. The wrists must always be loose and flexible; in most cases the ball will rebound from the hands of the player with rigid forearms and wrists.

Proper use of the glove and hands in fielding grounders and in catching low thrown balls is a very important asset to the infielder. The face of the glove and the palm of the other hand both face the ball as it comes. Thus the greatest possible area is presented to stop the grounder or pick up the low thrown ball. Practice fielding balls with a flat catching glove or new catching glove. This will help teach the proper movement of hands, wrists, and arms.

The good infielder has keen, accurate eyes and is capable of quick and sure foot movements. He can throw with great accuracy and considerable speed, even in a quick play which gives him little opportunity to set himself for the throw after receiving the ball.

the infielder's game

primary duties of the infielder

As is true of almost every team sport, expert play in baseball, regardless of the position, requires more than simply talent and desire. Certainly a combination of these qualities is essential, but other factors are involved in developing good infield play. It is probably more true of infield than outfield play that the player must strive not only for individual excellence, but also to learn to play "team ball." He needs to know the fundamentals of infield play and to master the particular techniques of his own position. For example, the double play is the type of individual and team play that is perhaps the most important and exciting to execute and watch. Generally speaking, it requires from 3.3 to 5.0 seconds for a player to run from home plate to first base, with the average speed varying from 4.2 to 4.5 seconds. This means that a double play cannot take more than from 3.5 to 4.5 seconds. Such skill and coordination do not often come naturally, but require a lot of practice and hard work.

Some of the important fundamentals all infielders should know and attempt to master follow.

The condition of the field, the wind, and the sun. The decision of where to play—deep or shallow—and whether to drift to the right or left, is affected by the playing surface, the direction and speed of the wind, and the position of the sun.

A dry, hard infield, or one on which the grass has been cut very close, is likely to cause a ground ball to travel faster and hop higher. Under these conditions, it may be necessary for the infielder to play a little deeper than he normally would. On the other hand, a wet, soft infield, or one on which the grass is relatively high, will play "slow"—that is, the ball will take longer to get to an infielder if he is playing his normal position. In this case, the infielder may have to move in closer in order to make a rapid and accurate play, especially if the batter is a fast runner.

The wind can also complicate the work of the infielder—especially in the case of high pop flies, which are difficult to judge in a stiff, shifting breeze. The direction and velocity of the wind should be checked every inning as the wind can shift in a matter of a few seconds. The most common way to get this information is by observing a flag flying in the park. This will give a pretty accurate idea of the direction of the wind, and the flapping motion of the flag will also tell whether the wind is blowing steadily in one direction, or in gusts, and whether it is a mild or a stiff breeze. Another common practice of the infielder is to toss some dirt or grass into the air from his position, and observe how it behaves.

A third condition that can be serious is the position of the sun. In playing balls hit into the sun, most players have found that the best way to shade their eyes is with the glove rather than the hand, and instead of facing the ball as it drops, they prefer to turn the body sideways to make the catch. It is wise to have the infielders decide ahead of time how they will play pop-ups hit into the sun. It is usually much easier for the infielder who is moving sideways toward the pop-up to make the play than for the infielder who has to look up into the sun, even though he may be closer to the play. Examples are balls popped up behind the first baseman or third baseman near the foul line. These are taken by the second baseman or shortstop in most cases.

If the sun is low and directly behind the batter, an infielder should play the sun rather than the batter. In other words, instead of playing the batter normally, the infielder should move to the left or right, depending on the batter's strength. This may mean the infielder will be playing out of position or away from the spot where the batter generally hits. In this case, the infielder must be ready to break for the spot he vacated in order to avoid looking into the sun. This also holds true for outfield play.

Before the pitch is made to the batter, an infielder should decide what to do with the ball, depending on what kind of hit is made, should also be thinking about the speed of the batter and any other runners already on base.

The position of the body at the time the pitch is made to the batter and before the ball is hit is extremely important: (1) the hands should be kept off the knees and held low and in front of the body; (2) the feet should be about shoulder width apart and pointing straight toward home plate with the toes turned slightly in; (3) the weight of the body should be on the balls of the feet; and (4) the knees should be bent slightly and the tail kept down in order to be able to break in any direction (see Figure 13).

An infielder should not let the ball play him, nor should he wait for the ball to come to him. On the other hand, he should not charge the ball before it is hit. What he can do is take a short, choppy 1-2 step just as the pitcher throws: the first step coming and landing as the pitcher strides, and the second as the pitcher takes his follow-through step. This 1-2 step can be taken at the infielder's position or slightly in front of it.

The infielder keeps his eyes on the pitcher until the pitcher makes his stride to the plate, at which time the infielder's eyes should move to the area of home plate where the ball will meet the bat. He then watches the pitch to the batter out of the corner of his eye. By looking at this area the fielder actually sees the ball meet the bat. He can then determine more easily the direction in which the ball will be hit. *Remember, the eyes move, not the head.*

If the infielder watches the catcher's signals, he can often come up with balls that might have gone for base hits. However, the infielder must be careful not to move so quickly as to give away the sign to the

figure **13**   figure **14**

batter. Actually, good timing by the infielder is more the result of his mental anticipation than of his physical movement to where the ball is likely to be hit.

After the pitch has been made, an infielder should keep his eyes on the ball, expecting not only that every ball will be hit to him, but also that they will all take bad hops. This is just another way of saying that an infielder should be prepared for any kind of ball hit to his position.

When fielding a ball, the infielder's wrists should be relaxed. He should watch the ball all the way into his glove, and instead of fighting it, should let it settle into its nest. Many errors result because the infielder raises his head and eyes just at the moment he is fielding a ground ball. In the case of the right-handed infielder, his legs are spread and his left foot is forward of his right foot. He fields the ball toward his right leg. Spreading the legs keeps the glove down and the knees out of the way (see Figure 14).

Another general fielding tip for the infielder is to keep his hands well out in front of his body; he should never attempt to field a ball under himself. He should keep his glove low and "dig dirt": it is much easier to bring the glove up on a ball than down on the ball.

Control of throws. The infielder makes a number of throws during the course of a game and it is important that he throw the ball where it should go. This means having control of the ball before throwing it. After catching the ball, he should step in the direction of the target, bringing the ball close to, but not against, his body before throwing. Although the overhand throw is the strongest, most accurate, and least strenuous to make, it is not the only throw "in the book." At times, it will be necessary to throw sidearm or even underhand; the main thing is to be fast and accurate. On double plays, the infielder should practice until he can make any and all types of throws from whatever position he is in when he gets the ball.

During infield practice, the infielder should make all the throws he might make during the game. On the double play from the first baseman, for example, it is a good idea for the shortstop to practice throwing to third base instead of always to first. This routine serves as practice for catching the runner who was on second base and rounds third too far in a double play situation where the batter cannot be put out at first after the force has been completed at second base.

A cardinal rule for the infielder is never to throw the ball if there is no chance to put out the runner. It is better to bluff the throw and try to catch another runner attempting to take an extra base on the throw he expected you to make. Always be alert for the alternative play, especially when an error or a wrong judgment has been made. For instance, many players overrun bases when expecting an infielder to throw to first base; as a result, numerous base runners are thrown out at second or third base by the alert infielder who makes the alternate play.

"Heads up" baseball is just as important as throwing and catching the ball. An infielder, for example, should never leave a base uncovered. This is especially important when a base on balls is given to the batter because, if second base is not covered, the runner may break for and reach that base. With a runner on third base, it is important to be alert for a possible overthrow of the pitcher to the catcher. When your teammate goes out for a fly ball be certain all bases are covered.

The good infielder must have no fear of a sliding base runner. The infielder should never go after the runner—he lets the runner come to him. On tags, go for the base where the runner must come.

When making the tag on the base runner, the bag should be straddled if possible, and the tag made by dropping the gloved ball to the bag so that the runner tags himself out. The ball should not be in the palm of the glove facing the runner, but in the web, with the back of the web and the thumb facing the runner. This will prevent the ball from being kicked out of the glove by the sliding runner. It is advisable to hold the ball approximately twelve inches above the base and to bring it down just as the runner approaches the bag. The glove and ball are brought up and away from the slider upon contact (see Figure 15).

If there is a runner on second base, it is often advantageous to dive and try to knock down ground balls that cannot be fielded with normal effort. While no putout may result when the infielder knocks the ball down, he may have prevented a run from scoring. This, again, is one of those "team plays."

On hits to the outfield, the infielder should hold his hands high to give the outfielder a good target to throw to. The throw from the outfield should be taken by the infielder on his glove side, about head-high whenever possible. The outfielder should make his throw head-high and about two to three feet out from the relay man on the glove side. This allows for an inaccurate throw. Should the throw come closer than this distance to the relay man, he is still in a good position to throw. If the throw is further away than three feet, it is a simple matter for the relay man to move toward the ball and he can still make a good throw.

On extra base hits, the second baseman goes out to act as the relay man whenever the ball is hit to right and right center fields, with the shortstop covering second base. On balls hit to left or left center field, the shortstop goes out to act as relay man and the second baseman covers second. In the case of balls hit directly to center field, the infielder with the best throwing arm acts as relay man. The first baseman, if he has a good arm, acts as relay man on all extra base hits along the right field foul line if there is a possibility of a run scoring on the hit.

Pop flies. The shortstop takes most pop flies behind third base and the second baseman takes most of the pop flies behind first base. It is easier for them to make these plays since they are moving toward the line and the ball. The first and third basemen have more difficulty because they have to back up on the ball. Each infielder calls for and handles pop flies in his area. The infielder should not call until he is certain of making the catch.

figure **15**

Outfield flies can be very tough to handle unless the infielder works together with the outfielders. As far as the infielder is concerned, every outfield pop fly is his play unless the outfielder calls him off. Although concentrating on making his play, the infielder should always be listening for the outfielder calling, "I have it!", or "Take it!". The outfielder should make this call several times and loud enough for the coach or the manager on the bench to hear. A third player should never do the calling on these outfield pop flies. An infielder can simply wave his arms if he can catch the ball, and the outfielder should control the play from his vantage point of coming in on the play. If the outfielder calls for the ball, the infielder steps out of the way and yells, "Take it!".

The infielder can use his voice to great advantage. He should continually call the number of outs to his teammates, chatter to the pitcher, and remind other players of specific defensive moves.

All of the foregoing points up the fact that the infielder's choice of position—deep or shallow—depends on a number of factors. These include the fielding and throwing ability of the infielder; the condition of the field, the wind, and the sun; the game situation; the speed of the batter; the type of hitter; and the position from which the infielder can best cover the most ground to field the ball.

The advantages and disadvantages of playing deep or shallow can be demonstrated by the coach. By placing one infielder about ten or fifteen feet in front of another during practice, he can show them how much ground can be covered from each position. The ball can be hit to their right and left, with both infielders breaking for the ball. The infielder playing in should be able to make a play on practically every ball the deep man can get, and perhaps on even more. It is understood that the deep man will probably catch more balls, but he will not be able to make a successful throw.

catching runners off base

The key to all run-down plays is to get the runner moving at full speed. He, therefore, must be chased at full speed. Only infielders should handle the ball when runners are caught off bases. Three men should be engaged in the play, and the unvarying rule should be this: Every time one player throws the ball to another, the one making the throw takes the position left vacant by the one receiving it. The following examples illustrate this rule:

When a runner is caught off first base. The first baseman starts the runner toward second base. The second baseman breaks for and protects the first baseman's position. Should the second baseman fail to get to first base, the pitcher must cover it. The shortstop, protecting second base, catches the ball thrown to him by the first baseman and again starts the runner in the opposite direction, making the putout at first base. The first baseman passes both the runner and the shortstop on the side opposite his throwing arm, and takes the protecting position at second base. The putout should be made at the base from which the play started.

When a runner is caught off second base by either the shortstop or the second baseman. The player catching the ball starts the runner toward third base and throws the ball to the third baseman, who in turn chases the runner back toward second, where the putout is made by the other infielder who remained there. The player making the throw to the third baseman takes the protecting position at third base.

When a runner is caught off third base. The third baseman chases the runner toward the plate and the shortstop takes third base. The former throws the ball to the catcher, who in turn chases the runner almost back to third and makes the assisted putout at that bag, the third baseman protecting the plate.

When a runner is undecided. When a runner stops between bases, apparently undecided as to which base to approach, the infielder having the ball should rush directly at him and attempt to make the putout at the base which the runner left when the play began. If the putout is not made at this base, the infielder who threw the ball to the base takes the baseman's position when that basemen chases the runner in a run-down play. It should be noted that whenever the basemen, without the ball, exchange positions, caution should be used not to interfere with the runner. Interference here will allow the runner to advance one base.

notes on the infield game

Whenever a defensive player takes a step to complete a play, a base runner is also taking a step to reach his base. Every possible time saving and movement saving tactic should be used by the defensive infielder.

With two out, an infielder should never make a long throw for an assisted out when a short throw will retire the runner; and it is preferable, whenever possible, for the fielder to tag the base instead of throwing the ball.

Fly balls caught or relay throws received should never be thrown by an infielder unless he is instructed to do so by another infielder. The player catching a relay throw should run toward the infield but he should never "challenge" a runner to advance a base on the "afraid to throw" play.

Infielders should always play ground balls instead of allowing ground balls to play them—by coming in rapidly toward the ball and catching it on a good, straight bound, if possible. Don't overcharge the ball, but never lay back.

Infielders should watch any runner approaching a base, and be sure he touches that base. If a runner misses any base, the umpire's attention should be called to the fact by going to the bag with a ball that is still in play (or with a new ball put in play by having the pitcher step on the rubber, back off, and throw it to a player who touches the bag missed). The player must, with his voice, call the umpire's attention to the play.

When there is a runner on third, the infield is playing close, and a putout is attempted at home plate, the catcher may have a run-down play to make. In that event it is advisable for the infielder making the throw to the catcher to continue to the plate in order to protect that position. There is, however, an exception to this rule: if the ball is hit to the pitcher, then the first baseman protects the catcher's position at the plate and the second baseman protects first base. Years of college coaching have proved to us that an infielder will make a better throw to the catcher if he knows that he must cover the plate for the possible run-down play. There may also be an occasion when the third baseman throwing the ball will have to cover third base. The runner may not be making an all out run for home plate.

Infielders should understand and be sure of the catcher's signals to the pitcher. When the catcher is in a squatting position, every infielder should be looking at him in order to obtain the signals, as these will help them in covering their respective territories. For example, if the catcher shows by his signal that a curve ball is to be pitched to a left-handed batter, and if the curve ball is pitched correctly, right field will be the only place where the ball normally can be hit—a wonderful thing for the players playing in the right field territory to know. They can get a start on the ball even before it is hit. It is a real asset to know when a change up or slow ball will be thrown: this pitch is normally pulled. If the third baseman or first baseman can't see the signs—and usually they can't—the sign can be relayed by the other infielders by a code word.

Infielders must be sure that the bases are within the boundary lines of the diamond. This is very important, especially for the first and third basemen. Both of these players should, before taking their positions, kick the base bags into a position so that the outer edge of the bag coincides with the outer edge of the base lines—the chalk or line markings designating the boundary lines of the playing field. According to definition, a batted ball that touches first base or third base is a fair hit. If any part of either first or third base happens to be outside the boundary lines and is hit by a batted ball, the umpire must declare it a fair hit.

Infielders sometimes find, after a run-down play has been completed, two base runners occupying the same base at the same time. The defensive player must not forget that the runner who originally was on the base is entitled to it. Often a defensive player can, after tagging both runners with the ball, say "you are out" to the runner entitled to the base and cause him to step from the bag. Retouching this player with the ball, after he steps off the base, completes a double play which otherwise could not have been completed.

All infielders should watch the following play, which often comes up in a ball game. When there is a runner on first base and a long fly ball is hit to the outfield (probably an offensive hit-and-run play), on which the runner passes second base before the ball is caught, he must make an effort to return to first. In so doing he often fails to touch the bag at second base. This case is covered fully in the rules, which state that a base runner returning to a base while the ball is in play must touch intervening bases in reverse order or be declared out upon the ball's being held by a fielder on any base he failed to retouch or on being touched with the ball in the hands of a fielder.

infield fly rule

All members of the baseball squad should know when an infield fly is hit. Many players have a mistaken impression that the infield fly rule is operative with a runner on first only, or with runners on first and third bases—this is not so. The rule was made to prevent a player from trapping the ball and starting a double play. When there is a runner on first base only and a batter hits a high fly which can be caught by an infielder, there is a certainty that one player will be put out, but with a runner of ordinary speed, there is practically no chance of two men being put out.

The rule, a very important one, states that: "The batter is out if, before two are out, while first and second, or first, second, and third bases are occupied, he hits a *fair* fly ball, other than a line drive, that can be handled by an infielder. In such cases, the umpire shall declare it an infield fly; but the runners may be off their bases or advance at the risk of the ball being caught, the same as on any other fly ball. Provided that, with first and second bases occupied, or first, second and third bases occupied, with less than two out, any attempt to bunt which results in a fair fly ball shall not be regarded as an infield fly."

It is important to note, first, that for any fly ball to be considered an infield fly by the umpire, the fly must be a fair ball. Then note that the runners may be off their bases, or that they may advance at the risk of the fly being caught, the same as on any fly ball. Also, note that an attempt to bunt which results in a fair fly ball is not to be considered an infield fly. The umpire must immediately declare a fly ball an infield fly if he thinks such a batted ball is an infield fly and will drop in fair territory.

1. What are the qualifications which should decide the selection of a man for an infield position?
2. How should an infielder field ground balls?
3. If a defensive play catches a runner off first base, how shall the putout be made in the resulting run-down play?
4. Suppose a base runner is caught off second base, how should the putout be made in the resulting run-down play?
5. If a runner, caught off third base by a throw from the catcher, starts for the plate, how should the putout be made?
6. How should an infielder tag a runner coming into the bag which he is protecting?
7. What should be done with a runner who stops half way between bases?
8. What should an infielder do the moment a batter steps up to the plate?
9. What should be done on all infield fly balls? State the infield fly rule.
10. If an opponent makes a three base hit, what are the duties of all the players within the diamond? Why is this so important?
11. If there is a runner on third base, state every infield play which can be made on this runner and the final position of each infielder.

True and false

1. The third baseman takes all pop flies on the third base side of the field.
2. Infielders make all their throws overhand.
3. Infielders should make their tag plays with the ball held firmly in the hand.
4. Infielders should shield their eyes from the sun with their gloves.
5. Infielders should always watch outfielders make their plays.
6. Infielders should never watch base runners.
7. Infielders should always have their feet together when fielding ground balls.
8. Infielders should always lift their heads before fielding a ground ball in order to see where the runner is.
9. Infielders should always try for a possible force play on a fumbled ball.
10. Infielders should always allow their pitcher to catch all the fly balls he can catch.
11. Infielders should allow their catcher to catch fly balls which they themselves could catch.

The old saying that first base is the easiest position to play is not true. A first baseman should be of medium size or tall, with a good reach, and he must have extraordinary ability to make pickups of low thrown balls from the infielders. He must at all times maintain perfect balance on his feet.

playing position of the first baseman

The first baseman never plays so far away from the first base bag that it is difficult for him to reach it in time to catch a throw. His feet are stationary, with heels touching the corners of the bag, a little before a thrown ball reaches him, and he is ready to shift them instantly if the throw happens to be wide of the base. The first baseman should stretch out as far as possible in order to meet the ball. In the case of a good throw or a pickup on which the first baseman has to stretch, his eyes should never be taken from the ball.

A low thrown ball, a pickup, or an inaccurately thrown ball coming to the first baseman on a long bound, are fielding plays in which good judgment must be used. For a pickup, the body is stretched forward as far as possible, with the pivot foot on the bag. The striding foot is extended toward the fielder throwing the ball, and slightly to the side of the path of the ball. The hands are in proper position, the fingers pointing toward the dirt and the ball. For really bad throws that bounce some distance

playing first base

figure **16**

from the base, the first baseman often has to back up, and with one foot on the bag, catch the ball in foul territory. Practice on such low, bounding throws coming from different angles, with the coach throwing balls at the first baseman standing against a fence, should make the first baseman proficient.

For a throw to the left side of the bag, the first baseman changes the position of his feet so that his right foot is in contact with the bag and his left foot far enough away to guarantee his catching the ball. For a throw to the right side, the first baseman changes the position of his feet so that his left foot is in contact with the bag and his right foot is extended far enough to catch the ball. For all throws directly in front of the bag, the right-handed first baseman places his right foot in contact with the bag and extends his left foot as far as possible in the direction of the throw. The left-handed first baseman keeps his left foot on the bag and extends his right foot. The first baseman will thus be able to reach farther toward the ball and will be in correct position to make a quick throw to another infielder if the situation demands it (see Figure 16).

Should the first baseman not be able to shift easily, it is perfectly all right to let the right-handed player tag the bag with his right foot at all times and stretch from there. The left-hander tags with his left foot. If they use the corners of the bag on throws to the side, they will be able to cover more territory and still do a good job.

The actual tag of the bag should be made by throwing the foot sideways with the inside of the ankle pointing toward the ground (Figure 16). This helps keep the toe in contact with the bag on a long stretch. In the stretch for the ball, the best way to insure not coming off the bag on the catch is to have the toe of the pivot foot in contact with the bag, then step toward the ball, and have the ball come in contact with the glove just as the striding foot hits the ground. Often, on a long stretch, when the striding foot hits the ground before the ball hits the glove, the pivot foot will be pulled off the bag. The first baseman will then have to kick back at the bag. In the kick back, the bag is frequently missed.

The first baseman, who has to handle and catch more bad throws than any other player on the team, should be able to catch balls thrown to him by fellow players with the gloved hand alone. Constant practice should be given to catching the ball with the gloved hand, but the gloved hand alone should never be used when both can be put on the ball.

Many times the throw comes to the first baseman on the left side of the bag directly in the path of the runner coming from the plate. This is the first baseman's hardest play. He must catch the ball with his gloved hand, and with almost the same motion, pivot on his striding foot, and, changing feet, jump away from the base line into the infield. It is advisable, if there is time enough, to step completely off the bag to catch the ball and to touch the runner with both hands. Whether the tag is made on the runner's back or front, the first baseman pivots counterclockwise with the runner. The runner may stop and go back toward the plate, but he is not out until he has been legally retired. This can be done by touching the runner with the ball, by stepping on first base, or by chasing the runner back beyond his legal base running lines. It is advisable either to touch the runner with the ball or to retire him legally at first base, whichever gives any other opposing runner the least possible chance of advancing a base while the putout is being made.

The first baseman makes every possible effort to get a ground ball that comes into his territory, but he should not go so far away from his position in fielding ground balls as to invade the territory of the second baseman. Fielding practice should teach the first baseman just how far he may go for grounders. Whenever the first baseman goes after a ground ball, the pitcher covers his base for him. In this event, the first baseman should make his throw to the pitcher so that it can be caught about shoulder high, at least two steps from the bag. This throw is very important as the pitcher must catch the ball on the run and then tag the bag. The pitcher cannot catch a low thrown ball and make this play successfully. The first baseman never tosses the ball to the pitcher unless he is very close; he throws it. Any player can throw a ball more accurately than he can toss it. The first baseman should set himself for this play and then throw the ball at the pitcher with some speed on it. The speedy throw is much easier to catch than a mere lob of the ball. Most pitchers prefer this kind of throw when the first baseman is some distance from the bag.

To prevent a runner on first base from obtaining a big lead toward second, the first baseman stands with the right foot firmly on the ground near the front corner (the one nearest the pitcher) of the bag and the other foot out in front (the part nearest the catcher and the foul line) of the bag, facing the pitcher, so that the weight of the body maintains a perfect balance. This is not exactly the starting position recommended for a sprinter's feet, but it is very similar to it. The first baseman must be able to make a quick break off the bag down the line toward second base to be in a fielding position for the batted ball. He does not break until the pitch is made. He breaks by taking two large jump steps, and faces the hitter. Caution should be used to keep the runner from getting between the hitter and the first baseman.

Often the pitcher makes an attempt, with a quick throw, to catch a runner off first base. The first baseman then catches the ball and puts it on the runner with almost the same motion. Go to the bag with the ball.

Going after the runner gives him an opportunity to slide around the ball. If at any time a runner is caught off the base so far away from the bag that he practically decides to give himself up for an out, the first baseman must be careful to tag the runner and not let him make a slide around him and into the bag safely. The first baseman gives the pitcher a target on pick-offs by holding the glove just off his right knee.

first base strategy

When a runner is on first base and the situation prompts a bunt. The first baseman comes from the bag toward the plate, but not too quickly. The batter may be expected to tip-off the bunt, by dropping the bat, just as he is attempting to bunt. If and when he does so, the first baseman charges quickly toward the plate for the possible forced play at second base. The catcher gives instructions in regard to this play. If the ball is bunted toward third base, the first baseman, if possible, returns to the first base bag for the putout. However, he should never interfere with the second baseman. As soon as the putout is made, he rushes into the diamond toward third to be in a position to stop any attempt of the sacrificed runner to advance to third.

When a runner is on first base, not a bunt situation. The first baseman holds the runner closely to the base. At times very hard balls are hit toward the first baseman, and the runner on first cannot judge whether the ball will be caught on a pickup or on the fly. If the first baseman makes a pickup, he touches the runner with the ball and then the bag—for a double play. If the first baseman touches the bag and then the runner who has returned to the bag, it is not a double play.

Many games have been lost in late innings because a first baseman, after fielding a ground ball, touched the first base bag before throwing to second base in an attempt to make a double play. When the first out is made at first base, the force is off at second. The runner may slide safely into second or get himself into a run-down until another runner scores. The first thought of the first baseman should be to keep the winning run as far from home plate as possible. Thus, the first out should always be attempted at second base, provided the ball hit to the first baseman is not fielded directly over the first base bag. The first baseman throws to shortstop, at second, on the inside of the diamond, taking care not to hit the runner. Any time the first baseman tags the bag first, he must yell loud and clear to the shortstop or second baseman to tag the runner.

When a ball is hit to the outfield, the first baseman plays his base until all possibility for a play to him has vanished. He then gets in a cut-off position, backs up second base, or trails the runner into second base on obvious extra base hits. Should the runner round the base too far, the first baseman could receive the ball from the relay man for a pick off play.

If the runner starts to steal second base, the first baseman should call out, "There he goes!", as loudly as possible. These three words will inform the catcher that the runner is stealing, and he will throw the ball directly to the bag at second.

In the event of a base hit to the outfield, the first baseman plays the bag for a possible run-down play.

If a runner caught off first base breaks fast for second, the first baseman throws the ball immediately to the shortstop, who is covering that bag, and returns to first for the putout in the run-down play. The second baseman protects the bag left vacant by the shortstop. If the runner breaks slowly, the first baseman runs him more than halfway to second base and then throws to the shortstop at second base, who in turn chases the runner back to first base for the putout there, the second baseman or the pitcher protecting that position (or possibly the catcher, if this is the only runner on base). The first baseman, after throwing the ball to the shortstop, takes the latter's position on second base.

With a runner on second base. The first baseman plays his position on base hits to the outfield. He backs up third base, however, whenever possible, on all fly balls to the outfield *which should be fielded*. If the throw goes from the outfielder to second base, the first baseman is in a position to back up that base without much lost motion on his part. If an out is attempted on the batter at first base, the first baseman should, as soon as he catches the ball for the putout, rush toward third base or the catcher, depending on where the runner is at the time of the putout, thus defending against a possible attempt by the base runner to advance.

With a runner on third base (close infield). If the runner attempts to score on a ground ball hit to the first baseman, the latter, after fielding and throwing the ball to the catcher, runs on to the plate in order to protect that position for a possible run-down play if the catcher chases the runner back to third.

The first baseman also backs up home plate whenever a ground ball is hit to the pitcher while a runner is trying to score from third base, the second baseman protecting first base. He should not break for home until he is certain the pitcher is throwing to the plate.

When a fly ball is hit to either right field or center field, the first baseman takes a position in the diamond such that, when the. ball is thrown to the plate, he can catch it in the air. In other words, the position of the first baseman in the diamond should be such that if he side-steps the throw by the outfielder, at the call of the catcher, it will make a perfect hop from where it hits the ground to the plate. If the first baseman is in the proper position, a good throw will bring about the desired result. The first baseman should, without any instructions whatever, catch all balls which are wildly thrown to the position he has taken. In the absence of instructions from the catcher, however, the first baseman should take the throw in order to attempt any other play that may be available. Whenever the cut-off man, in this case the first baseman, allows the ball to go to the catcher, he should make a fake catch of the ball, thus decoying the batter and/or other runners. Often this keeps them from attempting to advance another base.

When a fly ball is hit to left field under the same conditions, the first baseman, together with the pitcher, should back up the catcher.

With runners on first and second bases. If the situation prompts a bunt, the first baseman plays off the bag about halfway between the pitching box and first base. If the bat drops, indicating the batter's intention to bunt, the first baseman rushes toward the plate for the bunt and throws the ball as directed by the catcher.

If the situation does not prompt a bunt, the first baseman plays off his base just as he would without a runner on first base. The one exception to this rule is when the batter is a sure left-field hitter. In that case, the first baseman should hold the runner as closely as possible to the first base bag by standing a few feet behind the base line, not on the bag but in a direct line with his regular position. If the batter is a sure right-field hitter, the first baseman stands in his regular position behind the base line.

If a double play is being attempted from second base, the first baseman does not wait for the umpire to make his decision at either second or first base. As soon as he catches the ball, he rushes toward home plate and, if possible, makes a play on the runner who was on second base. The same play attempted by the first baseman when only second base is occupied and the putout is made at first.

If a double play is attempted on a ground ball to the first baseman, the first baseman should be sure that his throw to second base is perfect for the first putout. When the first baseman is back in a deep position, he throws to the outside of the diamond, taking care not to hit the runner in the back. In nearly every position the throw should be made overhand. However, there are times when the throw must be made sidearm or underhand. As the ball leaves his hand, the first baseman starts for first base for the completion of the double play, first to second to first. Many times the first baseman will make the first part of this play and find himself at an unaccustomed angle to the position of the first base bag—that is, in a position on the field from which he must see the bag before running to it. It is a good idea for the first baseman, as soon as he has thrown the ball for the first putout, to glance at the bag and then return his eyes to the throw coming from second base. Practice on this play will teach the first baseman how best to look at the first base bag as he starts for it and to see the thrown ball as it comes toward him.

With runners on first, second and third bases. If a double play is being attempted from an infielder to the catcher to the first baseman, the first baseman should take the throw from the catcher on the inside of the first base bag. He should use his voice, yelling, "Inside, Inside." His left foot should be against the bag and his right foot on the infield.

With runners on first and third bases. If a pitchout is called for on a double steal attempt, the first baseman follows the runner toward second base as soon as the ball has left the pitcher's hand. The first baseman should run as rapidly as the runner, so that if the runner stops before reaching second base, the first baseman will be in a good position to receive the ball from the shortstop or second baseman covering second base, make the putout, and throw to the catcher before the runner on third can possibly cross the plate for a run. The pitcher, immediately after throwing the pitch out, breaks for first base and protects it for a possible run-down play.

If the runner on third starts for the plate and stops between bases, the first baseman, if he has the ball, should rush at him and make the assist for the putout at third if possible. He should not throw the ball until the runner has committed himself to a base.

In all other situations, the first baseman plays his position as though there were a man on first base only.

Quiz on first base playing

1. What are the natural requirements for a first baseman?
2. Describe the position of the feet when a first baseman is taking a throw from another infielder.
3. State the duty of the first baseman when a runner is caught off first base.
4. What should a first baseman keep in mind when giving the ball to a pitcher covering first base for an attempted putout?
5. List the duties of a first baseman when a runner is on first base and the situation prompts a bunt. When runners are on first and second bases in the same situation.
6. With a runner on second base and an out being attempted at first, what should be the uppermost thought in the mind of a first baseman?
7. With runners on first and second bases and an out being attempted at first, what should be the uppermost thought in the mind of the first baseman?
8. Describe the action of the first baseman when a ball is hit hard to his right. When a slow ball is hit to his right.
9. What is the position of the first baseman when, with a runner on third base and one out, a fly ball is hit to right field?
10. State the play to be made when a ground ball is hit to the first baseman with a runner on third base attempting to score.

11. How should a first baseman play a ball which is thrown into a base runner coming toward first from the plate?
12. What should the first baseman do when the pitcher makes a wild throw to the plate with a runner on second base?
13. With a runner on first base, none or one out, what play should be made on a slow hit ball to the first baseman? A hard hit ball? A hard hit ball which is fumbled?
14. In what manner should a first baseman play a ball, thrown by an infielder, which hits the ground and makes a long hop? A wide throw? Short hops?
15. When a runner is advanced to second base on a sacrifice bunt, what is the duty of the first baseman if he has made the putout at first base?
16. With a runner on first base, two men out, the batter hits a ground ball to the first baseman. What is important?
17. With runners on first and second bases, a ground ball is fielded and thrown to the shortstop at second base for the start and completion of a double play. What should the first baseman do?

the second baseman

The second baseman, without regard to stature, should be fast on his feet and able to throw from any position. He must be a good judge of fly balls, and he must be able to catch balls that are thrown low. He must have a strong throwing arm and be able to pivot—the move upon which the success of a double play often depends. His natural throw should be sidearm across the chest, but he must be able to make the throw—whether overhand or underhand—that is fastest in the situation. The second baseman must also be a very quick thinker who can anticipate every sort of play.

second base strategy

With a runner on first base and none out, the situation prompting a bunt. There is a defense play which can be made in this situation, provided the runner is lax in his base running, when the first baseman goes toward the plate for the attempted bunt. By a prearranged signal between the catcher and the second baseman, a waste pitch is thrown. The moment the first baseman starts his break toward the plate, the second baseman starts for first and reaches that bag at the time a throw from the catcher arrives. The waste pitch, if a curve ball, may make the batter reach out farther toward the ball, thus fooling the base runner.

playing second base 5

The second baseman plays his regular position and watches the batter closely. If the batter drops his bat, the second baseman breaks for and covers first base for the putout. As soon as the putout is made, he rushes toward third base to be in a position to stop the sacrificed runner's attempt to advance to third. It is best for the second baseman to come to first base from the outfield side of the diamond near the line, rather than directly from his position. Doing so gives him a chance to meet the throw coming directly toward him, instead of taking the ball on the run at an angle to the throw. This position also gives the second baseman an opportunity to shift his feet to catch a wild throw at first base. If the first baseman comes back to the bag for the putout, the second baseman immediately vacates the bag and backs up the play. It must be assumed that the right fielder will also be backing up this play at first base.

If a runner is caught off first base by a pitcher's quick throw and the first baseman chases the runner toward second, the second baseman protects first base on the run-down play which naturally follows. There is one exception: if the runner breaks fast for second, the first baseman throws the ball to second base just as soon as the shortstop gets there, and returns immediately to first for the attempted out on the run-back by the shortstop. The second base bag, in this case, is protected by the second baseman.

With a runner on first base; a base hit to right field. The second baseman goes toward the outfielder in order to receive a possible relay throw. If the hit is fielded cleanly, the second baseman shouts throwing instructions to the outfielder and covers second base or backs up the short-stop, who may be making a play on the batter at second base on a throw from right fielder to third baseman to shortstop. If the base hit goes to left field, the second baseman covers his base for a possible play on the batter similar to the play made by the shortstop on a base hit to right field.

With a runner on first base; a fly ball to the outfield. If the ball goes to left field, the second baseman covers his base until the shortstop comes to take that position, and then backs up the throw to that bag.

If the fly ball goes to right field, the second baseman should go out for a possible relay. If the ball is fielded cleanly, the second baseman returns to the bag and takes the throw from the outfielder.

With a runner on second base; a base hit to the outfield. Prior to the pitch, the second baseman and shortstop must keep the runner close to the bag by making fake runs to the bag. The second baseman protects the bag in the case of all hits to left field. He goes out toward the outfielder on all hits to right field, but returns to the diamond, if the ball is properly fielded, to back up the shortstop for any play which may be made at second base by the infield cut-off man. On a base hit to center field, the infielder closest to the play goes out and the other infielder covers second base.

With a runner on second base; a fly ball to the outfield. The second baseman protects his base whenever a fly ball is hit to left field until the shortstop comes to the bag for a possible throw, and then he backs up the shortstop. The second baseman goes out toward the outfielder for all fly balls to right field in order to receive a possible relay. If the outfielder is set for the catch, the second baseman returns and takes the throw at the bag, or he stays in a position to protect the bag in a possible run-down play which may arise on the throw from the outfielder to third to second base. On a fly ball to center field, the shortstop lines up the throw to third base and the second baseman covers second base.

With a runner on second base, the situation prompting a bunt. The second baseman should play this in the same way as with a runner on first base in a situation prompting a bunt.

With a runner on third base; a fly ball to the outfield. The second baseman protects his base on all fly balls driven to the outfield, except when the ball is hit to right field. The second baseman then goes out for the relay throw.

With a close infield. If the second baseman fields a ground ball hit by the batter, he throws to the plate and then takes the catcher's position, protecting a run-down play. If the ball is hit to the first baseman or to the pitcher, the second baseman protects first base because there may be a run-down play at second base on a throw from an infielder to the shortstop protecting that bag. Whenever the ball is hit to the left side of the diamond, the second baseman protects second base.

With runners on first and second, the situation prompting a bunt. The second baseman does not leave his position until the batter drops his bat for a bunt, and then he covers first base as in the play with only first base occupied by a runner. As soon as the out is made, he rushes into the diamond to stop any attempt of the runner who was on second base to score.

With runners on first and second; a base hit to the outfield. The second baseman takes the same positions as with a runner on second base only.

With runners on first and second; a fly ball to the outfield. The second baseman takes the same positions as with a runner on second base only.

With runners on first, second, and third bases; a base hit to the outfield. The second baseman takes the same positions as with a runner on second base only.

With runners on first, second and third bases; a fly ball to the outfield. The second baseman takes the same positions as with a runner on second base only, unless there is a close infield. In that case, he plays as if there were a runner on third base only.

With runners on second and third bases; a base hit to the outfield. The second baseman takes the same positions as with a runner on second base only.

With runners on second and third bases; a fly ball to the outfield. The second baseman takes the same positions as with a runner on third base only.

With runners on first and third bases. On all balls hit to the outfield, the second baseman ignores the runner on third base. (He should make any play as though only first base were occupied by a runner, unless the situation calls for a close infield.) The one exception to this rule is when a double steal is attempted. Three plays are then possible: (1) When there is a clean or delayed steal without the runner on third base attempting to score; (2) when there is a steal, either clean or delayed, and the runner on third base attempts to score; (3) when there is a steal, clean or delayed, and the runner coming from first stops before he reaches second base. In the case of (3), a run-down is made, but the players in the run-down remain in a position to throw home in the event the runner on third attempts to score.

If a double steal is attempted and the second baseman is to cover second, he waits until the pitched ball is past the batter, then breaks for a spot three or four feet in front of second base. Almost simultaneously he glances at third base to see whether the runner is going home. If the runner starts for home, the second baseman moves in, cuts off the catcher's throw, and fires it home. If the runner on third base does not go home, the second baseman holds his position in front of second, takes the catcher's throw, and pivots to make the tag at second.

Although less effective, another method is advisable if the second baseman has a weak arm. In this instance, before the ball has passed the batter, the second baseman breaks for a position about halfway between the mound and second base, directly in line with the throw from the catcher. In this position he can cut off the catcher's throw if the runner at third attempts to go home. However, if the runner does not break, the second baseman lets the ball go through to the shortstop, who has straddled second base to make the tag on the runner from first base.

These cut-off plays are used to great advantage when the winning or tying run is going home. However, it is not advisable to let the winning or tying run go to second base while an attempt is made, on a close play, to put the third base runner out at home. When there is doubt about making a successful play at home, the play should be made on the runner at second to stop the threat. The inning and score should decide, in all cases, when to cut off the throw or complete the play at second base.

suggestions for the second baseman's game

The second baseman should try for every ball hit to the right of second base. If he can't catch it, he will be in position to help in any play that might follow: backing up the first baseman on all balls hit to him, or taking a relay throw from an outfielder.

When only first base is occupied by a runner, the second baseman should start toward second base after each pitched ball has passed the batter, in order to prevent the runner from making a delayed steal.

If the man at bat is a sure left-field hitter, the second baseman covers his base on all attempted steals. If the batter is a right-field batter, the second baseman plays his regular position and the shortstop covers second base.

It is advisable for the second baseman to cover his base for an attempted steal when a curved ball is pitched to a right-handed batter as a curve ball, which has less speed than a fast ball, is almost always hit into left field.

If the batter is a straightaway hitter—hits the ball according to the way it is pitched—the second baseman should inform his pitcher when he is going to protect the bag for attempted steals. The pitcher should pitch so that it is impossible for the batter to hit into right field when the second baseman is covering the bag.

Whenever a waste pitch is called for and delivered to a left-handed hitter, the second baseman should cover his bag for the play. The waste pitch should be outside for the batter and impossible to pull. The second baseman should run to the bag the instant the pitcher starts to pitch a waste pitch. The second baseman then has ample time to get in position to catch the ball if it is thrown by the catcher. The proper position is with both feet straddling the second base bag and the body parallel to an imaginary line drawn from first to third bases. On a perfect throw from the catcher, the second baseman swings his body around to face first base, with his left foot remaining on the outside of the diamond, his right foot on the inside of the diamond and the bag between his feet. The base runner is then tagged as described on page 40. If the ball is thrown inside the diamond, the second baseman can reach forward or step forward to get it and with one motion swing backward toward the incoming base runner for a putout.

Whenever the first baseman goes into the diamond on an attempted fielding play, the second baseman should back him up. It would be an exceptional play if the second baseman made a putout on the first baseman's assist, except in playing a bunt. The second baseman must protect first base on this particular play for a possible opportunity of making a putout.

When a runner is on first base, the ball is hit to the first baseman,

and the latter touches the bag before relaying the ball to second for the attempted completion of a double play, the second baseman must be sure to touch the runner coming from first base.

In almost every game a fly is hit just outside the diamond at second base. Both second baseman and shortstop go for it, neither knowing which can catch it. If the shortstop shouts for the ball, the second baseman rushes back to second to keep the runner who hit the ball, if it is not caught, from reaching second.

With a man on first base, a double play in sight, and a right-handed batter at the plate, one defense is for the second baseman to move toward the plate two or three steps, rather than toward second base. The other defense is to move back a few steps and closer to the bag. Both methods can be practiced to determine which works best for the player concerned. Either of these procedures can be used at all times, except when the batter is a definite pull-hitting left-hander. In this case the second baseman should consider himself the starter for the double play.

starting the double play

When the second baseman starts a double play, he should not be afraid to throw the ball. He should keep it in the shortstop's eyes, and not hang it in the air where he has to grab for it. He should not fool the shortstop

figure **18**

figure **17**

with a fancy toss. As a starter on double plays, the second baseman must use different pivots and different throws according to his position when fielding the ball. Some descriptions of fielding positions are as follows:

When a ball is hit directly at him, the second baseman should field it with his right foot slightly behind his left, legs spread, and both feet planted. He should *pivot his hips* and throw overhand or three-quarters sidearm to the shortstop. There should be no pivot of the feet (see Figure 17).

A ball hit to the second baseman's right should be fielded with the feet in approximately the same position as above, except that the second baseman may be facing the bag more or he may be on the move. The ball is tossed with a backhand sidearm motion directly from the glove. The palm of the hand should be facing the ground and should rotate counterclockwise as the ball is thrown to the shortstop (see Figure 18).

When a ball is hit to the second baseman's left where he can get in front of it, he should pivot in a snappy jump motion. His right foot should pivot back behind his left, and his left foot should pivot toward second base. The ball is thrown either three-quarters or sidearm (see Figure 19).

A ball hit to the second baseman's left where he cannot get in front of it but fields it on his left side is a difficult play. Often it is much

figure **20**

easier to pivot forward counterclockwise, crossing the right foot in front of the left and planting it out toward the right field foul line, and then to throw the ball as the left foot steps toward second base. Sometimes it is necessary to jump into the air and throw as soon as the body pivots into a throwing position (see Figure 20).

the pivot play

The pivot as the middle man on the double play is an individual problem. Very few second basemen make the play in exactly the same manner. In fact, no good second baseman makes the play the same way every time: if he does, smart base runners will knock him over on every slide.

There are several methods of making the double play—all of them should be tried, and the ones which come naturally should be practiced, practiced, and practiced. Double play practice is a daily duty during batting

figure **19**

practice and fielding practice. The shortstop and the second baseman must work together on this play until they can practically do it blindfolded. To make the pivot and throw, all throws should originate from the right foot, except when a player has to throw off his left foot in order to make the tag and get the ball away in a hurry. The second baseman should get to the bag as quickly as possible and complete the tag of the bag before the ball has actually been caught. The easiest way to do this is to arrive early at a point about one foot behind the bag and in a direct line with the throw. The second baseman's feet point toward third base and his upper body faces the throw. He then moves toward the bag, completes the pivot, and throws to first base. An ideal practice situation is to use a thirty gallon oil drum to stimulate a sliding base runner. Practice with the oil drum will give the second baseman and shortstop the correct moves (see Figure 21).

To pivot on the right foot, the second baseman moves toward second base, getting there as early as possible, steps on the bag with his right

figure **21**

foot, and throws from there. As his left foot hits the dirt on the stride to-ward first base, his right foot should come up and over the sliding runner, with a slight jump off the left foot. This seems to be the most popular and fastest method. The second baseman should not plant his left leg into the dirt, but should keep it relaxed in case the runner slides into him (see Figure 22).

The crow hop step is a popular pivot. The second baseman steps on the bag with his right foot, crow hops from six to twelve inches off the bag on his right foot, and throws from that position. The left foot steps toward first base (see Figure 23).

figure **22**

figure **23**

The hardest pivot play is for the second baseman to take the throw on the dead run, tag the bag, pivot, and throw. A good procedure is for the second baseman to step just in front of the bag with his left foot, dragging it across the bag for the tag as the right foot is planted on the other side of the bag. The left foot is pointed toward first base on the throw.

In another popular way to pivot the throw originates from the left foot. The second baseman may have to take the throw a few steps before he hits the bag with his left foot, and will then throw as he comes across the bag, leaping and throwing at the same time to get accuracy and something on the ball (see Figure 24).

The second baseman tags the bag with his left foot, backs up and throws when his weight has been shifted to his right foot. The tag of the bag is complete before the ball is received (see Figure 25).

The second baseman drags his left foot over the bag, plants his right foot toward the mound, and throws from there (see Figure 26).

The second baseman straddles the bag and uses a shift similar to that of a first baseman. When the ball is to his left, his right foot tags the bag, and he throws. With the ball to his right, he tags the bag with his left foot, shifts his weight to his right foot and throws.

If there is no chance of getting the runner at first base, the ball should not be thrown there. If first and second base are occupied, and a double play cannot be completed, look for the second base runner to round third, expecting a double play throw to first. This throw must be made without hesitation and before the second baseman knows the runner is off base far enough for a pick-off. The third baseman must always be alert for the play.

figure **24**

figure **25**

figure **26**

figure **27**

Tagging the runner coming from first base on the baseline and throwing to first to complete a double play can be a very difficult play. The runner has one thing in mind: to jar the second baseman loose from the ball. The best procedure here is to receive the ball and make a complete fake of the backhanded toss toward the shortstop covering second base. This fake move makes the runner think about taking the shortstop out instead of the second baseman. The second baseman, holding the ball firmly in his hand, makes a sweeping tag of the runner and throws to first base (see Figure 27).

If the runner stops, the second baseman moves him toward first base but throws the ball to the first baseman, covering first base, before the batter reaches first base. The runner who was on first base is now caught in a run-down play between the shortstop and first baseman, or between the second baseman and first baseman, providing the second baseman was far enough from the runner when the run-down started. If the second baseman was close to the runner, he continues to first base and protects that bag. The shortstop is backed up by one of the outfielders or by the third baseman, who covers second base while the shortstop chases the runner.

Quiz on second base playing

1. What are the requirements for a second baseman?
2. When the batter makes a base hit to left field with runners on second and third bases, what are the second baseman's duties? Why?
3. With runners on first and second bases, the situation prompting a bunt, what is the second baseman's duty?
4. With a runner on second base and a fly ball (that will be caught) to right field, what are the second baseman's duties?
5. State the three possible situations on a double steal with first and third bases occupied.

6. When should the second baseman cover second base for an attempted steal?

7. With a runner on third base and the infield close, the batter hits a ground ball to the second baseman and the runner attempts to score. What should the second baseman do? Suppose the runner stops on the base line?

8. What are the second baseman's duties on a long hit ball into right field? On a long hit ball into left field?

9. What is the second baseman's duty when a runner is on first base and a hit into right field is fielded cleanly? Why?

10. What is the second baseman's duty when a runner is on second base and a hit is made into left field? Why?

11. How does the second baseman attempt to stop an effort for a delayed steal?

12. How does a second baseman play ground balls for the start of a double play, second to short to first? Describe the position of the feet on every kind of hit ball.

13. How should the second baseman come to the bag at second for a throw from the shortstop starting a double play? What are his various pivot steps? What should be done if the runner does not slide?

14. What is the most important thing about a relay coming from the right fielder on a long hit ball? Why is it so important?

qualifications of a shortstop

Many authorities on the national game say that the shortstop has the most important fielding position.

The shortstop must be fast on his feet, capable of making fielding plays in a wide range of territory, very strong in his throwing arm, and able to throw accurately with either a sidearm, underhand, or overhand movement. He should be a man quick in his body motions, with an alert brain able to anticipate plays. The tall man, all things being equal, has an advantage in the shortstop position.

strategy of the shortstop's game

With a runner on first base. The shortstop, regardless of the number of outs, protects second base on all balls hit into right field or bunted in front of the plate. If the second baseman comes to the bag for a throw from the right fielder, the shortstop backs him up.

The shortstop goes out into left field for a possible relay whenever a ball is hit into that field. If the outfielder is set for a catch or fields a base hit cleanly, the shortstop should return to the bag and take the throw from the outfielder or line up the throw to second base. The only possible exception to this rule arises when the left fielder, on a playing field with

the shortstop's game

a long left-field foul line, is playing near the line and takes the ball deep in his territory. In that case the third baseman usually has to relay the ball.

With a left-handed batter at the plate, a base runner on first, and a double play in sight, the shortstop should move a few steps directly toward home and slightly toward second. This is his position before the pitch.

When a runner is on first base, the shortstop covers second for an attempted steal whenever the pitcher is in a "hole." This is one situation in which the hit-and-run play—in which the batter tries to hit behind the runner into the second baseman's territory—may be expected.

A left-handed hitter may try to hit the ball through short, especially when he has the "hole" advantage on the pitcher. The shortstop, therefore, should not leave his position too quickly in order to cover second base for the attempted steal, but should wait until the ball has either been hit, missed, or taken. The shortstop can protect himself on this play by moving a couple of steps nearer the second base bag before the pitcher has taken his proper pitching position. His movements should not be so conspicuous that his opponents know he is going to cover the bag for an attempted steal.

With a runner on second base. The shortstop goes into left field for a possible relay whenever a ball is hit into that territory. If the ball is a base hit and fielded cleanly, the shortstop returns immediately to the diamond and backs up the second baseman for a possible play coming from the infield cut-off man to the second baseman.

Whenever a fly ball is hit into left field, if he is sure that the ball will be caught and that all chances for a relay have vanished, the shortstop immediately goes toward third and takes the throw from the outfielder to that base. The third baseman backs up the play.

The shortstop protects second base on all base hits to right field. If a fly ball to right field is to be caught, the shortstop lines up the throw from the outfielder to third base. The third baseman covers third; the pitcher and left fielder back up the play.

If a runner is caught off second base by some defense play which finds the runner going toward third and the shortstop holding the ball, the shortstop starts the runner for that bag while the second baseman protects the bag at second, and then the third baseman concludes the play as described on page 43. If the second baseman starts the runner toward third with the ball in his hands, the shortstop protects the bag at second.

Frequently a batter hits a ground ball to the third baseman on which a run-down play may be started on the runner occupying second. In this case the shortstop protects third base.

With a runner on second base, a left-handed batter at the plate, and a close score, the shortstop must shorten his position and fake the second base runner back to the bag. His main job is to keep the runner close to the bag to prevent a steal of third or a score on any easy single.

With a runner on third base. The shortstop protects second base whenever a ball is hit to the outfield, except when a fly ball to left field is to be caught by that outfielder. Then the shortstop comes to third and protects that base for a possible run-down play.

If the catcher makes a throw to third base for an attempted putout and a run-down play follows, the shortstop protects the bag at third base.

If the team's defensive play brings the infielders into the diamond, a ball is hit to the shortstop, and the runner attempts to score, the short-stop fields the ball, throws it, and continues to the plate in order to pro-tect the catcher's position for a possible run-down play.

If a ground ball is hit to the third baseman and the runner attempts to score, the shortstop protects the bag at third base for a possible run-down play.

With runners on first and second bases, the situation prompting a bunt. The shortstop keeps the runner at second base as close as possible to the bag without leaving his fielding position too open. On a bunt, the shortstop must be alert for the ball that might get past the pitcher. It may be possible, beforehand, to get the runner off balance, and this should be attempted. The shortstop starts the runner toward second base in order to retard his break for third on the expected bunt. The pitcher should never pitch while the infielder is faking the runner back to the bag: he waits until the infielder is near his fielding position.

When the situation does not prompt a bunt, the shortstop plays his regular position for a possible double play. If the batter gets a base hit or hits a fly ball to the outfield, the shortstop plays his position as he would with a runner on second base.

With runners on first and third bases. The shortstop proceeds as he would with a base runner on first base only, ignoring the base runner on third base, unless the situation prompts a close infield. The exception to this rule is on a double steal with a straightaway hitter or a pull, or op-posite-field, hitter at bat. It must be understood that some hitters hit to all fields (straightaway hitters), and some hit to only one field (the pull, or opposite-field, hitters).

In the first situation three plays are possible: (1) when there is a clean or delayed steal and the runner on third base makes no attempt to score; (2) when there is a clean or delayed steal and the runner on third base does make an attempt to score; (3) when there is a clean or delayed steal and the runner coming from first base stops before he reaches second.

The shortstop must protect the bag at second base in all three cases. He must catch the throw from the catcher and tag the runner coming from first base, provided the second baseman does not cut off this thrown ball. The second baseman has by this time assumed a position either backing up second base, or about halfway between the second base bag and the pitcher's box, in line for the throw coming toward the bag. The shortstop must be very careful on a steal in situation (3), when the runner stops before reaching second base, depriving him of the opportunity to tag him with the ball.

When a right-field hitter is up and a double steal is attempted with men on first and third bases, the shortstop, taking the throw at second base, should break from his position to a spot about three or four feet in front of second base. He must take a look at third base and decide whether the runner is going home or holding third. If he goes home, the shortstop should move in to meet the catcher's throw, cut it off, and fire the ball home to cut down the base runner. If the runner on third holds, the shortstop should take the throw and pivot to make the tag at second. This is probably the best method. However, if the shortstop has a weak arm, he can break to a halfway position between second base and the mound. Then, if the third base runner does not go home, the shortstop lets the ball go through to the second baseman, who is straddling the bag and tags the runner coming from first base. In either situation, the second baseman can and should help the shortstop by shouting either, "home, home, home," or "second, second, second."

When two or more runs ahead, always play for the runner coming from first base.

With runners on second and third bases, a base hit to the out-field. The shortstop takes the same positions as with a runner on second base, unless the situation prompts a close infield—in which case he plays as when a runner is on third base.

With runners on second and third bases, and a fly ball to the outfield. The shortstop takes the same position as with a runner on second base only.

With runners on first, second and third bases. The shortstop should play his regular position unless his team's defense prompts a close infield. Otherwise, he plays his position as he would with a runner on second base only.

as a starter on a double play

The shortstop must give the ball to the second baseman as quickly as possible, chest-high, and to the side of the base desired by the second baseman. When possible, the throw should be overhand. However, there are times when a sidearm or underhand throw or toss is necessary to get the ball away quickly and accurately. The underhand toss should never be made flat-footed. With the toss, there should be a follow-through toward the base.

When the ball is hit to the shortstop's right. He should attempt to get in front of it. The ball should be fielded with the right foot slightly

figure **28**

in front of the left. This opens up the shortstop's hips toward second, placing him in a throwing position in which he will not hide the ball from the second baseman (see Figure 28).

On a ball hit to the shortstop's left. He should attempt to get around it to be in a better position to make the underhand toss of the ball to the second baseman. The toss should be a firm one that will stick in the second baseman's glove.

On a ball hit directly to him. He can field it with his feet in a normal fielding position, but it is better to move the right foot up even with the left foot or slightly forward of it, as shown in Figure 28. He will thus be in a better throwing position for the double play.

when he is the middle man in the double play

The following methods are used:

The right foot drag. The shortstop runs toward the bag, and places his right foot just short of the bag before or after receiving the ball. Then he steps out of the base path with his left foot and drags his right foot across second base for the out. He hops or skips to his right foot after

figure **29**

dragging it over the bag, plants it behind his left, and throws off his right foot (see Figure 29).

When receiving the throw from the first baseman. The shortstop comes to a stop three to four feet behind the bag, lining up the throw from first base. He faces the first baseman with his feet spread, ready for a bad throw to either side of the bag. This position can also be taken if the second baseman fields the ball in the base path. As the throw comes, he should take a little crow hop with his right foot behind the bag, catch the ball, and throw from behind the bag. He throws off his right foot, stepping on the bag with his left foot. His momentum from throwing the ball and a jump off the left foot carry him up and over the sliding runner (see Figure 30). The shortstop should make sure he has not thrown the ball before he hits the bag with his left foot. He can also throw by placing his left foot against the bag and pushing back after the throw. In either case, he is using the bag to protect his legs from the runner. If the throw is to his left, he tags the bag with his right foot. If it is to his right, he tags the bag with his left foot.

Using the left foot. The shortstop moves across the bag, hitting it with his left foot, and then pivots his right foot behind the left and plants it to make the throw. His momentum should carry him toward right field —avoiding the runner and using the bag for protection (see Figure 31).

Planting the right foot. If the shortstop has time, he can receive the ball, plant his right foot on the bag, and throw from that position. He tags the bag as he catches the ball. The throw and stride are directly down the base path toward first base.

The left foot back off. The shortstop moves over to meet the throw, tags the bag with his left foot, and steps away from the bag to his right to deliver the ball.

Never throw the ball if there is no chance to complete the double play. If first and second base are occupied and he knows there is a doubtful double play, second to first, the shortstop should look for the runner

figure **30**

who was on second to round third, where he might be picked off. It is often best to assume that the runner will round third. The throw should be made without looking to see whether the runner rounded third. The third baseman must always anticipate this play.

In any method, the main thing is to get the job done, and sometimes there is no time to be selective about how to do it. However, practice on the plays will show the value, in most instances, of dragging the right foot over second base. The shortstop and second baseman should never attempt to throw the ball around the runner. They throw down the base path through the runner. This makes the runner slide early and prevents bad throws.

figure **31**

pick-off plays

Any good keystone combination will have some pick-off plays which have proved successful. In this play, as a general rule, the second baseman is used as a decoy. Although pick-off plays take considerable practice, when successful, they take a great deal out of an opponent's rally. The short-stop is the key man in the pick-off play. He signals when the play is to be attempted, receiving an answer from the pitcher, or from the catcher in case of a catcher pick-off. Several methods are used, some of which we shall describe.

Count System. The shortstop or second baseman decoys the runner, so that the runner may be leaning toward third base after the decoy. Then the pitcher whirls. The count play, which is the easiest, starts when the pitcher looks away from the shortstop toward home. It is either a 1-2 or a 1-2-3 count, depending upon practice. The pitcher whirls on the count of 2 or 3. The throw should be low on the third base side of the bag. The shortstop breaks for second when the pitcher looks away from him and at the batter, and the pitcher counts when his head faces the batter.

Another Count System. This method is the same as the first one, except that the count starts when the pitcher's hands meet on his chest. The pitcher looks toward home during his stretch and the shortstop breaks when the pitcher's hands meet. The pitcher whirls and throws on the count of 2 or 3, depending on practice.

Daylight System. This set-up is also similar to the first method, except that instead of counting the pitcher looks back and waits until he can see daylight between the shortstop and the runner on the second base side of the runner as the shortstop breaks for the bag. The pitcher then turns his head toward home, whirls completely around, and throws to the shortstop covering second base.

The shortstop gives the signal to the catcher, who then answers and calls for a pitchout. The shortstop holds his natural position until the ball is ten or twelve feet from the batter. At this time the shortstop breaks for the bag, and the catcher throws to second base for the pick-off. The advantage of this method is that most coaches and the runner are watching the pitch. Also the shortstop has a good jump on the runner, who, anticipating a pass ball or a base hit, has started his lead toward third base.

In all of these plays the shortstop can get a better jump on the base runner by being up on the line behind the runner, perhaps a little on the second base side of him. It is good strategy to talk to the runner and back up—at an angle toward center field—as the pitcher is getting the pitch sign from the catcher. Thus by the time the shortstop is ready to break for second base, he will have a step or two jump on the runner.

suggestions for the shortstop's game

A deep position is the most elastic for covering ground, but it cannot be considered the best for all players. The player must neither overestimate his arm nor underestimate the runner's speed. The biggest fault of most shortstops is in overcharging the ball or not charging it at all. In either case, the shortstop should use a shorter position, where he does not have to cover as much ground, as in the deep position, to get the same hit ball.

The shortstop should go for every ball hit to the left-field side of second base. He will then at least be in position to do his part in any play that might follow: to back up the third baseman on a grounder or to relay a throw from an outfielder.

In a double play begun by the first baseman, who steps on the bag and throws to the shortstop at second, the latter *must* touch the runner at second base. This is not a force play.

Prior to making the routine throw to first base, the shortstop, when fielding the ball, should have his right foot slightly behind his left foot and his legs spread. As he throws overhand to first base, he steps directly toward the first baseman with his left foot, and follows through with his delivery after the throw.

The shortstop's hardest fielding plays are made (1) when a hit ball bounds over the pitcher's head and (2) when a ball is hit to the left of the third baseman and to the shortstop's extreme right.

In the first case the ball must be fielded by the shortstop on the run. He throws to first base, under full speed, from the position in which he fielded the ball. It is impossible for the shortstop to set himself for a perfect throw, but practice will aid him materially in perfecting this play. In the second case, the shortstop must go after the ball at full speed. As he fields it, he braces himself, throws most of his weight on his right foot, and stops or slides on this foot. His momentum may cause his right foot to slide some distance in the dirt—on the inside of the foot, not flat-footed. The ball meets the glove at almost the same time the right foot begins to plant for the slide. As quickly as possible, he balances his body for an overhand throw to first base.

When a ball is batted over second base in such a way that the short-stop has to make a long and hurried throw to his first baseman, he should make the throw on the run with a sweeping underhand movement.

This play occurs in almost every game. A fly is hit behind second base, too close for an outfielder to catch it. Shortstop and second baseman both run for it. If the second baseman shouts for the ball, the shortstop rushes back to second to keep the runner from reaching second if the ball is not caught. If neither fielder comes back to protect the bag, it is the duty of the pitcher to get there, or of the third baseman or first baseman, if there are no runners on those bases.

1. What are the qualifications of a shortstop?
2. What are the shortstop's duties when there is a runner on first base and the situation prompts a bunt? When the situation does not prompt a bunt, and a batter makes a base hit into right field?
3. With a runner on second base, what would be the shortstop's duty on a fly ball that will be caught in right field? On a base hit to right field? On a base hit to left field? On a fly ball to left field?
4. With a runner on third base, what would be the shortstop's duty on a fly ball to left field? On a base hit to left field?
5. With runners on first and second bases, if the situation prompts a bunt, what should the shortstop do on the defensive play?
6. When runners are on first and second bases and a fly ball is hit to the outfield, what does the shortstop do? On a base hit to right field?
7. The defense team is playing the batter as a sure right-field hitter, and the ball is hit to the first baseman, who touches the bag at first before throwing the ball to the shortstop for the completion of the double play. What should be done in this situation? What should the shortstop do? Why?
8. How should the shortstop receive a throw from either the first or the second baseman for the start of a double play?
9. When does the shortstop give instructions to the other players?
10. With a runner on second base, the batter hits a ball to the shortstop, who fumbles it. Is there a play which can sometimes be made, and which the shortstop should always keep in mind? If there is such a play, describe it in full.
11. What is the hardest fielding play(s) a shortstop has to make?
12. How should the shortstop relay a throw from the outfielders?
13. A fly ball is hit behind third base. Either the shortstop or the third baseman can catch it. Which player should catch the ball? Why?
14. Does the shortstop back up any fielding plays? If so, what are they?
15. If a runner is caught off second base—by either the shortstop or the second baseman—and starts for third, what are the duties of the shortstop in both situations?

the third baseman

The third baseman should be a good fielder on slow and hard hit balls, and especially on slow swinging bunts. He must be able to throw the ball from the position in which he fields it for forced plays and assisted putouts.

A very strong arm is not so essential to the third baseman as it is to other members of the infield. He has less call for powerful throwing. The closeness of his position to the batter gives the third baseman more time to make his throwing plays. Balls hit in his direction are driven either very hard or very slowly—hence the expression, "you do or you don't."

third base strategy

With a runner on first base. In bunting situations, the third baseman plays well inside the diamond. When the bat drops for a bunt, the third baseman starts toward the plate and the possible play. If the ball is fielded by the pitcher, the catcher, or the first baseman, the third baseman returns immediately to his bag and gets set for a possible play on the runner attempting to come to that base on the putout at first base.

When a batter has had two strikes called on him, the third baseman plays back in his regular position, for a batter usually will not bunt after two strikes.

playing third base

On base hits to the outfield, the third baseman plays his bag for the throw from the outfielder. If there is no chance of getting the ball in time to tag the runner who was on first as he comes to third, the third baseman rushes for the ball, catches it on the fly, and gets in position to make a play on the batter in case he tries to make second base on the throw by the outfielder.

When a fly ball is hit to right field and the runner on first does not attempt to go to third base, the third baseman backs up second base on the return of the ball to the infield.

With a runner on second base. On a base hit to center or right field, the third baseman plays his bag for a possible run-down play if the runner attempts to score on the hit. The first baseman cuts off the throw in front of the catcher. On a base hit to left field, the third baseman takes the cut off in front of the catcher. The shortstop covers third base for a possible run-down on the player attempting to score.

The third baseman plays as he would with a runner on first in a bunt situation. He does not, however, leave his position as quickly as he would with a runner on first only because a play might be made at his base if the runner comes from second upon the sacrifice bunt. The chances of completing this play are very remote and the assisted out, in most cases, is made at first base. Exceptions may be when the ball is bunted hard at the pitcher or the first baseman.

The third baseman should watch for the runner on second to steal as the batter bluffs a bunt. This is another reason why the third baseman should not leave his position too quickly as the batter drops his bat for the attempt to bunt.

Many times a batter will hit a ground ball to the third baseman with a runner on second, upon which the runner makes his start to third. If the runner stops, the third baseman should immediately chase him toward second and complete the play at that bag, before the player who hit the ball can reach second base. Often a quick bluff throw to first base, signifying that an attempt is going to be made on the batter, will pull the runner on second into the play. But one thing must surely be done, and that is to *get* one of the two runners. Most times the third baseman will have to bluff the runner back to second, then throw to first base.

With runners on first and second bases. In a bunt situation, the pitcher will attempt to make the assisted putout at third base, and thus make it necessary for the third baseman to protect the bag. The third baseman must be sure to have an understanding with the pitcher about this play. If the ball is bunted into the third baseman's territory, he must field it and throw it to first base for the putout. This play is one of the hardest a third baseman has to make, as it demands excellent judgment of the speed of the bunted ball. If it is bunted so hard that the pitcher cannot field it, then the third baseman must. In other words, if the bunted ball passes the pitcher, the third baseman must field it and make the assisted out at first. In either case, the third baseman must talk to the pitcher telling him what to do. If the pitcher is to field the ball, the third baseman will yell, "third," or possibly, "first." If the third baseman fields the ball he yells, "I have it." Some coaches have the catcher call the play. On a base hit to the outfield, the third baseman plays his position as suggested with a runner on second base.

On a fly ball to the outfield, the third baseman proceeds in the same manner as with a runner on second base.

A ground ball hit to the third baseman, with none out in the first half of a game and the score close, calls for a double play—second to first. There is, however, one exception: When the ball is fielded by the third baseman near the bag, he touches the bag with his right foot and attempts the double play on a throw to first.

In the last three innings of a ball game, with none out and the score tied, the first out should be made at third, then a possible double play attempted.

With one out, the double play, second to first, should always be attempted except when the ball is fielded by the third baseman near the bag. He should then step on the bag and attempt the completion of the double play on a throw to first.

With two out, the third baseman merely steps on the bag with the ball, retiring the side.

With a runner on third base. Whenever third base is occupied by a runner, the third baseman plays his position and protects his bag on all balls hit to the infield. He also plays this position on all balls hit to the outfield, except when there is a runner on third and a fly ball is hit to the left of an imaginary line drawn directly from home plate through second base to center field. In that case the third baseman goes into the diamond to act as cut-off man for a possible throw from the outfielder to the plate.

If a ground ball is hit to the third baseman, he must be sure that the runner on third is going to attempt to score before he throws the ball to the catcher. If he does throw to the catcher, he follows the throw and protects the plate in the possible run-down play, while the shortstop protects third base—unless the runner is close to home and the third baseman near third base when he throws the ball. In this case the third baseman will cover third base for a possible run-down play. If the runner makes no attempt to score, an out should be made at first base. With two men out, the third baseman normally makes the easiest out possible.

A play can be made to retire the runner between third and home on a ground ball to the infield, which, if properly executed, will always keep the batter from reaching second base during the run-down play. In this play the ball is hit to an infielder, the runner starts for home, and the third baseman instantly follows him. The runner, seeing that he is caught, stops in the hope of getting into a run-down play. The catcher quickly throws the ball to the third baseman, who is very close to the runner. The third baseman tags the runner out and throws to second base for a possible play on the batter.

There are very few third baseman who can properly execute this play and, consequently, it is not recommended for amateur players.

With the bases full. If possible, the third baseman starts the double play by throwing to the catcher for the first out. If the third baseman is forced out of position in fielding a ball, he may start the double play at second base instead. The third baseman must use his judgment on this play.

With runners on second and third bases. A run-down play on the runner on third attempting to score may terminate with both runners—the one who was on second and the one on third—occupying the base at the same time. The defensive player who has the ball at this particular time should know that the bag belongs to the runner who occupied it when the play started. He should tag both runners—the runner in back first—and yell, "You're out!". If the first runner steps off, he should be tagged for a double play.

On a base hit to the outfield, the third baseman plays as he would with a runner on second base.

fielding bunts

The so-called swing bunt calls for a very hard fielding play by the third baseman—a play with the fewest possible body motions. The third baseman has no opportunity whatever to set himself for the throw to first base if the batter, now a runner, is to be retired.

As the ball rolls slowly toward the third baseman, he rushes toward it, scoops it up in his bare hand, and with an underhand throw tries to get it to the first baseman before the runner reaches that bag. This play needs much practice. Most important are the eyes and the relaxed open hand. The eyes must not leave the ball until it is in the bare hand, and only then may the third baseman raise his head to see where to throw to the first baseman. The hand is open and acts like a cup, letting the ball roll into it. Once the ball is in the hand, the grip is taken for the throw (see Figure 32).

When the bunted ball stops rolling, the third baseman approaches the ball as quickly as possible. He places his left or right foot (whichever is easier) close to the ball, bends over, and pushes the ball into the grass

figure **32**   figure **33**

to assure a good grip. The hand is set in the throwing grip with the palm facing the ball as the third baseman approaches it (see Figure 33).

suggestions for the third baseman's game

The third baseman must be alert to cover second base. For instance, many times when the ball is hit behind second base but too near the infield for an outfielder to catch it, the shortstop and the second baseman both go for it, neither knowing which can make the out. It would be impossible for either of them to return in time to make a putout on the man who hit the ball, should he attempt to stretch his base hit to a two bagger. On this play the third baseman should protect second base. With his team ahead in late innings, the third baseman, as well as the first baseman, must protect the line against a possible double or triple down the foul line. He will catch all ground balls that would go that way. All ground balls through the infield should now be singles, thus giving the defense an opportunity for a force play or double play.

Quiz on third base playing

1. What are the requirements for a third baseman?
2. With a runner on first base and the situation prompting a bunt, what are the duties of the third baseman?
3. With a runner on first base, a base hit is made to the outfield. State every play the third baseman might expect at his corner.

4. With a runner on second base and the situation prompting a bunt, what does the third baseman do?

5. With a runner on second and a fly ball to the outfield to be caught, what does the third baseman do?

6. With a runner on second, the ball is hit to the left side of the diamond. The third baseman cannot field the ball, but the shortstop does. What is the duty of the third baseman?

7. When a runner on third attempts to score on a ground ball hit to the second baseman, what does the third baseman do?

8. With a runner on third base, what is the third baseman's duty when a fly ball is hit to left field? To right field?

9. With runners on first and second bases and the situation prompting a bunt, state exactly what the third baseman has to do.

10. How should the third baseman start a double play with the bases full?

11. With runners on first and second, how should the third baseman start a double play when a ground ball is hit to him?

12. What should the third baseman do if a ground ball is hit to him and a runner starts for third base and then stops between bases?

13. If a high fly goes up near the pitcher's box, what should the third baseman do if the sun is in the eyes of the first baseman? If the catcher comes out for the ball?

14. What should the third baseman do if, after a run-down play, he finds two runners on third base at the same time?

15. Why should the third baseman always protect his base when runners are in a scoring position?

16. Describe the methods used by a third baseman to field a slow rolling bunted ball. A ball that has stopped rolling.

requirements for the successful outfielder

The most successful outfielders are players who hustle every moment they are on the field, who back up every throw and base hit possible, and who throw the ball to the right base at the right time.

Outfielders should protect their arms and do all within their power to retain their throwing ability. They should not have too much throwing in practice. Many outfielders, who think they should be pitchers, fail to make an important throw to a base from their position in the outfield when such a throw would have been very easy for a fresh, strong arm. It is best to be careful in the limbering up. It is a good idea to have a relay player half way between the "fungo" hitter and the outfielders during outfield practice. The outfielder should never handicap himself through overexertion. His body and arm muscles are continually called on to do their part in defensive baseball. If these muscles are overworked, they will be unable to respond in an emergency. On cool or cold days, it is advisable to throw a ball between innings just as the infield does.

The fundamental requirements for a good outfielder are hitting, overhand throwing, and fielding ability. If an outfielder possesses the first two of these qualifications (and they are necessary for any outfielder), constant practice on fly balls and grounders will make him proficient in his fielding work. Plenty of infield ground balls are good for an outfielder.

Outfielders need very strong, accurate throwing arms—particularly the

the outfielder's game

right fielder, for on his throwing arm depends the success or failure of an opposing runner in advancing from first to third base on a base hit into right field territory. This throw is the most frequent and possibly the most important one that this fielder has to make.

The center fielder must be fast on his feet; in fact, he should be the fleetest player in the outfield, because he guards more territory than any of his teammates and has to make the greatest percentage of putouts in a series of games.

The left fielder must have a strong throwing arm. He must also be fast on his feet and a good fielder of ground balls. These qualifications enable him to protect the left field foul line on balls hit directly over the bag at third base. He must make quick, accurate throws to keep batters from making extra bases.

If a team has a left-handed and a right-handed outfielder of equal throwing ability, it is best for fielding and throwing advantage to put the left-hander in right field and the right-hander in left field.

important defense plays

The right fielder backs up first base on all bunted balls and on all plays attempted from the catcher to first—in fact, on every play at that bag when there is a possibility of the ball coming into his territory on an error or a wild throw. He backs up second base on all balls thrown from the left side of the diamond.

The center fielder backs up second base on all bunts, and also on all attempted outs at that bag.

The left fielder backs up second base on all attempted outs from the right side of the diamond, and backs up third on all attempted outs at that bag. These may include the following situations:

A runner on first base attempting to go from first to third on a hit to right field.

A runner on first base attempting to go from first to third on a bunt.

A runner who has made a long hit to right field trying to reach third on it.

A runner on second attempting to reach third after a fly ball has been caught in right field.

A runner caught between third and home plate.

A runner on second base attempting to reach third base on a bunt.

A runner on second attempting to steal third.

Outfielders, especially those playing amateur baseball, should study opposing batters during batting practice to find out to which field they naturally hit the ball. They should also note very carefully the physical strength of the hitters. It would be folly for an outfielder to play deep in the outfield for a small player who does not have the strength or the ability to hit long drives. It would likewise be ridiculous for an outfielder to play close to the infield when the batter is a big, robust fellow who has the ability now and then to hit the ball over the fence and out of the ball park. Professional players make a complete study of the hitting ability of their opponents, but since they play against much the same men year in and year out, they do not have to make such an important survey before each game. They have observed the hitting ability of each batter in previous games. As each opponent steps into the batter's box, they know how to play him—deep or short, right or left field. The amateur must make his observation and decisions before each contest because different players make up the teams against which he plays once or twice a week. But whether a player is a professional or an amateur, it is to his advantage to know the hitting ability of the man swinging the bat.

The straightaway hitter does not, as a general rule, hit the ball very close to either foul line unless he is badly fooled by a pitch. Thus for this type of batter, the outfielders should divide the space between the foul lines about equally between them, neither the left nor the right fielder playing very near the foul line.

Changes in the outfielders positions according to the natural ability of the man at bat are relative to the positions that they assume for a natural straightaway hitter. A left field hitter is a batter who usually hits the ball into left field. The outfielders shift toward left field with this type of batter. The left fielder plays deep, near the foul line; the center fielder moves into left center field, rather deep; and the right fielder changes his position into right center field, not too deep.

For a right field hitter, the right fielder plays deep in right field near the foul line; the center fielder moves rather deep into right center field; and the left fielder shifts into left center field, not too deep.

The outfielder watches the wind and judges his plays accordingly. If a hard wind is blowing toward the infield, he plays close to the infielders. If a hard wind is blowing toward the outfield, he plays deep. A cross wind will cause a fly ball or a thrown ball to curve.

In catching fly balls, the outfielder should never unconsciously regulate his speed so that he arrives at the point of making the catch just in time to meet the ball. When the ball goes into the air, he starts fast after the ball and sets himself for the catch in a throwing position. The start on a fly ball is thus very important to any outfielder, except when he must make a long throw. In this case a timed, running catch is preferable, because it enables the outfielder to put more on his throw. This can be done only when the outfielder has plenty of time to catch a fly ball, so that he can come toward the oncoming ball in almost a direct line toward the base to which he must throw. The ball should hit his glove just as his pivot foot hits the ground. He now crow-hops on his pivot foot and throws the ball. In all cases the outfielder must get around the ball and move toward it so as to be in a good position to throw to the proper base.

Before each pitch, outfielders should get set as follows: (1) Hands on knees as pitcher gets his sign. (2) Hands off knees as pitcher begins his movement to take wind-up or set stance. (3) As pitcher picks up his striding foot and steps, outfielders shift their eyes from the pitcher to the area where the bat will meet the ball, stepping in place or slightly forward with either foot. The flight of the pitched ball and the pitcher's delivery are seen out of the corners of the eyes. (4) As pitcher's pivot foot steps forward, the fielders' other foot comes up even with his striding foot. He is now in good position, on his toes, ready to break for a batted ball.

Outfielders must back up all throws from one infielder to another, if at all possible. The outfielder should know when a waste pitch is to be thrown, so that he can get a running start for the base which he must back up. He receives this information from the infielder designated to convey it.

The outfielder must not form the habit of holding the ball after he has made a catch or fielded a ground ball. The ball should be returned to the infield immediately.

Outfielders must remember that normally the first throw of a relay must be the short accurate throw, and the second throw, which is made by an infielder, is the long one. The outfielder makes the first throw of the relay in such a manner that the infielder receives it about shoulder high on the glove side, thus saving as much time as possible for the second throw to some base. If two outfielders are in position to field the ball starting the relay, the player nearest to a good throwing position is the one to do it.

Outfielders always try to field fly balls and grounders in a throwing position. Whenever a runner sees an outfielder at a disadvantage in his fielding, he will—or should, at any rate—attempt to take an extra base on his hit.

The outfielder who is a novice in the game usually feels more secure and has more confidence in himself if, in catching fly balls, he extends his arms upward so that the back of the glove and the back of the bare hand are toward his face. This position of the hands is easier for a young player as it leaves his wrists more flexible and allows him to watch the ball more closely. If a low line drive comes toward him, however, the backs of his hands are toward his lower limbs. As the player gains experience he will find that he can catch fly balls with the backs of his hands toward the ground, and his arms well extended from the body. This type of catch must be made when the outfielder is forced to extend himself to one side as he runs under full speed in order to catch a fly ball. Experience will also teach the young player that he can reach further with one hand— the gloved hand—and catch fly balls which would be impossible for him to catch with both hands. Practice in catching fly balls with one hand is necessary, but in a game an outfielder should never catch a fly ball with one hand when he can use both hands.

Inexperienced outfielders should practice catching fly balls over their heads in such a manner that they must run some distance in order to make the catch. Many young players make a common error in attempting to catch such fly balls: instead of turning their backs to the oncoming ball and running naturally for the catch, they back up—run backwards. The moment an outfielder judges a fly ball to be over his head, he should turn tail and run. If possible, he swings his body around so that he is facing the ball as he makes the catch, but many times he cannot do so and must make the catch over his shoulder. But he should always try to catch the ball facing it. With practice, the outfielder will develop skill in running for the ball without looking at it and turning at the proper time for the catch. It is better, however, for a young player to run for the ball with his eyes upon it from the time it leaves the bat until he catches it. If an outfielder is weak on this type of fly ball, it is best for him to play deeper in his outfield territory. A player can catch an oncoming fly ball or line drive much faster and more easily if he runs toward it than if he runs away from it.

Practice on the following breaks for the ball will help the outfielder catch balls hit directly over his head. In the case of the right-handed outfielder, the moment he knows the ball is over his head, he pivots on his left foot with the right foot stepping back. As he runs back, he curves to his right, looking over his left shoulder at the ball. As the ball falls to where it will hit the earth, the outfielder curves in toward that position. He makes the catch with his glove side turned toward the ball and his throwing arm toward the fence—this puts him in the best throwing position. The left-hander turns and curves the opposite way (see Figure 34).

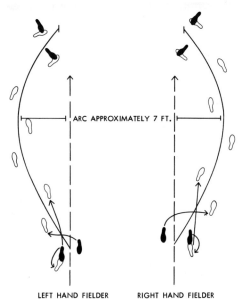

ARC APPROXIMATELY 7 FT.

LEFT HAND FIELDER   RIGHT HAND FIELDER   figure 34

Should the ball be a line drive or fly ball dropping in front of the outfielder, he will have two alternatives: (1) Hold up and catch the ball on a long hop, (2) Continue in for a shoestring catch or block of the short hop. In method (1), the outfielder must be certain not to hold up so long as to get a bad bounce of the ball and he must be certain he could not have made a catch of the fly ball. In method (2), the outfielder must make certain the ball will not get past him. He must field the ball on the glove side in front of his body. As the outfielder approaches the ball, he extends his glove hand and gets in a position so that his extended arm and glove are in line with the path of the ball. The arm is held stiff, never scooped forward at the ball or brought back to soften the catch. The glove should be right on the ball, which is either caught or rebounds from the stiff arm and wrist. The rebound is normally in front of the outfielder's body and in the direction he is moving—if his fielding arm is held rigid.

Outfielders should bear in mind that it is sometimes best to throw to a base to keep a runner from getting into a scoring position even if such a throw lets another man score a run. *The percentage of put-outs at the plate on throws from the outfield is very small.* The number of runs ahead or behind, the number of innings played, and the number of outs should always be borne in mind by the outfielder before the ball is hit, so that the right throw to the right base will be made on any hit ball. If the infielders are playing their positions so as to give a run, the outfielders should make their throws accordingly.

On catching a fly ball close to the infield, when there are runners on the bases, the outfielder immediately runs toward the infield, so that runners cannot advance on the catch. An outfielder, however, never challenges a runner to try to advance to another base. He throws the ball one base ahead of the runner for protection. Fly balls which both an outfielder and infielder can catch should always be taken by the outfielder. The outfielder informs the infielder that he is going to attempt the catch. "I have it!", shouted loudly a number of times while going for the ball, should keep the infielder out of the way and avoid a collision. The outfielder should also expect to hear instructions from the infielder attempting to catch the ball as to whose ball it is. Whenever a ball can be caught by either the outfielder or infielder and there is a runner tagging up to advance, the outfielder should always make the catch.

An outfielder should never attempt a shoestring catch (almost touching the ground) unless, in the last inning of a game, the winning run will cross the plate on a given base hit. The outfielder should be very careful in making or attempting to make this kind of a catch. In many cases he will show better judgment by giving the batter a safe hit rather than by giving him an opportunity to make a two or three base hit if he himself makes an error of judgment in fielding the ball.

Many times a foul fly cannot be caught by an infielder. If it is caught by an outfielder, a runner occupying third base would have a good opportunity to score after the catch. If the runner on third base is likely to score the tying or winning run in the eighth or ninth inning on such a caught ball, it is advisable for the outfielder to make no attempt to catch the foul fly. The left and right fielders should judge the chances of the runner on third base to score on such a caught ball, and play accordingly. Runs ahead should always prompt the attempted catch unless such a catch would allow runners other than the one on third to advance a base or bases to the scoring position for the tying or winning run. The catch, therefore, depends upon the number of innings played, the score of the game, and whether the outfielder is within safe throwing distance of home plate.

An outfielder should always wear sunglasses when the sun will bother his fielding. The outfielder never flips the sunglasses until he sees where the ball is going. Much practice is necessary to learn this difficult sun position. The eyes can be shielded with the glove, and the outfielder can turn his body sideways as he is receiving the ball, to get the sun out of his eyes (see Figure 35). If the sun is directly behind the batter, the outfielder can move in the direction of the batter's power so as to get a better jump on the ball.

Catching a ground ball can be a simple matter if the outfielder works hard enough. He will have two methods of handling a ground ball. (1) With a play to make, such as trying to throw a runner out at home, and (2) With no play to make, such as holding the batter to a single by merely getting the ball into second base. In method (1), the outfielder charges the ball as quickly as possible. When he gets within fifteen feet of the ball, he uses short choppy steps such as a football tackler uses when approaching a ball carrier. This keeps him in balance should the ball take a bad hop sideways. He now approaches the ball as an infielder, picking the good hop and throwing as he moves in. Should the ball be skidding rather than bouncing, the outfielder should attempt to scoop the ball up on his glove side. The approach to the ball in method (2) is the same as in method (1). If the ball is bouncing true and he can pick up a good hop, the outfielder fields it like an infielder and throws the ball into second base immediately. If the ball is hugging the ground or not bouncing true when he is about ten feet from the ball, he gets down on the knee of his pivot foot to block the ball. In the case of a right-handed thrower, he gets down on his right knee. His right leg is extended out to his right and his body faces the ball. Many balls are blocked this way which ordinarily would go through the outfielder for extra bases. By charging the ball and blocking it, thus

figure **35**

figure **36**

keeping the ball in front of him, the outfielder will keep the batter from taking an extra base (see Figure 36).

playing the outfield fences

Two innovations for outfielders came about because of injuries received by outfielders crashing fences. One is the dirt warning path next to the fence, which should be at least ten feet wide and extend along the entire fence line. Another is the mats or cushions for concrete fences which protect the head and body of the outfielder.

Several methods of approaching the fence can help the outfielder play the ball better and avoid injury.

Fielding fly balls at the fence. If the outfielder knows the ball is going to be near the fence, he should go to the fence as quickly as possible. Once at the fence, he should turn sideways. If a throw has to be made after the catch, the outfielder should try to field the ball with the gloved hand side of the body away from the fence. If no runners are on base, the catch can be made with the gloved hand side of the body next to the fence. Catching the ball with the glove side away from the fence keeps the outfielder in a good throwing position. After the catch, the pivot foot merely steps forward or hops forward to make a strong throw. Catching the ball with the glove side next to the fence makes the outfielder pivot his whole body before planting the pivot foot for the throw. This takes too much time, thus giving the base runner two to three extra steps toward the base to which he is advancing.

Another reason for turning sideways is to avoid having the buttocks bump the fence as the outfielder crouches to make the jump for the ball. Standing with the back to the fence is the worst way to play a fly ball next to the fence. A slight bump of the buttocks against the fence can cause poor timing in making the catch.

Crashing the fence. Many balls hit to the fence must be fielded the best way possible and no time can be given to get in the preferred position. The warning track usually tells the outfielder how close he is to the wall. Once he hits the track, he knows that in the next two steps he must be ready to leap for the catch and brace himself for the crash against the fence. If there is no warning track, it is difficult to know how close one is to the fence. The outfielder, when he thinks he is approaching the fence, must take a quick look to see where he is.

As the outfielder approaches the fence, he must feel for the fence with the hand nearest the fence. When he jumps for the ball, he should straighten the leg nearest the fence, tighten the leg muscles, and push the leg out and away from his body toward and against the fence. His shoulders should remain square or perpendicular with the fence to protect his head if he crashes. Hitting the fence as described above will have the foot, hip, and shoulder hitting the fence in that order.

Climbing the fence. There are balls hit to the fence which can be timed and caught by actually climbing the fence. Any fence—whether of concrete, brick, wood, metal, or wire—can be used to reach balls which otherwise could not be caught. This ball is normally a high fly ball which

figure **37**

gives the outfielder time to get under the ball and see the fence in time to guage his stride for the step onto the side of the fence.

As the outfielder approaches the fence, he times the ball so that his last step will be made up and on the fence just before the ball reaches the fence. He watches the flight of the ball until he takes his last step up on the fence. At that time, he must look at the fence. Just as his foot hits the fence, he must look up for the ball. His spikes are dug into the fence for the spring into the air.

On a concrete or metal fence it is possible to get as much as two to three feet higher than the normal jump. On a wire fence, and some wooden fences, an outfielder can get as much as four feet higher than normal (see Figure 37).

If the fence is low enough there is nothing wrong with using the top of the fence for an extra shove or pulling with the hand to get additional height.

Breaking away from the fence. In the event the outfielder sees he cannot make a catch on the fly ball, he must break away from the fence in the direction he thinks the ball will rebound off the fence. He then plays the ball off the fence, pivots after the catch, and throws to the relay man or proper base.

Playing rebounds. The outfielder must play rebounds according to the composition and angle of the fence. He must study the fence by observing the behavior of balls hit against it by a fungo hitter hitting from the direction of homeplate.

Concrete, brick, and stone walls will rebound balls very fast and at an angle depending on the position of the fence and its shape. Wooden fences will not rebound a ball nearly as fast as a concrete fence. Metal fences usually do not rebound as well as wood, but they sometimes rebound at odd angles depending on their texture or surface. If the fence is of a corrugated metal, the outfielder should expect anything. Wire fences usually do not rebound a ball very fast except if they are tightly hung, in which case they rebound nearly as well as a wooden fence. The angle of the ball rebounding off a wire fence is not always the same. Here texture and the mesh opening play an important part.

Playing the ball lying against the fence. Very often an outfielder must field a ball which is lying near the fence. The proper way to pick this ball up for the quickest and most powerful throw is to get the pivot foot to the side of the ball and close to the fence. Example: right-handers, as they face the ball lying against the fence, place their right foot to the right of the ball. This puts them in excellent position to pick the ball up and either throw from that position or crow hop on the right foot for a little extra on the throw. To pick it up by placing the other foot next to the fence would make the outfielder pivot his whole body before he can

figure **38**   figure **39**

get set to throw. Getting the pivot foot on the correct side may seem to cause the outfielder to take an extra step sometimes, but it still beats the time required to pivot his whole body to throw (see Figures 38 and 39).

All the above methods of playing the fences can be learned by much practice. To begin the early fundamentals, someone should throw the ball for the outfielder to field. After the outfielder learns the fundamentals, the ball should be hit with a fungo bat from the direction of home plate.

Quiz on outfield playing

1. What are the important requirements for the outfield position?
2. What is probably the most important throw a right fielder has to make? Why is it so important?
3. Describe every situation which will bring the left fielder from his position to back up third base.
4. Should the outfielder notice the direction of the wind? If so, why?
5. How does an outfielder start a relay throw?
6. With runners on bases, what thoughts should be in the minds of the outfielders the moment the batter takes his position at the plate?
7. If an outfielder catches a fly ball near the infield, what should he do?
8. How should an outfielder make his throws to bases? Why?
9. When should an outfielder attempt a shoestring catch?
10. Should the right and left fielders always attempt to catch foul fly balls? Why?

the outfielder's game   **97**

11. What is meant by the phrase, "An outfielder at a disadvantage"?
12. Discuss the proper manner in which an outfielder should catch a fly ball.
13. When should the timed catch be used?
14. What is meant by the phrase, "Challenge the runner"?
15. If the infielders play a particular batter as a right-field hitter, what should the outfielders do?
16. What should an outfielder do when a fly ball is hit over his head?
17. How would you play for a right-field hitter? For a left-field hitter?
18. How should an outfielder pick up a ball lying against a fence?
19. How does an outfielder catch a fly ball that would hit the fence?

basic principles

Defensive tactics in baseball hinge upon two factors: (1) each player in the right place at the right time; (2) each player aware of what he must do with the ball when he gets it.

Every position on the playing field has certain fundamental defensive requirements which must be followed by all players.

Whenever possible, base runners must be kept from getting into scoring positions, either at second or third base. It is impossible, however, to lay down an ironclad set of rules with regard to defensive tactics. Every phase of the game—the ability of the pitcher, of the batter, and of the fielder, the speed of the runner, and any likely fumble or error—must be taken into account. Each defensive player must know what to do when he takes his position on the playing field. Upon each man playing as he should depends a very definite part of the success of his team's defense.

All defensive players should be careful not to throw the ball too much or too often, for every time a throw is made there is a chance for an error. Every player should have a good reason for throwing the ball whenever he does so. *To attempt an impossible play is nothing short of foolishness.*

The first and third baseman protect the lines in late innings if the defensive team is ahead, and the outfield plays deep. The theory here is to give opponents a single rather than an extra base hit, thus setting up a force situation and possible double play.

defense strategy

foundations of the defense game

Every baseball game depends upon three self-evident facts: the number of runs ahead or behind, the number of outs, and the number of innings played. Three questions in regard to the defensive game are often asked by ball players:

When shall a team play with a close infield?

When shall a team give a run?

When shall a team not give a run?

A close infield is advantageous to the offensive team for the infielders are unable to protect as wide a range of territory when they play close as when they play back in a deep position. It has been estimated that a man with a .250 batting average, for example, becomes a .500 hitter the instant the infielders come into close formation.

The defensive team never plays a close infield when a run can be given which will not necessarily mean the loss of the game; in other words, a close infield should be played only when a run cannot be given. Any club which makes a practice of playing a deep infield and is willing to give a run—even though it may be the tying run—to prevent another runner from getting into position to score the winning run, is a hard club to beat. Its defensive tactics are fundamentally sound.

examples of good defense

Infield defense with the bases full in the first inning; one out. The defensive team should play a deep infield and make a double play from second base to first. If the ball is hit hard at the pitcher or the third baseman, the double play must be to the catcher to the first baseman. The only exception to this rule is this: if the batter is a sure left-field hitter, the first baseman plays a close infield and his play, if the ball is hit to him, is to the catcher instead of to second base. The third baseman plays deep and would probably start his double play to second base.

With runners on first and third bases in the second inning; none or one out; no score. The infielders should play deep.

With runners on second and third bases in the third inning; one out; the defensive team leading by one run. It would not be unsound baseball to give the run, and it should be given if there is a very hard hitter at bat. If the batter is a weak hitter, it is advisable to play the infield moderately deep.

With a runner on third in the seventh inning; none out; the defensive team ahead by one run. The run may be given, but in this inning it is better that it should not. The infielders play close or moderately deep, according to the ability of the man at bat.

With runners on first and third bases in the seventh inning, none out; the defensive team leading by one run. The run can be given in order to keep the possible winning runner from getting into a scoring position. There is also an opportunity for a double play from second base to first. The infield should play moderately deep. It might be advisable to keep the third baseman close to protect the bunt possibility.

With runners on first and third bases in the seventh inning; one out; the defensive team leading by one run. The infield plays moderately deep. A double play is attempted if the ball is hit to either the shortstop or the second baseman. The play in this situation depends on the hitting ability of the batter and the pitcher's success with this particular batter.

With a runner on third base in the seventh inning; one out; the defensive team leading by one run. The infield should play close.

With runners on first and third bases in the eighth inning; the defensive team leading by two runs. It would be unsound baseball, regardless of the number of outs, to play a close infield. The runner to be kept away from the scoring position is the one on first base. Every effort on the part of the defensive team is made to keep this runner away from second base, the scoring position. Even if the ball is hit back hard at the pitcher, it is fundamentally correct to attempt a double play, pitcher to shortstop to first base. In the run-down play between the catcher and third baseman, if the pitcher attempts to get the runner who is trying to score from third base, the chances favor the runner on first base reaching third and the batter going to second base. In such a case a base hit, an error, a passed ball, or a wild pitch might then give the offensive team two runs; as a consequence, instead of the defensive team having a lead of one run and an opportunity for completing a double play, the offensive team will have tied the score.

With runners on first and third bases in the eighth inning; none out; the home team on the defense leading the visiting team by one run. It would not be bad baseball to give the run, thus allowing the game to be tied, in order to avoid a possible winning run through the man on first base getting to second, the scoring position. The second baseman and the shortstop, playing deep on the defense in anticipation of a double play, would lose on their strategy play only if the batter made a base hit or hit a slow grounder to some infielder. If a slow grounder is hit to the pitcher, or to the first or third baseman, the out should be made at the plate, as a force play is impossible at second on a slow hit ball. Every possible effort should be made to keep the runner on first from reaching second base, where he would probably score the winning run on an error, a hit, or a wild pitch. If the tying run were allowed to score, the home team would have an opportunity to break the tie in the last half of the inning, and the batting ability of players coming to bat for the home team must be considered in reaching a decision for the defense tactics of the infielders.

With a runner on third base in the eighth inning; one out; the defensive team one run behind. The infield should play close. The run cannot be given.

With runners on first and third bases in the eighth inning; none out; the score tied one and one. Assuming that runs have been very hard to score in this game, it is advisable to play the infield moderately deep. If the ball is hit to the pitcher, to the third baseman, or to the first baseman, the play is at the plate. If the ball is hit to either the shortstop or the second baseman, an attempt should be made for a double play, second to first.

With a runner on third in the ninth inning; one out; the defensive team leading by one run. The infield plays close, stops the runner who is attempting to score, and if possible, keeps the batter from getting into a scoring position.

With bases full in the ninth inning; none out; the defensive team leading by four runs. The infield plays deep for a possible double play. The runner to be kept off the base is the man at bat, for his is the tying run. If the ball is hit to the pitcher, or to the first baseman playing his position for a left field hitter, the double play is to the catcher to first base. Three runs can be given, and these runs should be given if defensive tactics can keep the tying run from being scored or the runner from reaching second base, from which he might score.

With runners on second and third bases in the ninth inning; one out; the defensive team leading by two runs. The infield plays deep and tries to keep the batter from reaching first, thus eliminating the possibility of his making the winning run. If the ball is hit to the pitcher or the third baseman, or to the first baseman playing the batter as a left field hitter, an attempt should be made for an out at the plate.

With bases full in the ninth inning; one out; a good hitter at bat, the defensive team leading by one run. The infield plays deep and attempts a double play. If the ball is hit to the first baseman, who would probably be playing a close infield, to the pitcher, or to the third baseman, then the play is to catcher to first baseman for a double play. A good .250 batter becomes a .500 hitter when the infield plays close.

With a runner on third base in the ninth inning; none out; the defensive team leading by two runs. The run should be given, with the infield playing deep. It takes two runs to tie and three to win, and it is up to the defensive team to keep the tying runner off first base.

With bases full in the latter part of the game; none out; the defensive team leading by two runs. The infield plays deep. If the ball is hit to the pitcher, to the third baseman, or to the first baseman, provided he is playing for a left field hitter, a double play should be made to catcher to first. If the ball is hit to the shortstop or the second baseman, the double play should be to second base to first.

With a runner on third base in the top of the ninth inning or any extra inning; none out; a tie score. The infield should play close and cut off the runner who is attempting to score. It is not advisable to fill the bases in this situation because the defensive home team has an opportunity to go to bat in the last half of the inning. If the bases are filled and the visiting team gets a base hit or an error is committed, they could score two or more runs. It is better to keep runners off base at this time. It is easier for the home team to score one run than two or more in the last half of the ninth.

If the score is tied in the last of the ninth inning, or any extra inning, and the lead off man triples. Fill the bases with intentional bases on balls. The infield plays close and the outfield moves in to where it can absolutely throw the runner out at home on a fly ball. All plays call for a throw home.

With a runner on second base, the ball is hit between the infielders. Every effort should be made to knock the ball down to keep the runner from scoring on a base hit through the infield. This may mean a dive at the ball and a quick scramble to pick it up after it is knocked down.

With the winning run or tying run on second base, the infield should play deep. However, with less than two out, thought must be given to a possible bunt play. The shortstop and second baseman must play deep and protect the area through the middle of the infield. They must not let a base hit go to center field. The only logical men to throw the runner out at home are the left fielder and right fielder. Thus, if a hit is to get through the infield, it should go to the right fielder or the left fielder.

TWO

the
offensive game

A good batter is a good hitter naturally. Every young player should realize that the art of batting does not merely mean swinging at the ball to see how far it can be hit, but rather meeting the ball squarely with a natural swing. Of course, a coach can do much to eliminate poor technique in a naturally good batter. He can train any batter to be a better hitter. But unless the coach has good natural batting material in an otherwise good player, he cannot possibly make a good batter out of him.

Each player has his own batting style and should be encouraged to continue in it unless he has developed certain detrimental habits, such as pulling away from the plate, dropping one shoulder in the swing of the bat, an exaggerated crouch, turning the body, standing in the extreme rear or the extreme front of the batter's box, or taking too long a stride. Good batters do not allow themselves to develop these habits.

The good batter is ready to hit the ball every time the pitcher makes his delivery. The swing must be started with every pitch. If it is a bad ball, the swing is stopped. High school and college players are apt to develop unconsciously the habit of allowing the ball to be on its way from the pitcher's hand toward the plate before an earnest attempt is made to hit it. Each batter should be in his proper stance and *ready* to hit at the time the pitcher's delivery is to be made. Great batters in our professional game are never lax at this point. Prior to the delivery, however, they are completely relaxed from head to toe.

batting

qualifications of a batter

A good batter must have good eyes, a comfortable stance, concentration, a perfect stride or step, and a faultless swing. These qualifications are of no use to a batter who does not make the pitcher pitch. One swing of the bat at a good ball over the plate is far more important than random swings at all sorts of balls delivered by the pitcher. The batter should leave all pitches above the strike zone alone. There is only one place the average batter can hit a high ball—into the air. And it is frequently missed. If the batter is a natural up-swinger, he must never swing at a ball in the high strike zone or above.

A good batter may, at times, get into what is called a "batting slump." He is unable to hit a ball beyond the imaginary lines of the infield, and when he does hit the ball, it is almost always a pop fly or a weak grounder. The real cause of this slump is that the batter is out of time. He is not meeting the ball at the instant when the weight of his body is changing from one foot to the other—his bat is coming around either too fast or too slow. The only remedy for this poor timing is to have a pitcher throw, in a long batting practice, nothing but fast, straight balls to the batter until he has again coordinated his stride and swing. It sometimes takes much earnest practice for him to regain confidence in his batting. A change in the weight of the bat he is using may be helpful. A swing hitter may aid himself by "choking" his bat a little. Bunting practice sometimes makes him follow the ball better. The difficulty sometimes lies in the fact that the batter's eyes are not following the ball. There are many causes for a batter's slump, but at the bottom of them all lies his difficulty in timing.

five essentials in batting

A good eye is the most important thing in batting. The batter should keep his head still, both eyes level and looking at the pitcher, while he is in a batting position. His eyes follow the ball from the time the pitcher starts his delivery until the ball has been swung at or caught by the catcher. The batter never turns his head to follow the direction of the bat as it comes around for the swing. His eyes should see the bat hit the ball, so closely should they follow the ball. *A motionless head, with watchful eyes, is the greatest asset of any batter.* A good way to follow the ball is to look for the stitches.

The proper grip of the bat. It is impossible to be a good hitter unless the grip is comfortable and the bat is positioned in the hand so as to allow an explosive swing at the ball. Too many young players grip the bat too tightly prior to the delivery and swing. The bat must be held in such a position that the hands and wrists have freedom of motion on contact with the ball.

To get the bat in proper position in the hand, one must visualize the bat, in the case of the right-hander, as a tennis racket in his right hand. The head of the bat should be placed on the ground in front of the body, with the rest of the bat leaning toward the body so that the knob points toward the stomach. Place the hands at the sides of the bat with the palms facing each other and grip the bat lightly. The bat should now be positioned diagonally through the palm from between the base and first knuckle of the index finger to just behind the base knuckle of the little finger. The actual grip is now with the little finger, ring finger, and middle finger (see Figure 40). The index finger and thumb are held loosely around the bat (see Figure 41). Prior to the pitch, the grip is very relaxed. If the coach can see white on the knuckles, the bat is gripped too tightly. If pulled, the bat should come out of the hands very easily. As the pitch is delivered the grip becomes more firm until, during the swing, the bat is held very tightly. The top hand, when the bat meets the ball, should be in position so that if the hand were open the palm would face the ball. This is very similar to the grip of a tennis racket or golf club.

Proper position of the hands on the bat can be checked by looking at the relationship between the knuckles of the two hands. At no time should the middle knuckles of the top hand line up beyond the base knuckles or middle knuckles of the bottom hand. The middle knuckles of the top hand must line up either with the middle or base knuckles of the bottom hand, or somewhere between them.

figure **40**   *figure* **41**

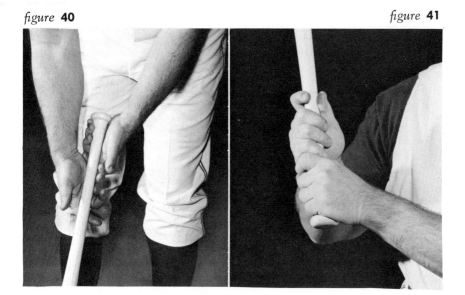

figure **42**

A proper stance. A good stance ends in a good stride and a good swing. The batter stands a little nearer the rear of the box than the front of it, with both feet firmly on the ground in as comfortable a position as possible, and with most of his weight on the rear foot. The feet are as close together as an easy stance will allow. The front foot (the one nearest the pitcher) is closer to the inside line of the batter's box than is the rear foot. A good batter, as a rule, never pulls away or steps away from the plate, or from the line of the ball as it comes toward him. A single step forward will bring his front foot into such a position that the swing of the bat meets the ball when his body is nearly perpendicular to the path of the ball. His shoulders will be nearly parallel with the earth. His knees are bent slightly prior to the pitch to allow an easy stride or step.

As the batter waits for the delivery his elbows are away from his body and his forearms, wrists, and hands are in a very relaxed, comfortable position in front of his body, holding the bat slightly back toward the catcher. His arms are fully extended when he meets the ball (see Figure 42).

The stride or step. The batter's step is ordinarily straight toward the pitcher. Constant practice should determine the proper length of the step, but the average batter's stride is about eighteen inches or less. This step should be easy and so firm that the body, as the weight changes from back foot to the front, maintains a perfect balance. The bat should never meet the ball before or after the stride has been taken, but at the instant the weight of the body is equal on both feet. The drive given to the ball comes from the weight of the body as it changes from the rear foot to the front foot. If the bat meets the ball at this exact instant, it is perfectly timed. *Without perfect timing, no player can ever obtain great success as a batter.*

The stride should never be a high step, but merely a slide of the

front foot forward, just high enough so that the spikes of the shoe clear the ground in the batter's box.

A good way to tell if a batter is striding wrong is to study his shadow in the swing. The batter's back is to the late afternoon sun casting a shadow directly in front of him. The batter now assumes his proper stance and the coach puts his foot on the batter's head shadow. Now the player takes a good swing and follows through. If the coach's foot stays on the head or nearly on the head, the batter is striding and holding his head correctly. If the head moves forward or backward, the batter is striding and moving his head too far. He may be dropping his body by bending his knees in his swing.

The correct swing of the bat. The swing of the bat should be level and parallel to the ground on most pitched balls. Of course, it is impossible to have the bat swing parallel on a low ball. In this case, the swing should be down toward the ball rather than up. A down swing with the front shoulder held level with the back shoulder will give the batter a consistently better swing. Remember this is not a chop swing, but a hard even swing from level shoulders. Movements of the wrists and forearms upward from a level position will cause a clean miss, a pop fly, or a badly topped ball. The bat should follow through—that is, it should not stop when it hits the ball but should keep on going so that the top of the bat, at the end of the swing, is far beyond the side of the body nearest the pitcher, thus, nearer the back than the front of the body (see Figure 42).

The arm farthest from the pitcher gives impetus to the drive. The arm nearest the pitcher acts as a guide to keep the bat in a horizontal position, and also as a "puller" to help the other arm bring the bat forward. The arms should go back on the stroke, but the body is held straight and is never thrown backward in preparation for the swing. Very little waggling or false motion of the bat should be made after the pitcher takes his position on the pitching rubber. Backward or forward motions of the bat may throw the batter off balance. Unnecessary motion often causes movements of the head and arms which are hindrances to good hitting.

The foregoing advice for the correct swing of the bat is given in order that a coach may do everything possible to prevent the young player from swinging at high and low pitched balls which are not strikes. All young players and many older ones have a very strong inclination to swing at balls which come shoulder high or higher. It is for those who have this habit that the horizontal and down swing of the bat is so important. The pitched ball coming between the hips and knees of the batter does not give so much trouble.

"choke" versus "swing" hitting

The selection of a bat is very important. It must never be so heavy that it swings the batter instead of letting the batter swing it, nor so light that the batter cannot control his swing.

Length of the bat is also very important. A high school player should be using a 33 to 34 inch bat. However, a big strong boy could swing a 35 inch bat. The normal sizes for a college player are 34 and 35 inch bats. However, the small player might use a 33 inch bat. Many professionals use 33½ and 34½ inch bats. A 36 inch bat should never be used.

Some men prefer to *choke* the bat—that is, to hold it far up the handle and to swing with a short stroke. Others prefer a full swing, with the bat held at the very end. The success of either style depends wholly on the strength and natural ability of the batter. In any event, the bat must balance perfectly in his hands, whether they grip it far apart or close together, on the end or near the trademark.

The choke hitter seldom drives the ball very far; he merely pokes at it with a three-quarter swing, his hands far up on the handle of the bat. Such a batter does not strike out many times during the course of a season, and he is a very reliable hitter. The swing hitter is not so reliable as the choke hitter; he may strike out many times during the season, but he is always more dangerous than the choke hitter. The swing hitter is likely to hit the ball out of the park any time he swings the bat. It is impossible for him to place his hits; the only place hitting he can do is to drive the ball beyond the boundary of the playing field. The choke hitter, on the other hand, can be very skillful in the art of placing hits because of his greater control over the bat. There is a happy medium between the choke hitter and the end of the bat swinger. Many good long ball hitters choke up the bat about one inch from the knob of the bat. This gives them better bat control as well as good leverage for hitting the long ball.

Any type of batter can obtain good practice, in a way unnoticed by many players, in the following manner. Whenever a pitcher practicing on the side lines starts to throw a ball to his catcher, the batter can stand in about his regular batting position in front of the catcher. As he sees the ball coming, he should say to himself: "No good," or "Good ball." The batter can thus practice deciding which balls to swing at in a regular game, and which balls to let pass. With some help from his catcher, who can tell him whether or not the ball thrown was a strike, he should become a better judge of pitched balls in a regular game.

type of batters

The pull hitter. The batter who hits the ball with a full swing and follows through before the ball gets even with his body is a pull hitter. He meets the ball with his bat well ahead of the front foot, even before the ball has passed over any portion of the plate, and hits it into the field corresponding to his position at the plate; that is, a right-handed batter hits to left field and a left-handed batter to right field.

The straightaway hitter. The batter who hits the ball according to the way the pitcher delivers it is a straightaway hitter. He hits inside pitches to left field if he is right-handed and to right field if he is left-handed. When the ball is delivered directly over the plate, he hits it toward center field. On an outside pitch, he hits to the field opposite his position at the plate. These rules hold true for all pitched balls, with one exception: if a pitched ball completely fools the batter, then he is likely to hit it, if at all, into any field.

The slice or late hitter. The batter who continually swings late at the ball hits it into the field opposite his position in the batter's box. He is the real hit-and-run batter. To become a successful slice hitter, the player must stand far enough away from the plate so that a ball pitched to the

figure **43**

inside corner will not be hit on the handle of the bat. He must keep away from the ball so that he can hit it with a late stroke. It is almost impossible to slice an inside pitched ball unless the batter assumes the stance just described, and a batter with a natural talent for slicing should so protect himself against the inside pitch. A good way to learn to slice the ball, or opposite field hitting, is to stand very close (the toes are within approximately 12 inches) to a screen or net and swing a bat, leading with the hands so that the end of the bat drags behind on the net. Many swings like this will give the batter the correct swing and the idea of how the bat angles to hit the ball to the opposite field (see Figure 43).

bunting the ball

There are times when it is important to bunt the ball. Many batters make the mistakes of attempting to bunt bad balls—balls which are not strikes—and of trying to get away from the plate too quickly—starting to run as they start to bunt. Bunt the ball first.

figure **44**

Bunting need not be a lost art; it merely takes time and work. The bunter must visualize the top half of the ball meeting the bottom half of the head of the bat, with the bat angled so as to bunt the ball near a foul line or in the area desired. He must also realize that a position in the front part of the batter's box gives him a better opportunity to bunt the ball fair. All bunters could be aided by the use of an instructional bunting bat (see Figure 44). The batter should never fail to bunt when he is called upon to do so. He should perfect himself in this kind of hitting by constant practice, and should try at all times to assume a comfortable bunting position. He holds the bat loosely, the upper hand gripping it at about halfway up and acting as a fulcrum. The lower hand guides the bat. The more firmly his hands grip the bat, the harder he will bunt the ball. A hard bunt is not desirable. The bat must be under perfect control but very loosely held. The easiest way to teach the grip of the top hand is to lay the bat on the ground and pick it up without wrapping the fingers around the bat. Pick it up near the trademark where the top hand should grip the bat.

A properly bunted ball has little momentum as it settles on the ground. It will not go into the air. The good bunter picks out strikes, and does not attempt to bunt on just any ball delivered by the pitcher unless the signal for a hit-and-run squeeze play has been given. In that event he must bunt the next ball, no matter where it comes. If the pitcher expects a bunt, he will deliver the ball high; thus, it is to the batter's advantage to train his eye to bunt nothing but strikes.

The left-handed batter has an advantage over a right-handed man in bunting for a sure hit, as he is more than a full step nearer first base. A left-handed man who is fast on his feet and a good bunter is a player whom the opposing team must watch very cautiously when he appears at the plate. He may attempt either to hit or to bunt. When a left-handed batter bunts for a base hit, his first step is his left foot stepping over his right foot. However, some bunters prefer to take a short step with the right foot, and then step over with the left.

A drag bunt is a ball bunted on the ground between the pitcher and first base, just hard enough to be out of the pitcher's reach and slow enough to keep the second baseman from fielding it. With practice, a left-handed batter can develop an effective drag bunt. If he is very fast on his feet, his running advantage from his natural batting stance at the plate makes him a very dangerous offensive player with this particular style of bunting. The drag bunt is successful only when the defense is not expecting it.

The right-handed batter can make a similar play, but instead of dragging the ball, he must push it, so that it settles on the ground between the pitcher and first base. This offensive attack can be made if the defensive team is lax and off-guard. In this push bunt, the right foot steps first toward first base. Caution must be used so that the ball meets the

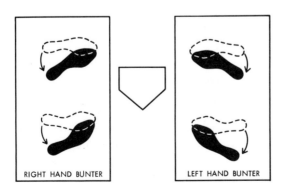

RIGHT HAND BUNTER   LEFT HAND BUNTER   *figure* **45**

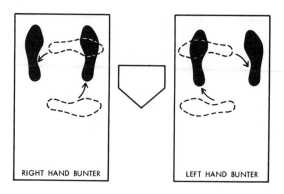

RIGHT HAND BUNTER   LEFT HAND BUNTER

figure **46**

bat before the right foot touches the ground. If it does touch the ground first, the bunter will be called out for stepping out of the box. After the ball meets the bat, he may step out of the box toward first base.

The bunted ball should be placed near the first or the third base line. A speedy left-handed batter should bunt outside balls to the third base line and inside balls to the first base line. The right-handed batter bunts inside balls to the third base line and outside balls to the first base line.

A comfortable foot position is important to place a good bunt. There are two positions that are acceptable to most coaches.

Pivot in tracks: The bunter stands in his normal hitting position, then pivots on the balls of his feet and faces the pitcher (see Figure 45). The bunter pivots as the pitcher cocks his arm for the delivery.

Square around: The bunter assumes his natural hitting stance. As the pitcher cocks his arm for the delivery, the bunter moves his front foot sideways away from home plate and moves his rear foot up even with the front foot. The feet are now spread comfortably for good movement and the bunter faces the pitcher (see Figure 46).

the hit-and-run play

The idea of the hit-and-run play is that the batter shall hit the ball into the territory of the defensive player who is to cover second base for the apparently clean steal by the runner trying for that base.

A base runner can assist a batter in the execution of this play. The runner, as the pitcher pitches, makes an earnest start for second base, stops instantly, and returns to first base. In a great many cases, the player who is going to protect second base for the attempted steal from first base will either lean or take a step toward second base. The batter sees this. Through a prearranged signal, the runner breaks for second base as the pitcher pitches to the batter; the ball is hit into the territory of the player who gave away his intentions unconsciously.

The batter has an advantage over the pitcher if he keeps this in mind: whenever the pitcher is in a hole, and there are runners in a scoring position, he should hit. The pitcher is in a *hole* when two balls and no strikes or three balls and one strike have been called. Under ordinary circumstances the pitcher in this position delivers a straight fast ball. The batter will not make a mistake in looking for this kind of pitch. It is good baseball to hit when the count is three balls and one strike, with one or two men out and no runners on bases. The batter should swing hard in an effort to make a long hit. He should have enough confidence in his own ability to hit and hit hard any strike delivered by the pitcher, whenever he has an advantage, or the pitcher is in a hole.

The hit-and-run play is one of the most dangerous and yet one of the best offensive attacks in baseball. The batter should make a study of the pitcher even while he is sitting on the players' bench during the course of the game. He should pay close attention to the defensive tactics of the opposing team. When called upon to make an offensive attack, he should know just what to do. A careful study of the opposing pitcher is very necessary to the success of the hit-and-run play.

Three balls and one strike is the only ideal hit-and-run situation. The batter can tell his base runner that he is going to hit the next ball pitched, provided it is a strike. He does this by giving the runner a prearranged sign. The pitcher's hands are tied: he must deliver a strike or give the batter the base on balls.

A count of two balls and no strikes, although not the ideal hit-and-run situation, constitutes a good opportunity for such a move. If the pitcher, with first base occupied by a runner, pitches the first ball to all batters for a strike, the hit-and-run play can be used. The offensive team must, however, watch the defensive work of the pitcher. The latter may change his defense after one hit-and-run play has been successfully made in the above manner. The hit-and-run play is a battle of wits between the pitcher and the batter.

It is not good baseball to attempt a hit-and-run play when more than one base is occupied by the batter's teammates. With two balls and no strikes or three balls and one strike, and with more than one base occupied by runners, one runner would be in a scoring position with the pitcher in the hole, and the batter should hit straightaway. Many a batter will hit the ball harder and use better judgment in his selection of strikes if he does not give the hit-and-run signal in this situation.

The batter should never take a long swing at the ball in his hit-and-run play; he must be sure to meet the ball squarely and, if he can possibly do so, slice it behind the base runner. If he knows who is covering second base, he attempts to hit the position left open. A batter who strikes out frequently is not a good hit-and-run man.

squeeze play

The squeeze play is really a sacrifice bunt used only when third base is occupied by a runner. If the score is close and one run is very important, this play is often used by the offensive team. When runs are hard to score, this type of a sacrifice bunt should be used only in the latter part of a game—the seventh, eighth, or ninth innings.

Bunt and run. The base runner on third knows by a signal that the batter is going to bunt, and he must attempt to score. The batter picks a good ball and bunts down either the third or the first base line. The base runner takes his lead off third in foul territory. The size of his lead will be determined by the position of the third baseman. The runner must be alert. He must not try to score before the ball is bunted, and he must protect himself from a quick throw by the catcher to the third baseman which might put him out, should the batter not bunt the pitcher's ball. The success of this play depends to a great extent on the base runner's break when the ball is bunted. If it is not bunted or is popped up, the runner must get back to third base.

The run and bunt, do or die, or suicide squeeze. This play is very similar to the bunt and run squeeze. The only difference is that the runner knows by a signal from the batter which ball is to be bunted. When the signal is given, the batter must bunt the ball regardless of where it is pitched, because the runner, as soon as the pitcher's striding foot hits the ground out in front of the mound, makes a sudden dash for the plate as in a plain steal. On this squeeze, the runner will score regardless of where the ball is bunted or hit, provided of course that the ball is bunted on the ground. For this play to succeed, the batter must bunt the ball for which the signal has been given and the runner must break when the pitcher's striding foot hits the ground. If the runner leaves too early, the pitcher will see this and throw a waste pitch which must be bunted if at all possible to protect the runner coming to score.

The double squeeze. The batter signals for the hit-and-run squeeze with runners on second and third bases. The runner on third base plays his part as he would on the run-and-bunt squeeze. The runner on second takes a big lead. As the pitcher starts his pitching motions, he dashes for third base, rounds the bag under full running stride, and continues on to the plate as some infielder or the pitcher throws the bunted ball to the first baseman for the putout on the batter. The runner coming to third must keep his eye on the bunted ball as a heady infielder might make a bluff throw toward the first baseman and get him in a run-down play at the plate. The success of this play depends wholly on the ability of the batter to bunt the ball so that the infielder fielding it will have his back to the base runner who was on second base.

1. What mistakes must a coach rectify in the average school player?
2. What are the qualifications for a good batter?
3. What are the five essential things in batting? Discuss each.
4. Is there a great difference between a swing and a choke hitter? If so, discuss the difference.
5. Discuss the types of batters a coach has to contend with.
6. Discuss how you would teach a youngster the art of bunting.
7. What does angle of bat mean in bunting?
8. Under what conditions would you advise your players to bunt?
9. Would you advise your fast runner to perfect the art of bunting? Why?
10. If you expect to employ the hit-and-run play, give a detailed description of how you will use it and why.
11. What "hole" situations would prompt the hit-and-run play?
12. Would you use the hit-and-run play when you are three runs behind? Why?
13. How many types of squeeze plays can you use in your offense?
14. Which squeeze play would you try to perfect? Why?
15. When would you use the double squeeze play? Why?
16. What two things are important to the success of the perfect suicide squeeze play?

The first rule for base runners is, *touch or tag every base; never miss a bag*. Every player should know thoroughly the rules which pertain to base runners.

The average baseball player finds it difficult to steal a base or to advance an extra base on a hit to the outfield. Base running should not be slighted by any player, for it is a real qualification in the make up of an expert in the game. Good base runners do not have to be fast on their feet, although speed is always a great asset; a greater test of ability is to keep the eyes open and the head up. A fumble, a hesitation, or a play that puts an outfielder in a non-throwing position gives the runner a chance to advance an extra base, and he must always be ready to seize such an opportunity.

Base running is not a simple part of the game. It requires much observation and study, especially of the opposing battery men and outfielders. Heady, alert base running wins many a ball game, and stupid, indifferent base running loses just as many.

One of the greatest errors of judgment a base runner can make is to let himself be picked off a "scoring position" base after reaching it safely. Such a misfortune means that the base runner is either not thinking or is overanxious.

The art of sliding makes good base runners out of average base runners. Most players will not advance to third base from first base or score from second base for fear that they will have to slide. Players who know how to slide like to run bases and take the extra bases.

base running 11

essentials of base running

The batter running to first base. The instant the batter hits the ball he is a base runner, and from then on he must never loaf. He should run out every hit, no matter where it goes. No matter how sure an outfielder may be, he may drop a fly ball. The best of infielders occasionally makes inexcusable fumbles and bad throws. *Nothing can be taken for granted in baseball.* First base is the batter's objective, and no player can be excused for not doing his utmost to reach it. The good base runner is never satisfied with one base, he is always looking for a break to give him another base.

Every batter, whenever he hits a ball to the outfield, gets away as fast as possible to first base and pivots on the bag, keeping his eyes on the ball as it is played by some member of the defensive team. On any fumble or fielding play in which the outfielder is at a disadvantage, the runner must try to make an extra base.

The batter never slides into the first base bag except to avoid being touched by the first baseman, in case the latter has had to leave the bag in order to catch a ball thrown wide of the base by an infielder. A slide under any condition means a loss of speed and time. The slide is made to avoid overrunning a bag, but the batter is allowed by the rule to overrun first base, and advantage should be taken of this rule. The batter, now a base runner, should do nothing to slacken his speed until the first base bag has been touched. If he runs hard and the throw is wild, there is no lost motion in his attempt to advance to second base. It is to the baserunner's advantage to tag the front edge of the base in attempting to beat out an infield hit. Never hit the middle of the bag or miss the bag on an obvious out. Hitting the middle of the bag adds distance to the run. Missing the bag is foolish because the first baseman may juggle or drop the ball.

The pivot. Going to first on a base hit or on a fly ball to the outfielder, the runner *pivots* directly on the inside edge of the bag to save time and yardage in his attempt to make second base. He should pivot sharply whenever he tries to go more than one base on a play or in rounding a base.

When a runner knows he is going to take extra bases, he should begin his circle early enough to keep him from making a large turn toward right field. He should concentrate on hitting the inside of the bag with either foot that gets to the bag in stride and keep the circle small. He does this by leaning in toward the infield and using the side of the bag to pivot in toward the next base.

Another method commonly used is as follows: When the runner is about four strides away from the base which he is rounding, the left leg crosses over the right leg, then the right foot hits the ground in front of his left foot and he throws his weight heavily upon it to begin his turn toward the next bag. He now swings his left foot in front of his right leg and his body turns toward the next base. When the left foot hits the ground, the body also leans in toward the infield. His next stride or two should put him close to the bag for the final pivot on the inside of the bag. This pivot is a hard pivot and lean toward second base. The smaller arc, made by pivoting on the last few steps toward a base, places the runner's feet in such a position that he hits the bag with either the left or the right foot (preferably the left) in almost a direct line to the base ahead. The runner should never shorten the last two or three steps just before reaching a bag. All pivoting is done at full speed and with a natural stride. If a runner on a long hit does not pivot, he may be compelled to run the bases just as he would a large circular track.

A runner must not be confused by the rule which forbids a base runner from running out of the base line. That rule applies only to a runner who goes out of the base line to avoid being touched by a player holding the ball.

The slide. The purpose of a slide is not to frighten an opponent, but to prevent the runner from overrunning his base and being tagged, and also to give the baseman as small a part of the runner's body as possible to touch with the ball for an out. *Any deliberate attempt on the part of a runner to spike or injure his opponent will never be tolerated. It is never necessary or justifiable. Slide low and slide hard.*

Here is a cardinal rule on sliding which never should be violated. When a runner has made up his mind to slide into a base, he should slide into that base. He must not listen to instructions given him in a friendly manner by an opposing infielder; nor should he listen to the advice of his coaches unless he is far enough away from the base to which he is going—never when he is about to throw himself into the air for his slide. More sprained ankles, broken legs, and other injuries are inflicted on base runners by this mental lapse than by any other playing action. "I will slide—no I won't," is worthless technique. Sudden stops, halfway slides into a base, and slides which carry the body over the base have caused much physical damage to ball players.

There are two ways of sliding into bases: head first and feet first. The head first slide is the most dangerous one and is very seldom used, except by expert ball players. Risk of injury to the head, arms, or hands is great. The player sliding head first throws his arms in front of him and slides into the bag on his stomach. If the baseman guarding that bag has to leap to get a badly thrown ball, he may come down with his spikes on the arms or hands of the runner. The runner would then be in danger, not only of being incapacitated for the game, but of being seriously and permanently injured. Should the baseman block the base with his legs, the slider can injure his arms or shoulders. The slide is used mostly for getting back to a base on pick-off plays or when a player has an injured leg.

We break the feet first slide into four methods. The hook slide, hook slide fade-away, bent leg and up, and bent leg and go.

1. *Hook Slide.* This slide can be made to either side; the side should be determined by the fielder. In order to decide which side to approach before the ball arrives, the slider should watch the fielder's eyes and go opposite where he is looking. A slider's feet and legs should be extended out in front of his body, but the leg tagging the bag should be bent, and the instep used to hook the bag. The foot tagging the bag leaves the ground last and is the take-off foot. This slide is more on the hip than on the calf of that leg. The slider's body should be in a rather prone position and turned to the outside, rather than perpendicular to the bag. His body should be carried to the side of the bag, and the instep of his inside leg (take-off foot) used to hook the bag. The outside extended leg should be bent slightly and kept away from the bag, giving the fielder only a foot to tag. Keeping the extended leg too straight often causes injuries (see Figure 47).

2. *Hook Slide Fade-away.* Basically, this slide is the same as the straight hook slide. The difference lies in the tag of the bag. A slider's hooking foot comes into the bag for a fake tag. When it is approximately three feet from the bag, it is thrown over his other leg and foot. This momentum carries his body and leg past the bag. As the slider comes in, he should grasp the bag with the hand nearest it, or he can continue past the bag and spin his body toward the bag, grabbing it with his outside hand, behind the fielder. He would now be lying on his stomach (see Figure 48).

3. *Bent Leg and Up.* A slider may execute this slide on either side, thus taking off from either foot. The first foot to leave the ground should be the one that is extended in front of the body. The foot from which he takes off should be bent in under the knee of the extended leg. The slider's body is going forward almost perpendicular to the base in a sitting position. The slide is made on the calf and hip of the bent leg while the other foot is carried in the air. Even if it is not necessary to get up in a hurry, the bent leg slide is basically the best slide into the bag. The momentum of the slider's body and the push of his bent leg against the bag or earth bounces him up on his feet. To get up quickly, he should start his push with the bent leg before he reaches the bag. The extended foot then hits the bag to aid in the push up. This slide is the fastest slide to a base and is used by most good base runners (see Figure 49).

4. *Bent Leg and Go.* While this slide can be on either side, preferably it should be made on the bent left leg. The bent leg and go should be executed exactly as described for the bent leg and up slide, except that the bent leg always pushes up before the slide is completed and this leg hits the bag. A slider's extended foot also hits the bag, making this slide fast and hard. The momentum generated by the slide, the push up on the dirt of the bent left leg, and the push up of the extended right foot on

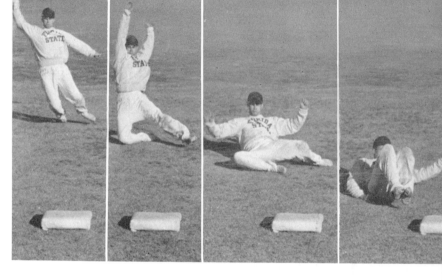

figure **47**

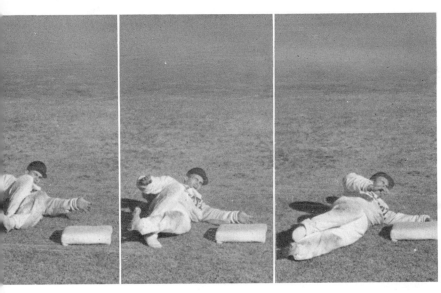

figure **48**

figure **49**

figure **50**

the bag spins the slider toward the next base (see Figure 50). There is no cessation of motion. Sliding on a bent right leg spins the slider toward the outfield and slows up his motion toward the advance base.

Only constant practice will make a player perfect in sliding. Timing is essential: the slide must not start too soon or too late. If a runner slides too late he will overslide the bag and probably be injured; if he slides too quickly, he will not reach the base and may be put out.

The ideal way of teaching sliding is to give your players a pair of old sweat pants to put over their baseball pants, have them remove their shoes, and make them slide in the grass (note Figures 47, 48, 49 and 50). Pick a well-sodded area and make certain there are no pieces of glass, sticks, or stones hidden in the grass. A sliding pit, filled with sand or sawdust, can be used to teach players, properly equipped with pads, how to fall, but the complete slide should be practiced only on grass.

The runner about to slide keeps his eyes on the man guarding the base. If the baseman goes to the base runner's left for a thrown ball, the runner slides on the right side of his body to the outside of the diamond, hooking the bag with his left foot. On the other hand, if the baseman goes to the base runner's right for the ball, the runner slides on his left side to the inside of the diamond and hooks the bag with his right foot.

It should be noted here that the slider in sliding feet first should keep his hands out of the dirt to prevent jammed wrists or other injuries to the hand or arm.

steals starting from first base

First base strategy. Base stealing does not necessarily call for a big lead off first base or any other base from which a steal might be attempted. Ability to make a quick get away, as a track man would term it, is the

main qualification of a good base stealer. Practice makes perfect, and much practice work is needed on this particular part of the game.

The cross over step is the fastest and most effective start, especially in stealing bases. It is accomplished by a quick spin of the head and shoulders toward second base and a quick pivot on the right foot, after which the left foot crosses over the right leg. Both feet dig into the ground for a good hold. The body remains low, particularly at the instant of the start when the head and shoulders are thrown toward second base, and then gradually assumes the natural running position. The form is very similar to that of the sprinter in track, picking up the knees and placing the toes out in front of his nose and leaning forward. Never run in an upright position.

The runner stays on the bag at first base until he is satisfied that the pitcher has the ball. He should either see the ball or see the pitcher step to his position on the pitching rubber. If the pitcher steps on the pitching rubber without the ball, he has made a balk. It is time for him to take his lead off first base as soon as the pitcher has come into his pitching position. The weight of the runner's body is distributed evenly on both feet, so that he has absolute control of his body. *A good safe lead does not take the runner away from first base so far that he could not get back to it with two steps and a slide or a head first slide.* This distance should not be increased until the runner is absolutely sure that the pitcher has delivered the ball to the batter. When the ball is delivered, the runner should be in motion on a direct line toward second base, but not too far to allow a safe return to first after the ball passes the batter. If the batter hits the ball, the runner has the necessary start toward second base.

Every player should study the peculiarities of the opposing pitcher, even while sitting on the bench. There are many pitchers against whom a big lead from first base can be taken safely, and there are others against whom the runner must exercise great caution. Left-handed pitchers should be watched very closely: they often use body and leg movements to pitch to a batter that are almost identical with their movements for throwing to first base.

A pitcher cannot possibly deliver a ball to the batter without bending his front knee a little from its natural position. Every offensive player should train himself to watch closely for this slight movement. There is a difference between the knee action accompanying a throw to first base and that for a pitch to the plate. There is also a big difference in the movement of the pitcher's front foot. The pitcher's glove and ball should rest on the front of his body, waist-high. If this position is not used, there is a great variation in the arm movement for the throw to first base and for the pitch to the plate. If the pitcher's feet are in any position other than the correct one described in Chapter 1, a throw to first base can be expected. All of these peculiarities should be studied. All of them tell the runner whether or not to increase his lead off first base. The longer this lead can be safely made, the easier it is to steal second or beat a force play.

All base runners must check the number of outs and know the score and inning. Prior to the pitch and after getting the signs, they should check to see where the outfielders are playing. This allows the base runner to know in advance what to do when the ball is hit to the outfield.

Varieties of steals from first base. There are several types of steals starting from first base: the plain, the delayed, the double, the forced balk, and the base on balls steal.

The plain steal to second base is the one most often attempted since, if it is successful, it brings the runner into a scoring position. The plain steal is never attempted unless it will benefit the offensive team. It is not advisable, under any situation, for a base runner to attempt to steal second base when a pitcher or a weak hitter is at bat and two men are out. Failure of a base runner to steal second base may cause the pitcher or the weak batter to become the first batter in the following inning. This would be very bad baseball.

If the offensive team is so many runs behind that a perfect steal, giving an opportunity to score one run on a base hit or an error, would not benefit the team, it is a stupid play. The runner should play safe and take no chances, as one run would not help the team; more than one run must cross the plate to be of any benefit. This precaution does not mean that the runner should not be ready to take advantage of wild throws or wildly pitched balls. He must be alert and ready to run on hits and fielding errors.

When the score is close, however, the style of running is quite different. When the offensive team is one run behind with a good base stealer on first, the situation calls for an attempt to steal second base, provided the pitcher is delivering balls which are difficult for the catcher to handle for his throw to second. The observing runner will have noticed, in different situations, which pitch causes the catcher difficulty in catching and coming back to his throwing position. If the runner can tell when a curve ball is to be pitched to the batter, this is another ball prompting a steal. A curve ball is naturally pitched low and obliges the catcher to go down for his catch and then to come back up again into his throwing position. The ball delivered high to the catcher does not put him so far out of his throwing position, and so diminishes the runner's chances for making a plain steal.

A delayed steal can be made only when the catcher, the shortstop, or the second baseman is lax in his fielding duties. If the catcher habitually tosses or lobs the ball back to the pitcher after each pitch, the runner, taking his regular lead from first base, can usually steal second base. The start for second is made the instant the ball is to leave the catcher's hand for the customary toss to the pitcher. Even if the catcher sees the base runner start on a delayed steal and is able to hold back his toss to the pitcher, he is bound to lose some time in assuming the correct position for throwing to second. Moreover, his throw will have to be a hurried one. If the shortstop or second baseman fails to take a few steps toward the bag at second base after each pitch, he has to catch the ball on the run and is consequently at a great disadvantage in tagging the base runner. Any of these acts on the part of the defensive team affords an opportunity to start a delayed steal.

The base runner has another way of attempting a delayed steal. He takes a big lead off the base after the ball has been delivered to the batter. The catcher, seeing this big lead, often makes the mistake of throwing to the bag occupied by the runner. The latter, seeing the motion for the throw to that base, makes a dash for the next one.

double steals

The double steal can be executed by runners on first and third, first and second, and second and third bases.

With runners on first and third bases. The double steal with runners on first and third bases is the one most often attempted, usually when the offensive team has a weak man at bat with two men out. It is also attempted even with a strong man at bat, but it would be unsound baseball to make the attempt before the strong hitter has had two strikes called on him.

The double steal usually is not attempted with fewer than two outs, as the runner on third has many opportunities for scoring which should not be endangered by taking a chance on a double steal in order to score one run. The double steal, if successfully made, means a run and another base runner in a scoring position, or another runner in scoring position, thus eliminating a force situation at second base. Close thinking is demanded in this play.

Knowing well that the other team has a defense for the attempted double steal, the runner on first base, from which the steal must start, can play his part correctly in one of five ways: (1) a plain steal; (2) a plain steal, stopping just before reaching second base; (3) a delayed steal; (4) by getting intentionally picked off; and (5) a base on balls steal of second.

The usual procedure is for the runner on first to start to make a plain steal, all the time watching the defensive player around second base. If the ball coming from the catcher passes the player who may be in the proper position for the cut off and is caught by the player at second base, the runner never deliberately gives himself up for an easy putout, but stops and retraces his steps toward first base. The reason for stopping is to give the runner on third base an opportunity to dash for the plate, provided he did not make his start when the catcher made the throw to second base. If the runner on third did not make a dash for the plate when the catcher threw to second, he should do so just as soon as the defensive player in the run-down play on the runner from first base is in a poor throwing position. For example, suppose the man who chases the runner back to first base is a right handed thrower. In his play on the runner when the chaser is going full speed he is in a poor throwing position. Or if the defensive first baseman is a left handed thrower and is chasing the runner toward second base, running at full speed puts him at a disadvantage in throwing home. He must stop and turn his body if he is to make an accurate throw to the plate to get the runner who is dashing home from third base.

If the runner on third has decided to score on the catcher's throw to second base, he must not be too far off third base when the play starts. A snap throw to third, or a bluff throw to second turned into a quick throw to third by the catcher, might get him. If the catcher makes a good bluff of throwing to second and the runner on third has made up his mind to score on the throw, the only thing for the catcher to do is to tag the runner who is almost on the plate. In this case, the runner must attempt to get into a run-down play so the runner on first can advance to third base should there be less than two out. If two men are out, the runner on first should stay on second base. The runner on third must be exceedingly careful; he must see the ball actually on its way to second base before he attempts to dash for the plate. He must also be certain that the ball will not be cut off by the pitcher.

The runner on first base can start his part of the double steal with a delayed steal. In this case the delayed steal is made just as if there were a runner on first base only. If the runner on first attempts a delayed steal and sees that he is caught for an out at second base, he should attempt to maneuver as a base runner would in a plain steal under the same conditions. The advantage of the delayed steal comes only when the short-stop and second baseman are very slack in their duties, failing to go toward the bag at second base after each pitched ball has passed the batter, or when the catcher lobs the ball back to the pitcher.

The most effective way to pull the delayed double steal is to have perfect timing. To get this timing the runner on first base takes a normal lead not indicating that he will attempt to steal a base. As soon as the pitcher pitches the ball, the runner begins to walk toward second base in a fast walk. When the ball hits the catcher's glove, the runner—walking all the time—counts to three and, on the count of three breaks for second as fast as possible. This timing throws the infielders off balance and gets the catcher in the act of throwing the ball back to the pitcher. It often catches him so much by surprise that he throws the ball into center field. His first instinct is to throw right away, but since neither the shortstop nor the second baseman have broken for the bag, he cannot. This hesitation often makes the catcher throw wild and makes the fielders catch the ball on the run, which is difficult if a tag has to be made.

A difficult steal to defend against is when the runner on first base gets picked off intentionally. He should do this with a left-handed first baseman, who he knows does not have a good arm. When the runner is picked off, he gets the first baseman to chase him at full speed. Once the first baseman is thus diverted, the runner on third base, who has been creeping cautiously toward home, breaks for home at full speed. The first baseman will have a difficult time stopping to make a strong, accurate throw.

A runner on first base can start the hardest defensive play in base-ball by stealing second while the defense is playing a close infield to stop the winning run at home plate. The defensive team's only solution to the stolen base is to walk the batter and take a chance on a force play at the plate. The motive for the steal is to draw a wild throw from the catcher, or to have the batter walked and replaced by a better one.

The forced balk steal is actually a steal by attempting to make the pitcher balk. Normally a pitcher in his stretch looks at the runner on third base, then at the runner on first. The runner on first breaks as soon as the pitcher, after getting his sign from the catcher, moves his hands at the sides of his legs to get set. The runner on third takes a good lead, one that would necessitate a dive back to the base should the pitcher attempt to pick him off. If the pitcher throws to second, the runner on third goes home. The base runners must run at full speed. The pitcher some-times gets his sign off of the rubber, then places his pivot foot on the rubber prior to his stretch. In this case, the runner on first breaks as soon as the pitcher's foot contacts the rubber, before he starts his stretch. The only way the pitcher can stop this play is to back off the rubber, pivot toward third base to drive the runner back to third, and then throw to second base.

The base on balls steal is used best when the offensive team needs a run and has a runner on third base with a poor hitter on deck. The batter gets a base on balls. He then begins to jog down to first base. As he approaches the bag, he sees that the shortstop and second baseman are not covering second and that the pitcher, who has the ball, is not looking at him. As soon as he hits first base he breaks for second base as fast as possible. The runner on third has a good lead, and waits for the pitcher to throw to second base so he can break for home. Should the runner at first base be caught going to second, he maneuvers as he would on other steals by getting into a run-down play.

With runners on first and second bases. A double steal is very seldom attempted by runners on first and second bases. One runner is in a scoring position, and a two base hit should mean two runs. A base hit would mean one run. If the defensive outfielder throws the ball toward the plate to catch the runner who was on second base, the runner who was on first base goes to third and the player who hit the ball goes to second, provided, of course, that the defense is lax. A base hit, an error, or a wild pitch would then score two more runs. The self-satisfaction of the base runners at being in such a strong offensive position does not often prompt a double steal. If a plain steal is attempted, the man on second base is the key runner. The whole attempt hinges on his having an extra big lead off second base. The runner on first base follows the lead of the runner on second: that is, if the runner on second does attempt to steal third, the runner on first goes to second. He must run hard because smart catchers often throw to second base rather than third base to catch the lax base runner.

During a game the catcher might throw to the first baseman to catch the base runner for an out (read the first paragraph on page 30). If this attempt is made, the runner on second should not hesitate to steal third. If the runner on second base is alert, it is impossible for the first baseman to put the runner out at first base and obtain an assisted putout at third base. If the runner on first base is alert, he may entice the catcher into throwing the ball and pull him into this play, which is a great help to the offensive team. The runner on first must play his part correctly and not be caught by the throw.

With runners on first, second, and third bases. The offensive team should not attempt a triple steal unless they are excellent base runners. This steal is usually attempted with two men out and a weak hitter at bat. All base runners should be wide awake and ready to advance on pass balls or wild pitches, which often occur when a defensive team has this disadvantage. A play which the runners should watch very carefully is a throw from the catcher to the first baseman or to the guardians of second base for an attempted pick off on the base runner. The runners should take a substantial lead from all three bases, but never be far enough from the bases to be caught. A runner caught by the defensive team when the offensive team has such an advantage can justly be called a "bonehead." Such a play is inexcusable.

With runners on second and third bases. It is very seldom that this particular double steal is attempted, on account of the great importance of the expected base hit, which should score two runs. As a matter of fact, this double steal, engineered by the runner on third base, can never be successfully made unless the pitcher's mind is on something far away from the ball game. It should not be attempted at all unless the runner on third has waited until two men are out and a very weak hitter is at bat. The many opportunities to score from third base should never be overlooked when this steal is contemplated.

stealing from second base

Occasionally a defensive team has a catcher who is fond of displaying his strong throwing arm. A steal can be pulled on such a catcher if the runner on second base can entice him into throwing the ball. The runner takes a big lead off second base, on the assumption that the catcher will be tempted to make a play on him. If he succeeds in getting the catcher to throw—here he must guard against being deceived by a bluff throw—the runner dashes for third base as soon as the ball leaves the catcher's hand.

A good steal can be made when a very good bunter is at bat. The batter signals his intention to bunt the next pitched ball. The ball is not bunted, but as soon as the third baseman sees the bat drop for a bunt, he must protect his position and will, in most cases, start toward the plate. Being drawn down out of position by the actions of the batter, he leaves the base open for a clean steal. This steal can be made very successfully when the pitcher is in a hole, but only when the defensive team knows that the batter is a sure bunter and a fast runner.

We favor the runner on second base assuming a normal lead off the bag but about six feet behind the baseline. The theory on this is not to remain at this position until the ball is hit, but to be in the baseline when it is hit. While the pitcher is looking back at him, the runner moves forward, on an angle toward third, toward the mound. By the time he is in the baseline, he will have a better lead than he would have gotten by shuffling off. He is also in a better position to move right or left. If he is stealing, he makes a little bigger angle toward third. To the pitcher, this does not appear to be an exceptional lead, but in reality the runner is getting a good jump.

stealing from third base

The steal from third should be called the "idiotic" steal, because no sane player will attempt it under ordinary conditions. There are times, however, when with two out the pitcher becomes lax in his movements and makes an unusually long windup. In such a situation, when a weak hitter is at bat with one or no strikes on him, an attempt to steal from third may be worthwhile. Ordinarily, however, so many opportunities are open for scoring a run when third base has been reached that it is foolish to risk being put out on a steal.

base running problems

An important cardinal rule: *A base runner should make every possible effort to reach third base when there is one man out, but he should never take the same chance to reach that base when no one is out or when two men are out.*

With a runner on second; a ball is hit to third base. The runner on second should have a safe lead. A safe lead would be three steps and the length of the body or three steps and a slide. He might go to third base as the third baseman throws to first for the attempted out on the batter. The runner on second base, if first or third is not occupied, goes to third on all balls hit to his left. If the ball is hit to his right, he waits for it to go out of the infield—as a hit or an error—before starting for third. If two men are out, he breaks for third on all ground balls. He knows where all the defensive men, particularly the outfielders, are playing before every pitch.

With a runner on first base; a hit to the outfield. Just before the runner reaches second base, he looks at the ball—if it is in front of him—or at the third base coach—if the ball is behind him. If the fielder is caught in a non-throwing or poor position, the runner attempts to go forward for an extra base. The batter rounding first base follows the runner ahead of him, unless he sees a defensive player in a position to make a play whereby he might be retired. In that case, he stops at first base.

There is a rule which states that a base runner shall be declared out immediately if he passes a preceding base runner before such a base runner has legally been put out. The base runner must watch this situation, especially the runner who hit the ball. The runner who was on first base might be undecided as to whether the ball will be caught by the outfielder and stop between first and second bases. If the batter, now a base runner, passes the runner who has stopped, he will be declared out immediately.

With a runner on first base; a fly ball is caught in the outfield on a hit-and-run play. The runner on a hit-and-run play, thinking a batted ball to be a safe hit, may be beyond second base when the ball is caught. He must be sure to touch the bag at second base on his return to first. The substance of the rule is: "If, when obliged to return to a base, while the ball is in play, the runner fails to touch the intervening base, he may be put out by the ball being held by a fielder on any base he failed to touch, or by being touched by the ball in the hand of a fielder."

With runners on first and third bases. The first thought of the runner on third base should be to attempt to score on any ball hit to the infield, in order to stop a double play if such is possible. If the ball thrown by the infielder reaches the catcher before the runner crosses the plate, the runner stops and runs back and forth until the runner on first has reached third base and the batter has reached second base.

With runners on second and third bases. The runner on third should try to score on any ground ball hit to the infield. If he sees that the ball thrown by the infielder is going to reach the catcher before he himself can get safely to the plate, he stops and gets into a run-down play so that the batter can get to second base and the runner who was on second can reach third.

With runners on second and third bases, a situation may arise in which the runner on third has a chance to score on a sacrifice fly. If the fly is caught, making the second out, the runner on second must be very careful in his attempt to reach third. The defensive team might make the play at third and the runner coming from second might be retired before the runner who was on third can cross the plate with a run. Both runners should tag up, and as soon as the ball is caught, they should start for the base ahead, but the runner on second should be sure that the throw cannot retire him.

With two runners on the same bag at the same time. If the runners are not certain which one of them is out, they should wait for the umpire to decide. For example, if two runners are on the bag at second, the one who came to second from first is not entitled to the base unless the one who was previously on that bag is off it and has been declared out, or has passed on to third base. If both runners are standing on the bag and both are touched with the ball by a defensive fielder, the runner who came from first base is out.

With a runner on third base only. When no one is out and the ball is hit toward an infielder, the runner must be sure that it goes by the infielder before he tries to score. If the ball is not hit hard, making a slow difficult play for the infielder, a good base runner could score if the infield is back.

If there is one out, the runner should try to score. If the ball reaches the catcher before the runner gets to the plate, the latter gets into a run-down play until the batter has reached second base, a scoring position.

The runner takes a lead of two steps and the length of his body from third base, his body in foul territory. Doing this prevents his being called out by the umpire if hit by a batted ball, as would be the case if his body were on fair ground. He comes forward two full steps toward the plate when the pitcher is making his delivery to the catcher. If the ball is not hit by the batter, the runner should return to the bag on fair territory. This will cause a handicap to the catcher in making a throw to the third baseman for an attempted pick off.

With a runner on any base. The runner should be on the bag at the base to which he is entitled whenever a long hit is made to the outfield which is an obvious putout. If the ball is caught, the runner may have a chance to advance an extra base after the catch. This, of course, he can never do if he is off his base when the catch is made. If the ball goes over the outfielder's head, the runner is in position to get away, taking no chances on a one hand catch for a possible double play.

The rule to follow is this: whenever an outfielder is going back for a ball, tag up. If the outfielder, on the other hand, is coming in for a short fly ball just back of the infield, take a safe lead off the bag. If the catch is not made, the runner has an opportunity to advance. If there is doubt on a catch, take a safe lead, except on third base. The third base runner tags up on all fly balls.

After three balls and two strikes, the runner has a chance to make a start from first base. It is inadvisable to make such a start with a weak hitter at bat. With one out, if the batter strikes out and the runner is thrown out on an attempted steal, the inning is closed.

Infield fly rule. Every member of the squad should know when an infield fly is hit. Many players have a mistaken impression that the infield fly rule is operative with a runner on first only, or with runners on first and third bases. The rule is made to prevent a player from dropping the ball and starting a double play. When there is a runner on first base only and a batter hits a high fly which can be caught by an infielder, it is certain that one player will be put out under usual circumstances, but there is practically no chance of two men being put out.

The rule reads as follows: "If, before two are out, while first and second or first, second and third bases are occupied, the batter hits a *fair* fly ball, other than a line drive, that can be handled by an infielder, the umpire shall declare it an infield fly; but the runners may be off their bases or advance at the risk of the ball being caught, the same as on any other fly ball. Provided, that with first and second bases occupied, or first, second and third bases occupied, with less than two out, any attempt to bunt which results in a fair fly ball shall not be regarded as an infield fly."

It is important first of all to note that to be considered an infield fly by the umpire, the ball must be fair. Then note that the runners may be off their bases or advance at the risk of the fly being caught, as on any other fly ball. An attempt to bunt which results in a fair fly ball is not to be considered an infield fly. The umpire must immediately declare an infield fly to be such.

coaching the runners

Coaches as advisers. The coaches at first and third bases are two very important factors in the offensive game and should thoroughly familiarize themselves with the coaching rules. Curiously enough, as a rule, coaches are regarded as figure heads by those watching the game. The general impression is that a runner can run the bases himself. But this is not always true; the runner often needs the aid and advice of another player. The coaches at first and third bases have real duties to perform. Idiotic actions and sarcastic remarks designed to annoy an opposing player should never be used by any coaches. The coach has other things to do, and his mind should be on his own game. His job calls for only such activities as will benefit the runner and his team.

Both coaches should know where the ball is after each play has been completed, and advise their base runners where it is.

The third base coach. The third base coach occupies one of the most important offensive positions on his ball team. Snap decisions with sound judgment must, in a great many cases, be made by the third base coach. He must remember that a runner coming toward third has his back to every defensive play, and the coach's own judgment must determine ultimately the real value of the situation.

The third base coach informs the runner just what he is to do in every situation. The runner must be informed of the number of outs and of every possible situation which may be expected to arise, such as, for example, the signal for a squeeze play. The runner must be cautioned to watch for a fly ball to the outfield and to remain on the third base bag until the ball either is caught or goes for a base hit; and also to watch the ball hit to the infield. Every offensive play should be very clear in the mind of the coach, so that he can keep his base runner fully informed.

Many a third base coach makes this great mistake: he does not place himself in a position to advise correctly a runner coming toward third base at full speed. When a runner is in scoring position or the batter has made a long hit, the coach should leave his lines and come up toward the plate, so that at the very last instant he can inform the runner what to do. Some-

times a base runner comes toward third base on a hit and the coach knows that he should not encourage the runner to attempt to score. Although ordinarily no chance should be taken under such circumstances, a defensive player's fumble may change the whole matter, so that a run can be scored if the coach is in the right position to inform the runner to that effect. The coach holds his hands and arms high if he wants the runner to stop. By waving them toward the plate, he urges the runner to attempt to score. By waving his hands down toward the earth and holding them parallel to the ground, he indicates a slide. By pointing at the bag, he indicates, "Hold the base." By bringing his hands in toward his chest, he indicates, "Make your turn." His right hand is for the runner on second who is rounding third. His left hand is for the runner who was on first rounding second base (see Figures 51, 52, 53, 54 and 55).

According to the rules, the coach must remain in the lines of his position, but he is allowed to move away from these lines after a ball is hit or when a play is being made, as long as he does not in any way thereby interfere with any defensive play or player.

Coaching a runner on second base. A runner on second base is aided by both the first and third base coaches as to what he is to do in any given situation. Both coaches watch for any attempt by the second baseman or the shortstop to catch this runner off the bag. We find it best to let the third base coach watch the shortstop and keep talking to the runner in a loud voice. The runner keeps his eyes on the second baseman and pitcher. Any movement by the shortstop is relayed by the third base coach to the runner. He tells him when to score on a base hit; in fact, he tells him everything he is to do offensively.

figures **51–55**

Coaching a runner on first base. Not so much depends on the coach at first base as on the coach at third, for nearly every play which is made or attempted is directly in front of the runner coming to first base. The real help that a coach at first base can give to a base runner is to urge him on to second base on a wild throw or in the case of an extra base hit down the left field line. When a runner is on first base, the coach steps up to him and whispers the number of outs, the play to expect, and whatever signal he should look for in that particular situation. This is a violation of the rule governing the coach's position, but it is almost universally permitted by umpires, provided the coach is within his proper territory when a ball is hit, when a play is attempted, or when the pitcher is in position to pitch.

When a runner is on first base and the first baseman is playing his position as he would without a runner on first, a play might be attempted from the catcher to the first baseman. The base runner has his back to the first baseman and cannot see any change in his position. The coach turns his back to the batter and watches the first baseman's actions. He talks to the runner, informing him of the action of the first baseman.

Quiz on base running

1. What is the first rule in base running?
2. Discuss the proper way for a base runner to pivot the bases.
3. What would be the proper form for a start from first base in an attempt to steal second base?
4. How many types of slides should the squad be taught?

5. Which are the most dangerous slides? Why?
6. What is the most essential thing in stealing bases? Why?
7. How many kinds of steals can a runner start from first base? When will he use them?
8. Discuss fully the types of double steals you would want your players to attempt.
9. When should players attempt to steal third base from second base?
10. What is the cardinal rule according to which a base runner should make an effort to reach third base?
11. When would you attempt to steal home?
12. Your team has runners on first and third bases and the batter hits a ground ball to the infield. Discuss fully just what you expect those runners to do.
13. Your team has runners on second and third bases. Discuss fully just what you would expect your base runners to do if the batter hits a ground ball to the infield. A fly ball to the outfield.
14. Your team has a runner on third base. What would you expect that runner to do on a ball hit to the infield with none out? With one out? Why?
15. What should the squad know about two base runners on the same base at the same time?
16. Discuss a base runner's lead off first base. Off second base. Off third base.
17. When can a base runner run out of the base line?
18. State the infield fly rule.
19. *A* is base runner on first base, *B* is batter. *B* on a hit-and-run play hits a long fly ball to the outfield which is caught. *A* was almost to third base when the ball was caught. What must *A* do?
20. What opponents will you study closely in order to help you in your base running?
21. Discuss one opponent having peculiarities which will be the most important to your success in base running.

Quiz on coaches

1. Why is the third base coach so important?
2. What great mistakes do many third base coaches make?
3. Who should coach a base runner on second base?
4. Is there any time during a game when the first base coach should pay strict attention to his base runner on first base instead of watching other offensive players?
5. Is it important that the coaches know the number of outs, the number of innings played, and the score? Why?
6. If a base runner is caught off any base by the hidden ball trick, whose fault is it?

The batting order is an important part of the team's offensive strategy, and much time and thought should be given to it. It is hard to make up a batting order when the team is made up of hitters who are all apparently of the same type. Usually, however, certain members of the team are better hitters than the rest, and they are given certain positions in the batting order.

the first batter

The first or lead-off batter is not necessarily a small, short man, though a small man is difficult to pitch to; but he must be a good "waiter," a player sound and quick in his judgment of all pitched balls. The duty of the first batter is to reach first base if possible, no matter by what means. He must have a keen eye. He seldom swings at the first ball pitched. If he is a good bunter and a good base runner, he will cause his opponents much anxiety. It is unsound judgment to play a heavy hitter in the lead-off position, because after the game is under way, the players coming to bat before the lead-off man are always those who get on the bases the fewest number of times. It is best to save the long ball hitter to come up when the good hitters get on base.

the batting order

the second batter

The second batter occupies what is often called the "sacrifice" position. Any player able to bunt and to make a hit-and-run play is eligible for the second batter's position. He should not be a swing hitter, but rather a choke, chop, or slice hitter. The swing hitter cannot successfully make the hit-and-run play. On the whole, however, it is well to have a good hitter in the second batting position. Many sound baseball men like to have a left-handed hitter in this position. If a runner is on first base, he will have a hole to hit at between the first baseman and second baseman. His speed will prevent any double plays.

the third and fourth batters

The third and fourth men in the batting order should be the real hitters —the sluggers of the ball club. These players drive in runs, either with hits or with long fly balls. Number three batter should be the faster of the two on his feet, even though their hitting qualifications are equal. The opportunity for scoring many runs rests upon the speed of number three. especially when the fourth batter is also a heavy hitter.

the fifth batter

The fifth man in the batting order should also be a real hitter, even another slugger, if it is possible to obtain such a player from the personnel of the team. His position is not so important as that of the third or fourth batter as regards to hitting ability; nevertheless, the fifth batter should be a long hitter.

the sixth batter

The sixth man is the same type of player as the lead-off man. His position is thought of by many authorities as the second lead-off position. It is important that a lead-off man reach first base. The second lead-off man should be a bunter and a good waiter, but it might not be bad judgment to have the stronger hitter of the two in the sixth batting position. The sixth batter has more opportunity to drive in runners than the first batter. The players coming to the plate as hitters before number six make more base hits than those who precede number one.

the seventh batter

The seventh batter is much like number two. Although not so fast on his feet as number two, he should be as good a hit-and-run hitter.

the eighth and ninth batters

It has always been the policy of most managers and men who know baseball to place the battery men (pitchers and catchers) in the eighth and ninth positions. Pitchers are not in the game regularly day after day, and the batting order would be broken up each time the team played a game if the pitcher was placed in any but the last batting position. Each of the first seven men in the batting order knows the playing style of each man preceding or following him at bat, so that a change in the batting order from day to day might break up an offensive attack. Good hitting catchers have often been moved up higher in the batting order.

In amateur baseball, there is no set rule as to the position of the battery men in the batting list. The ball team, as a club, plays against an opponent only once or twice a week, and its battery men are continually in the game. It is not necessary to confine them to the eighth and ninth positions. Instead, the weakest batters are placed in the last two batting positions, and the battery men, if they are good hitters, are placed higher in the batting order. The hitting power and strength of any ball team should be concentrated in the most important positions rather than allowed to go to the tail end of the batting order.

the batting summary with suggestions

The first man up in each inning should make every effort to reach first base. It is generally advisable to take at least one strike. If, however, the pitcher continually delivers the first ball for a strike and expects the batter to let it go by, it is a good idea toward the end of the game for the batter to hit it. If the batter has made up his mind to hit the first ball pitched, an effort to drive the ball for an extra base hit should be the thought behind the swing of the bat.

No one on bases; two balls and no strikes.
With no one out, as a rule, the batter takes the next pitched ball.
With one out, a good hitter should hit, if the ball delivered is to his liking. It is advisable for a weak hitter to take the next pitched ball.
With two out, it is proper for the batter to hit. His swing should

be hard; he tries to make a long hit in order to get into a scoring position, where his run might score on a base hit, an error, or a wild pitch.

No one on bases; three balls and no strikes. Under any conditions, the batter should take another pitched ball. Outstanding hitters are given the choice of taking the pitch or hitting it on rare occasions.

No one on bases; three balls and one strike.

With none out, the batter usually takes one strike.

With one out, the good hitter hits, and hits hard. The weak batter takes another strike.

With two out, it is advisable for both the good batter and the weak batter to hit if the pitcher can be expected to put a fast ball directly over the plate. However, if the pitcher in this situation has consistently pitched a curve ball for a strike, it is rather bad baseball for the weak batter to hit.

With a runner on first base; two balls and no strikes.

With none out, three runs behind, the batter should take the next pitched ball. If the batter has been instructed to bunt for a sacrifice, he does so if the next ball pitched is a strike. If the batter has been told to make a hit-and-run play, he now has one of the good situations. However, being three runs behind, this is not the best policy unless the batter is a good hit-and-run man.

With one out, the good batter should hit, possibly making a hit-and-run play. The hit-and-run play should not be attempted, however, if the offensive team is more than two runs behind. In that case, it is best for the good batter to hit straightaway at the first opportunity.

With two out, the good batter hits straightaway. The weak batter takes the next pitched ball.

With a runner on first base; three balls and no strikes. The batter, regardless of the number of outs, always takes the next pitched ball.

With a runner on first base; three balls and one strike.

With none out, the batter bunts the next strike pitched provided he has been ordered to sacrifice.

If the ability of the batter prompts a hit-and-run play, here is the only legitimate situation for it. It should be used unless the offensive team is more than two runs behind.

With one out, straightaway or hit-and-run tactics should be used. The number of runs ahead or behind and the ability of the batter determine the instructions to be given. The good hitter should hit, but the weak hitter and slow runner should, without doubt, take a strike.

With a runner on second base. The batter always hits straightaway unless ordered to sacrifice, and then he bunts the first strike. However, this rule does not hold true with the count at three balls and no strikes; in that case the batter always takes one strike.

With none out, all batters must attempt to hit the ball to the right side of the infield, thus advancing the runner on a ground ball out, an error, a base hit, or a fly ball to right field. Once advanced to third base, and with one out, the runner can score on a hit, an error, a wild pitch, or a fly ball.

With a runner on third base. Regardless of the number of outs, the batter should hit any time he has the pitcher in a hole, unless the count is three balls and no strikes, in which case one strike is usually taken.

With runners on first and second bases. The batter always hits a good ball—especially if the pitcher is in a hole—unless he is ordered to sacrifice, in which case he bunts the first strike. When there are three balls and no strikes, however, one strike should be taken.

Runners on second and third bases. The batter should hit unless three balls and no strikes have been called. The "hole" advantage on the pitcher should be a great help.

With a runner on first base. Pitchers will attempt to keep the ball low to make the batter hit a ground ball.

With a runner on second base. The pitcher will try to make the batter hit a fly ball or a ground ball on the third base side of the field.

With a runner on third base. The pitcher will try to make the batter hit the ball in the dirt, particularly when the infield is in close.

Knowing your bench strength. It is very important for a coach to know exactly who he has on the bench to call on for pitching, hitting, bunting, and base running. On the lineup card, he should indicate his long and short relievers and not use these fellows needlessly in a game that is one-sided in the opponent's favor. He should also indicate on the card good bunters and pinch hitters. He must be careful not to use his top hitters and best base runners early in the game, especially if the team is down a few runs. They should be saved for late or extra innings. The coach would use a younger player who needs experience in the early innings.

It is hard to pick the right man by looking up and down the bench. By having this information on a card in front of him, the coach will not overlook the right player in the right spot.

THREE

scoring

a mythical ball game

Now that we have in mind the essential tactics of defensive and offensive baseball, let us set up a mythical game. We shall bring up as many errors of judgment as could possibly occur during the course of a game, and discuss each one of them.

advice to the coach

First, a word with the coach. You know that your players will make many errors of judgment during your scheduled contests. You must go over these errors with them, showing them from your own experience what would have been the correct and logical thing to do in each case. During the game you unconsciously place yourself in the diamond as an infielder, and outside it as an outfielder, on all defensive plays. You cannot expect your young players to do exactly what you, with your years of experience, would inevitably do, for they are at best comparatively inexperienced youngsters. Here are three important facts to keep in mind: as a coach, you are expected to know the game expertly; you are, therefore, the adviser of your young players; and whether they win or lose, they are your boys, and you must bear with them in defeat as well as in victory.

Let us give a word of rather rueful testimony right here. When we graduated from college, we thought we knew baseball from A to Z, but to our chagrin we found out that we were very ignorant players when we joined a major league baseball team. We did know the fundamentals of

introduction 13

the game in a casual way—but many of our new teammates were experts. They had made a life study of the game and they knew it in a way we never dreamed of. They were seniors in our great national game and we were pretty green freshmen. There was only one thing for us to do: to forget that we knew anything about the game and then go to school all over again with these masters of the game as our tutors.

As to the errors in the mythical game which we are about to observe, we may as well admit at once that we made many of these same errors as players in amateur as well as professional baseball. We do not pretend, of course, to have catalogued all the errors possible in a game; there are many more which could not be crowded into one game of nine innings. Those which we have included are errors which we ourselves made and which we had to overcome through many years of observation and study. Lack of experience and cockiness are really the cause of these errors. Increased experience, confidence, and careful observation were the only cure for them.

preparation for the game

In laying out this game, we made our plans two days before the game, and formed our attack.

Advance planning. We decided that Martin would pitch for the visiting team and that Lee would pitch for the home team. Both men got a hard workout, pitching to the batters in their batting practice. We have found that a pitcher develops better control of the ball when he does some pitching to the batters during their batting practice. After these men had their workouts, we sent them to the showers.

Final work-outs. The next day, that is, the day before the game, we had the infielders and the outfielders, together with the utility men whom we thought we might use in the contest, take their batting practice in the proper batting order. The pitchers, Martin and Lee, joined them. We were very careful about the work given to the two pitchers on this day because we have found from experience that a pitcher cannot do hard work the day before a game and be a strong pitcher in the contest itself.

Batting practice lasted forty-five minutes. Then we sent the two pitchers to the clubhouse, letting the rest of the squad throw the ball around to limber up their muscles. For five minutes this work went on, and then the players went to their respective playing positions for a short workout on grounders and fly balls. With words of encouragement, we hustled them through the practice and sent them to the clubhouse for their showers, to report the next day an hour and thirty minutes before the time for the scheduled game to begin.

It is well for a coach to set some definite time for every item of work to be done on the day of the game. Amateur games are not governed by rules regarding time for batting and fielding practice for the contesting teams, but a gentleman's agreement should be made giving each team an equal amount of time for its workout.

The day of the game arrived. The game was to begin at 3:00 in the afternoon. At 1:25 all the home players came upon the field. Promptly at 1:30 a pitcher who had been warming up walked to the pitching box and the home team began its batting practice, which lasted thirty minutes. At 2:00 the visiting team came upon the field for its batting practice. At 2:30 the home players went out to their respective playing positions for infield work, and at 2:40 the visitors took their place on the field for practice. At 2:50 the ground crew went to work. At 2:55 the umpires appeared on the field for the discussion of the ground rules with the opposing coaches and captains. During this conference at the plate, the ground crew continued to place in proper position the foul lines of the diamond and to smooth the dirt part of the infield. Both had been somewhat disarranged during the practice of the two teams.

Meanwhile the pitchers for the game had been loosening up their pitching arms. They had gone into action at 2:45 P.M. when the visiting team took the field for its workout. This arrangement allowed them fifteen minutes for their work, which is ample time for what the pitcher ought to do. The game started promptly at 3:00 P.M.

Here is a hint to the coach. Do not allow your pitcher for any contest to start throwing the ball around with other members of the squad the moment the team comes on the playing field, that is, an hour before it

figure **56**

BIG TEN CONFERENCE OFFICIAL BATTING ORDER		
TEAM DETROIT		
HOME TEAM DATE 5-1-64		
	ORIGINAL	CHANGE
1	DAY 8	
2	LONG 4	
3	LOWE 6	
4	THOMAS 7	
5	TURNER 5	
6	SHORT 9	
7	HAYES 3	
8	PATTEN 2	
9	LEE 1	

figure **57**

BIG TEN CONFERENCE OFFICIAL BATTING ORDER		
TEAM NEW YORK		
VISITORS DATE 5-1-64		
	ORIGINAL	CHANGE
1	WHITE 4	
2	JONES 5	
3	SMITH 7	
4	COLLINS 9	
5	BLACK 3	
6	BUCK 8	
7	O'BRIEN 6	
8	HOYT 2	
9	MARTIN 1	

is time for the game to begin. Fifteen minutes and no more should be enough, unless the day of the game happens to be very cool, in which case the pitcher may well extend his warm-up period in a longer but easier workout. The visiting pitcher may start five minutes after the home team pitcher because the first half of the first inning will use up time.

Let us come back to the game. The ground rules had been given to the umpire and the visiting captain and coach by the leaders of the home team. Batting orders had been handed to the umpire-in-chief, and the batteries for the game had been announced as follows: for the visiting team, Martin pitching and Hoyt catching; for the home team, Lee pitching and Patten catching. During the announcement of the batteries, the following batting orders were handed to the press representatives. It should be noted that the home team always presents its batting order line-up card to the umpire-in-chief first (Figure 56). Then the visiting team presents its line-up (Figure 57).

Note that both batting orders were arranged to conform as nearly as possible to the suggestions given in Chapter 12.

The ability of each of these mythical players was carefully noted, and his position was arranged after much study with the idea of matching his qualifications with those necessary for his position on the list.

In the following chapter, we would like to use these mythical players to explain a simple method of keeping score and statistics.

scoring

Scoring is nothing more than a baseball shorthand that enables the scorer to record a great deal of information in a relatively small amount of space. This method is so complete that anyone familiar with baseball can pick up a scorebook twenty years after the game was played and replay the game from the information recorded exactly as it happened. In scoring, the players' positions are referred to by numbers instead of letters as illustrated in the following diagram (Figure 58). This numbering system is the basis for the whole system of scorekeeping.

First, let us consider balls hit on the ground. Two or three numbers will be used to record each out. The first number is the man fielding the ball and the second the man making the putout. Example: A ball hit to the shortstop who fields it and throws to first. This would be recorded 6-3. On double plays three numbers can be used. Example: A double play from second to short to first would be recorded 4-6-3.

Balls hit into the air can be designated by one of the following: F-9 for fly ball to right fielder; L-7 for line drive to left fielder; Fo-2 for foul ball to catcher; P-6 for pop fly to shortstop.

Hits are designated by a dash, or dashes, followed by a number. Examples: —7 = single to left; ≡8 = triple to center. In the event of a long inning in which more than nine men bat, simply renumber the innings and use two columns. Other symbols and their meaning are as follows:

scoring, statistics, and the game itself

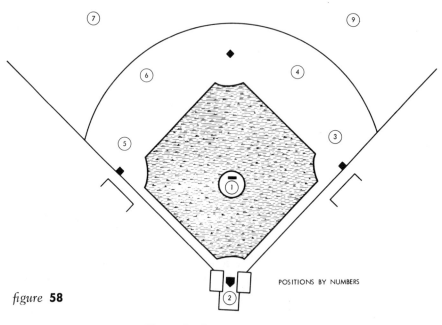

figure **58**

POSITIONS BY NUMBERS

K	Strike out swinging
Я	Strike out taken
FC	Fielder's Choice
BB	Base on balls
SB	Stolen Base
HP	Hit by pitcher
SH	Sacrifice Hit
SF	Sacrifice fly
WP	Wild pitch
PB	Passed ball
DP	Double play

One of the most important factors in scorekeeping is neatness. Be sure to have a good supply of sharp pencils available.

There are many types of scorebooks but we like a simple square type with a diamond insert. This type is excellent for simple scorekeeping and for compiling statistics.

Each player has an individual square for each time at bat. This square has a diamond inside and the player's performance at bat and progress on bases is shown with numbers. When a player advances, his advance is shown by the position number of the player who made this advance possible. Example: The right fielder (9) walked and advanced to third on a single to center field by the left fielder (7). He later scored on a fly ball to right field by the catcher (2). When a player (9) scores a run, the diamond is filled in so that it will stand out in the book for easy checks of the score during the game. Outs are designated by a number in the center of the diamond. The first out, a fly ball to right field, was made by the catcher (2). The second out, a strike out, by the first baseman (3). The third out was made by the second baseman (4), second to first (4-3). The diagonal line after the third out indicates the close of an inning (Figure 59).

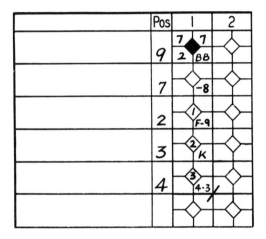

figure 59

the game itself

Now, using our mythical players, we will break the scoring down by half innings so that it can be followed.

THE FIRST INNING

The Visiting Team

1. White up. Knowing that the first batter in an inning should invariably take at least one strike, White looked at the first pitch. The umpire called a ball. The second pitch was also a ball.

Should the batter hit when he is a lead-off man with two called balls? The only times a batter should hit with two balls and no strikes are when there is an opportunity for a hit-and-run play, when with two men out he tries for a long hit and to get into a scoring position, or when his teammates are in a scoring position.

White took one called strike. The next pitch was a ball.

Should White hit with three balls and one strike? Not as a lead-off man in the inning. He should make every effort to get on first base. His chances of reaching first on a hit are less than one in three. He should take another strike.

White took the second strike, and with three balls and two strikes on him, he hit a grounder to Long at second base and was out at first.

One out (4-3).

2. Jones up. Jones took one strike, and on the second ball pitched hit a long fly ball to Day in center field.

Two out (F-8).

3. Smith up. The first ball pitched to Smith was a curve, which he let pass for one ball. The second pitch was also a ball.

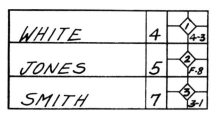

figure **60**

Should Smith hit with two balls and no strikes? Yes. He should swing hard, trying to get a long hit on which he might reach second base, from which he could score on a base hit, an error, or a wild pitch.

Smith did hit the next pitch, and Hayes at first base made a remarkable play on the ground ball. He fielded it perfectly and, after getting the ball firmly in his hands, threw it to Lee, who caught it at least two steps before he reached the bag. Lee had ample time to see that he properly touched the bag at first base.

Three out (3-1).

No runs, no hits, no errors. See top half of first inning diagram above (Figure 60).

The Home Team

1. Day up. Day employed the same tactics as White did in the first half of the inning and played Martin to a three ball and two strike situation. The fourth ball was called, and Day walked (BB).

2. Long up. What offensive attack should be employed? It is not good baseball to sacrifice and to play for one run in the early part of a ball game if it is at all possible to create a hit-and-run situation. The lively ball used today makes it necessary to get more than one or two runs to win a game. Very few games are won with this number of runs. If, however, the batter sees the defensive team playing out of position for a sacrifice bunt, he has an opportunity to bunt safely for a base hit. Such offensive tactics should be used when the defense is lax. An attempted sacrifice bunt may mean a base hit.

Long bluffed a bunt on the first pitch, which was called a ball. He bluffed a bunt on the second pitch, which was also called a ball.

Should Long make the hit-and-run play on the next pitch? He noticed that pitcher Martin was not putting all of his speed on every pitch, but that he was trying to aim the ball over the plate. He correctly elected to play hit-and-run on the next pitched ball, knowing that this was one of the hit-and-run situations.

Long singled to right field (—9). Day stopped at second.

3. Lowe up. What offensive attack should now be used? A sacrifice bunt means an opportunity for scoring two runs, whereas a hit-and-run play or a straightaway hit might mean a double play.

Lowe, with a count of two balls and no strikes, bunted in front of the plate for a sacrifice hit and was out by Martin to White, who covered first for the putout.

One out (SH 1-4).

4. Thomas up. How should the visiting team play the infield? The infield should play deep, willing to give a run in the first inning of the game in an attempt to retire the batter and perhaps to lessen the chances of the home team scoring more than one run.

With the infield playing deep, Thomas hit the first pitched ball to Jones at third.

Day had walked on four balls; Long, after two balls and no strikes, had used the hit-and-run; Lowe, with two balls and no strikes, had sacrificed. It may not have been good judgment on the part of Thomas to hit the first ball pitched. However, Thomas may have noted that the pitcher was letting up to get the ball over.

Jones fielded the ball cleanly and Day, trying to score, saw that he was caught. Consequently, he immediately stopped and began to run back and forth on the base line, doing his part to help Long and Thomas reach third and second bases respectively. Day was out, Jones to Hoyt to O'Brien, but Long reached third. Thomas overran first base, and when he finally woke up to the fact that there was a run-down play going on between third base and home plate, decided he should go to second. He made the attempt and was putout, O'Brien to White, completing a double play. This

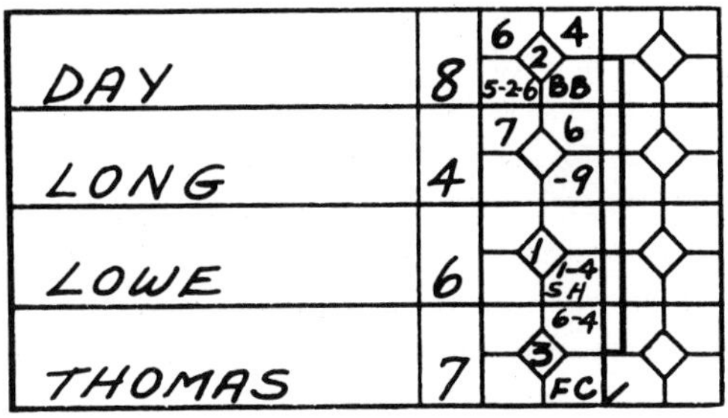

figure **61**

was very bad base running on the part of Thomas. He should have known that Day was going to attempt to score on his infield hit. There was no excuse for his stupidity.

Three out. See Figure 62 for use of the double play bracket.

Thomas reached first base on a fielder's choice (FC) and was out attempting to go to second (6-4).

No runs, one hit, no errors. See bottom half of first inning (Figure 61).

THE SECOND INNING

The Visiting Team

1. Collins up. Collins took a strike and then, with a count of two balls and one strike, hit to left field for two bases (=7).

2. Black up. Black usually hits into left field and would be considered a left-field hitter. If he were allowed to hit straightaway, the chances would be very much against Collins reaching third base. Only on a base hit or a long fly ball to the outfield would the runner be sure of reaching that bag.

Black bunted for a sacrifice hit and was out, Hayes to Long, Collins advancing to third base.

One out (SH 3-4).

3. Buck up. The defensive infield came in close but on second thought went back and played fairly deep. This was the correct thing to do, as the visitors hoped that the fairly good batter hitting in sixth position would hit a hard ball at one of them, giving an opportunity for a play either at the plate or at first base.

Buck hit a line drive into left field, where Thomas made a one-hand catch.

Two out (L-7).

Collins, thinking Buck had made an extra base hit, started for the plate as soon as he saw the ball hit. When Thomas made his great catch, Collins had almost reached the plate. He immediately sprinted back to third in order to tag up before making the attempt to score after the catch. He went back fast, and after the tag, broke for the plate, where he was an easy out on a perfect relay, Thomas to Turner to Patten. The double play was made possible by bad base running (7-5-2).

Three out (see Figure 62 for double play designation).

The stands began to jeer the third base coach for the bad base running of Collins. However, it was not the coach's fault. The runner had been told to make an attempt to score only on a ball hit on the ground to an infielder, and if he was caught, to run back and forth on the base line until the batter had reached a scoring position. If the ball was hit to the outfield, his instructions were to come back to the bag so that he might

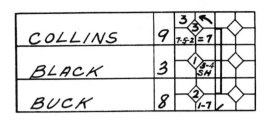

figure **62**

be able to score on a caught fly ball or trot over the plate with a run on a base hit.

No runs, one hit, no errors. See top half of second inning (Figure 62).

The Home Team

1. Turner up. Turner, with a count of one strike and no balls, hit a curve ball between the first and second basemen. Both Black and White tried to field the grounder. It passed Black and White got it. Martin forgot that the pitcher should start for first base on all balls hit to his left and failed to cover the bag. Thus Turner was credited with a base hit (—4).

2. Short up. The weak end of the batting order was coming up in the second inning. It would be good baseball to attempt to get the pitcher in a hole and to play hit-and-run, or to allow the batter, a right field hitter, to hit straightaway.

Short did not get the hit-and-run advantage. Consequently he hit straightaway, but behind the runner and was out, White to Black. Turner went to second base.

One out (4-3).

3. Hayes up. The batter should pick the ball he wants to hit, because a runner was in a scoring position.

Hayes with a count of three balls and no strikes, correctly took one strike. On the next ball pitched, he singled to left field (—7), Turner scoring from second base. Smith made his throw toward the plate in an attempt to get Turner, but the throw was wide and Hayes went to second, because the defense did not have a player in the cut-off position within the diamond. Hayes' advance to second is scored as a fielder's choice (FC).

4. Patten up. Patten, with a count of two balls and no strikes, correctly elected to hit the next ball pitched. He hit a slow grounder to the left of third baseman Jones and was out at first base. Hayes used very good judgment on the play, for as soon as he saw Jones going in for the slow grounder he went to third base. First baseman Black made his play correctly, for as soon as he caught the ball thrown by Jones for the putout, he rushed into the diamond toward third base in order to keep Hayes from scoring.

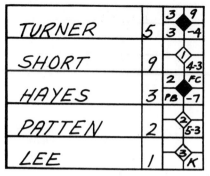

figure **63**

Two out (5-3).

5. Lee up. Lee had two strikes called on him, after which Martin, in his eagerness to strike him out, pitched a low curve ball which bounded from the mitt of catcher Hoyt as a passed ball. Martin failed to cover the plate quickly enough on the passed ball to keep Hayes from scoring. Lee struck out (*K*). Hayes scored on a passed ball (*PB*).

Three out.

Two runs, two hits, no errors. See bottom half of second inning (Figure 63).

THE THIRD INNING

The Visiting Team

1. O'Brien up. O'Brien took a strike after one ball had been called on him. He then singled into right field just out of reach of Long at second base (—9).

2. Hoyt up. The pitcher, Lee, did not realize that this was not a bunt situation, since his team had a lead of two runs, and he began to pitch high to Hoyt, expecting a sacrifice bunt.

After two balls, Hoyt elected to hit-and-run with his base runner. His effort was a single to center (—8) and O'Brien correctly stopped at second base. (*Take every chance possible to reach third base with one out, but do not make the same effort with none or two out.*)

3. Martin up. Lee pitched correctly for the bunt situation with a weak hitter at bat, but failed to go to his defensive position for such a play. Turner, the third baseman, quickly grasped the situation, fielded the sacrifice bunt, and threw to Long, who covered first base for the putout. Both runners advanced.

One out (*SH* 5-4).

4. White up. How should the home team play its defense? With two runs ahead, a run could be given—so the team played deep.

White hit a fly to Short in right field. Both O'Brien and Hoyt went back to the bags to tag up as soon as the ball was hit. Short caught the ball, and both runners started for the base ahead. Hoyt did not expect the throw to go to third base and, with two out after the catch was made, took a desperate chance, not realizing a run was going over the plate.

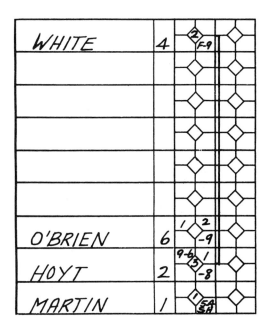

WHITE	4	②F-9			
O'BRIEN	6	1 2 -9			
HOYT	2	9-6 ③ 1 -8			
MARTIN	1	1 SA			

figure **64**

O'Brien, attempting to score from third base after the catch, looked over his shoulder, saw the throw going to third base, and decided to watch the play. Hoyt was thrown out by a fine throw from Short to Lowe, retiring the side before O'Brien had crossed with the run (*F-9*, see Figure 64 for double play scoring).

Three out, no runs, two hits, no errors. See top half of third inning (Figure 64).

The Home Team

1. Day up. Day made Martin pitch, and after bringing him down to a count of three and two, hit a high infield fly between third and home plate, which both Jones and Hoyt went after. They ran together but the taller man, Jones, made the catch.

One out (*P-5*).

Hoyt should have let Jones catch the ball without any interference whatsoever, since Jones was coming toward the fly ball while Hoyt was going away from it. Hoyt's catch would have been a rather difficult play for any ball player to make.

The player coming toward a fly ball should be the one to catch it.

2. Long up. Long noticed that pitcher Martin was trying to put the ball over the plate for a strike on his first pitch. He hit the first one into right field for a single (*—9*).

3. Lowe up. The first ball pitched to Lowe was called a strike. With one strike on the batter, amateur pitchers invariably pitch a curve ball. This

scoring, statistics, and the game itself **161**

is just what Martin had been doing throughout the game. A curve was pitched for a called ball. On the third ball, a fast one, Lowe singled to right field for a hit-and-run play (—9). Collins, in right field, picked up the ball in a throwing position and threw it toward third base in an effort to catch Long, who was correctly attempting to reach third base with one out. The throw was perfect but Long, having taken a running start, had almost reached the base before the ball arrived. Jones, seeing that it was impossible to get Long yelled, "Cut!". O'Brien cut the ball off and threw to White in an attempt to keep Lowe from reaching second. Lowe, running with his head down like a bull chasing a red flag, was thrown out by the defensive play, Collins to O'Brien to White (9-6-4).

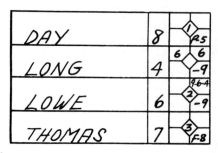

figure **65**

Two out.

4. Thomas up. Thomas swung hard at the first pitched ball and hit a long fly to Buck in center field.

Three out (*F-8*).

No runs, two hits, no errors. See bottom half of third inning (Figure 65).

THE FOURTH INNING

The Visiting Team

1. Jones up. Jones hit a terrific drive, on the third ball pitched, deep into right center. It looked like a three base hit. The ball was correctly relayed. Short made a short, accurate throw to Long, and Long made a long, accurate relay throw to Turner. As Jones rounded second base, Lowe, who was watching the runner to be sure he touched the bag, saw him step completely over it. The umpire's attention was called to this error in base running, and the ball was thrown to Lowe, who stepped on the bag. Jones was declared out (—9). The play was from Short to Long to Turner to Lowe (9-4-5-6). Three assists were made on this play.

One out.

2. Smith up. Smith hit the second pitched ball to Long at second, who fumbled and then threw wild to Hayes. Catcher Patten failed to back up first base on this play, so that when the ball was retrieved by him, Smith was on second (*E-4*).

The catcher must back up all throws to first base, unless there is a runner in a scoring position. In that case, he must not leave his position at the plate.

3. Collins up. Collins thought that he might catch Turner napping at third and bunted the first ball pitched. Turner fumbled the bunt and Collins was safe at first on the error, Smith moving up to third on the play. A sacrifice hit was scored for Collins (*SH E-5*).

4. Black up. Black hit the first ball high in the air for an infield fly very near the pitching box. Lee stepped to one side and let Lowe make the catch.

When the ball is hit high enough for an infielder to make the catch, the pitcher lets the infielder do it.

Black saw the ball go high in the air and saw Lowe get set for the catch, and then, in disgust, threw his bat toward the visiting club's bench and followed it. Lowe dropped the ball, picked it up and threw to Hayes at first base, who touched the base runner, Collins, then tagged the bag for the completion of a double play.

Three out (6-3-3).

If Hayes had touched the bag before he touched Collins, it would not have been a double play. Black did not hit an infield fly as he thought he had. An infield fly cannot be hit except when first and second, or when first, second, and third bases are occupied by runners with less than two outs. Black should have run out the ball; there probably would have been a forced play at second and a run scored.

No runs, one hit, two errors. See top half of fourth inning (Figure 66).

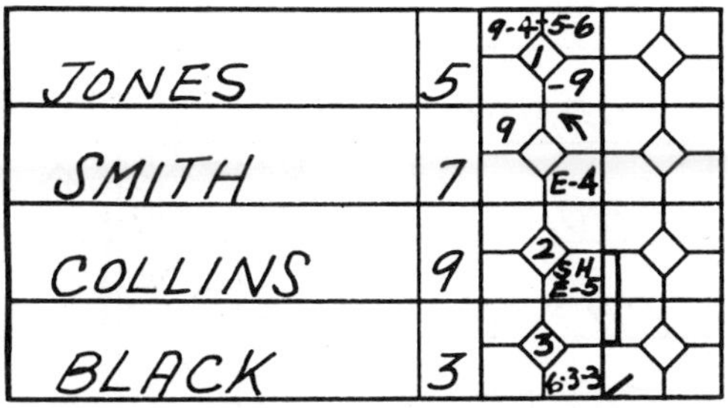

figure **66**

The Home Team

1. Turner up. Turner made Martin pitch four balls and went to first (BB).

2. Short up. The home team was two runs ahead, and it would be sound baseball to play for another run. The weak end of the batting order coming up might influence a player to do anything but bunt.

Short bunted for a sacrifice hit on the second ball pitched, after he had bluffed a bunt on the first pitched ball, which was called a strike. The ball was bunted hard at the pitcher who, on the advice of the catcher, threw to second base, where O'Brien had his foot off the base. Both runners were safe. (O'Brien's play must be placed on the score card as a fielding error: *E-6*. Martin's assist should be recorded in the assist column at this time since it is not shown in the box score. Short gets a fielder's choice: *FC*.)

3. Hayes up. Martin should have seen that a bunt situation was very much in evidence, but in his excitement, he pitched as if he knew nothing about the game. Black fielded the bunt and when he turned to make the throw to first base, there was no one there covering the bag. White, the second baseman, failed to grasp the bunt situation and Hayes' bunt went for a base hit (−3).

4. Patten up. The bases were full. The defensive infield played moderately deep, feeling that it would be lucky to get out of such a situation by giving the home team only one run. Patten, after two balls and no strikes, hit a hard grounder to Jones at third base. Jones correctly threw it to catcher Hoyt for the first out, and Hoyt relayed the ball to Black for the completion of a double play. Short went to third and Hayes went to second on the play.

Two out (5-2-3).

5. Lee up. Lee swung at the first three balls pitched and was out on strikes (*K*).

Three out.

No runs, one hit, one error. See bottom half of fourth inning (Figure 67).

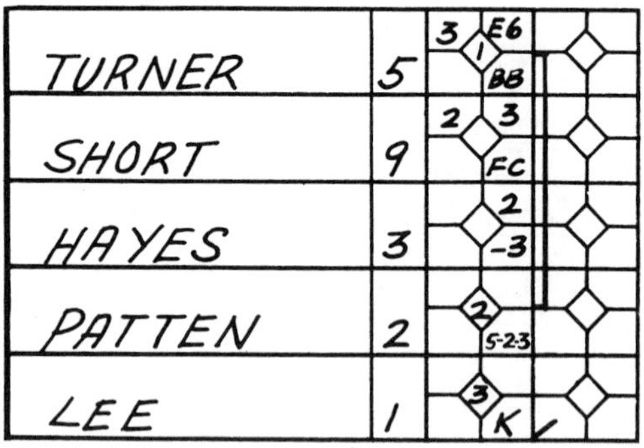

figure **67**

THE FIFTH INNING

The Visiting Team

1. Buck up. Buck hit the third ball to center field for a base hit (−8).

2. O'Brien up. How should the offensive team play the seventh player in the batting order? Two runs behind, the offensive team must get this batter on first base in order to get the tying runner in a position to score. The bunt must not be used as a sacrifice.

O'Brien elected to hit the first ball pitched and singled to right (—9). Buck knew that under the conditions of the game he should take no chances by trying to reach third base, so he stopped at second. That was the correct thing for him to do.

3. Hoyt up. Should this man sacrifice? With the tying runners in scoring positions, it is well to bunt.

Hoyt bunted for the sacrifice and was out at first base, Hayes to Long, who covered the bag. Both runners advanced (SH 3-4).

One out.

4. Martin up. Should a substitute batter be placed in the batting order for the pitcher? Martin was pitching very good ball and should not under ordinary circumstances be taken out in this early part of the game.

The defensive team played moderately deep. To do so was correct with a weak hitter at bat. A run could be given.

Martin hit to Lowe at short, who fumbled the ground ball (E-6). Buck scored and all of the runners would have been safe had not O'Brien, thinking the hit was a safe one, overrun third base. Lowe made a quick recovery and threw to Turner at third. In the run-down play which followed, O'Brien was out, Lowe to Turner to Patten, Martin going to second on the play (6-5-2).

5. White up. White, with two balls and no strikes on him, hit the next pitch into left center for a two base hit (=7). Martin scored the tying run. White, forgetting the rule that he should not take any chances by trying to reach third base with two men out, attempted to stretch his

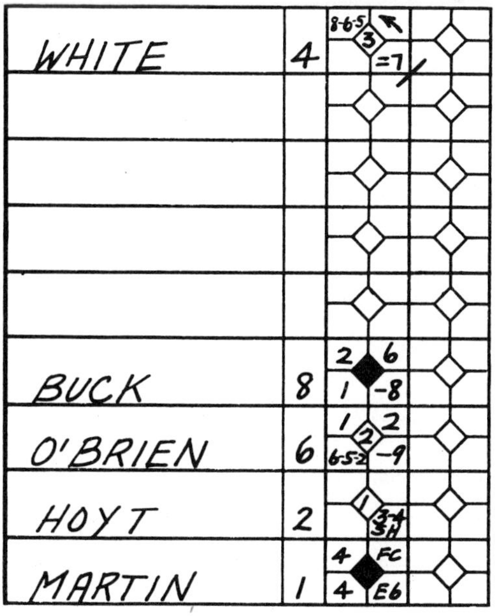

figure **68**

hit to a three bagger and was an easy out on a fine relay, Day to Lowe to Turner (8-6-5).

Three out.

Two runs, three hits, one error. See top half of fifth inning (Figure 68).

The Home Team

1. Day up. Day caught Jones napping and beat out a bunt along the third base line for a base hit. The ball was rolling into foul territory but Jones, for some unknown reason, picked up the ball without having an opportunity to retire Day at first base (—5).

2. Long up. Long bunted the second ball pitched for a sacrifice bunt down the third base line and was out, Jones to White (SH 5-4). Day, running around second, noticed that third base was not protected by the catcher, so he ran to third on the bunt. O'Brien, who was on the bag at second base for a possible play there, tried to get to third when he saw it was unprotected. White threw toward O'Brien, who was running for the bag, but the throw was wild (E-4). Smith, the left fielder, did not properly back up the throw. Consequently, Day walked into home plate with the third run for the home team.

One out.

3. Lowe up. Lowe hit a high foul fly to catcher Hoyt. Hoyt used good judgment and got under the ball so that it looked as though it would hit him on the head. He went back one step just before it reached him, and caught it solidly in his mitt (Fo-2).

Two out.

4. Thomas up. Thomas, with two balls and no strikes, correctly swung hard at the next ball delivered, sent it for a two base hit into left field, and reached the scoring position (=7).

5. Turner up. Pitcher Martin, hearing the third base coach plead with

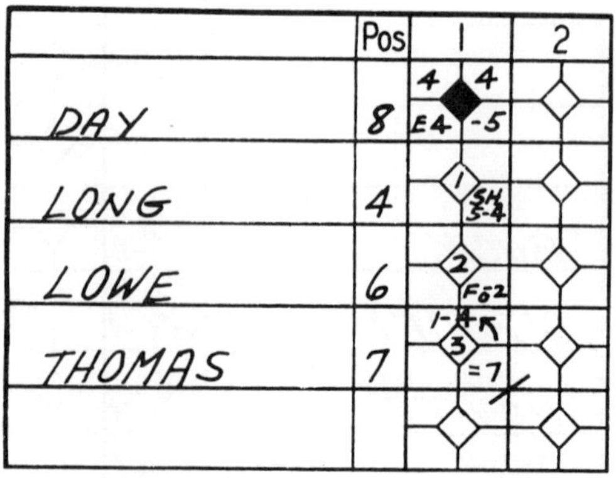

	Pos	1	2
DAY	8	4 4 / E4 -5	
LONG	4	1 / SH 5-4	
LOWE	6	2 / Fo2	
THOMAS	7	1-4 3 / =7	

figure **69**

Thomas to be sure to score on a base hit, pitched the first ball high to Turner. After he received a signal from the catcher for the next ball to be pitched, he took his stance on the pitching rubber but immediately whirled and threw the ball to White, who went to cover second base for a pick-off play. Thomas, thinking about scoring on a base hit, was out on a beautifully executed defensive play, Martin to White (*1-4*).

Three out.

One run, two hits, one error. See bottom half of fifth inning (Figure 69).

THE SIXTH INNING

The Visiting Team

1. Jones up. Jones hit a high fly toward right field. Long and Short each waited for the other to catch it. The ball fell between them for a base hit (—9).

The outfielder coming toward a fly ball should make the catch, if possible. The outfielder runs this play.

2. Smith up. How should the offensive team play this situation? For the visiting team it would not be unsound baseball to play for more than one run, especially with the third man in the batting order at bat. It would be good baseball to attempt to work the pitcher into a hole or into a hit-and-run situation.

After taking one strike, Smith hit the next ball into center field for a single (—8). Jones saw the ball go for a base hit but failed to recognize the fact that Day was fielding the ball in a throwing position, and overran the bag at second base. He was put out, Day to Lowe, Smith held first (8-6).

One out.

3. Collins up. Smith stole second on the first ball pitched (*SB*). He pulled a delayed steal which caught both second baseman Long and catcher Patten napping.

The second baseman should never forget to take a step or two toward second base after the ball has passed the batter. If the batter is a right-field hitter, the shortstop should take the steps toward the bag. This act of the infielders will often break up any ideas a runner may have about a delayed steal.

Collins singled to left field and Smith scored (—7). Thomas forgot himself for an instant and threw the ball toward the plate in an attempt to get Smith.

Outfielders should keep in mind that the percentage of runners thrown out at the plate on base hits is very small. It is usually better to keep runners from getting into scoring positions.

Collins failed to pivot correctly as he rounded first and, in his effort to reach second base, was an easy out on the defensive cut-off play, Thomas to Turner to Long (7-5-4).

Two out.

4. Black up. Black hit a terrific line drive down the right-field foul line for a two base hit (=9). Short's return of the ball to second base took a bad hop over Lowe's head, and the runner went on to third (E-9).

The left fielder, as well as the pitcher, should have been in the backing up position on this play.

5. Buck up. Buck hit the first ball back at Lee, and should have been an easy out at first base. But the coach at third base shouted, "Home!"; Lee forgot how many were out and instantly began to make motions to keep Black from scoring. When he woke up to the fact that two men were out, Buck was safe at first on a fielder's choice and Black was safe at third (FC).

Each player should know how many are out.

6. O'Brien up. O'Brien let the first pitched ball go for a called strike. The second ball pitched was also called a strike.

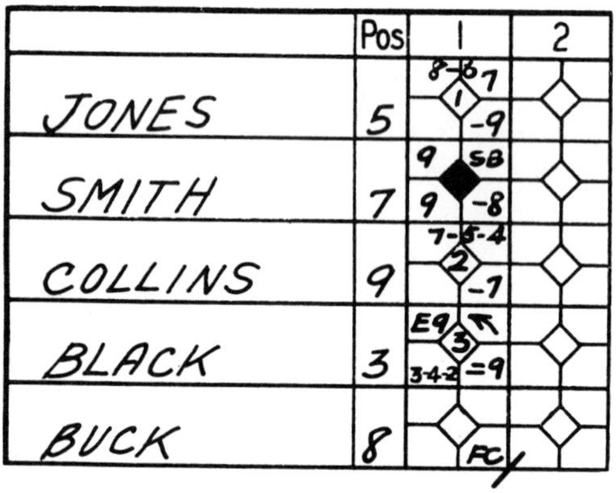

	Pos	1	2
JONES	5	8-6-7 (1) -9	
SMITH	7	9 SB 9 -8	
COLLINS	9	7-5-4 (2) -7	
BLACK	3	E9 (3) 3-4-2 =9	
BUCK	8	FC	

figure 70

With a fairly good hitter at bat, two strikes and two men out ought to prompt some base running, provided the runner gets a start.

Catcher Patten saw the situation and called for a waste ball. His throw to second was perfect. Long saw Black start for the plate and cut the ball off, as he was in the right position for the defense against a double steal. Black was out at the plate, Patten to Long to Patten (2-4-2).

Three out.

One run, four hits, one error. See top half of sixth inning (Figure 70).

The Home Team

1. Turner up. Turner got a base on balls (BB).

2. Short up. Short sacrificed and was out at first, Martin to Black. Turner got to second (SH 1-3).

One out.

It was not bad baseball to play for the winning run in this inning, but the weak end of the batting order, which was coming to bat, might make a batter change his mind as to the sacrifice, unless he knew that pinch hitters would be used.

I would have advised the batter, number 6 in the batting order, to get the pitcher into a hole if at all possible, and then hit straightaway or use the hit-and-run play.

3. Hayes up. Hayes hit a ground ball almost over the bag at second, upon which O'Brien made a remarkable play and threw Hayes out at first. Turner, thinking it was a base hit, rounded third base at full speed. The coach could not stop him, so he continued on to the plate and scored. Black, the first baseman, did not expect Turner to score from second base on the out at first and was not in position to throw to the plate (6-3).

Two out.

The first baseman must never forget that, with second base occupied by

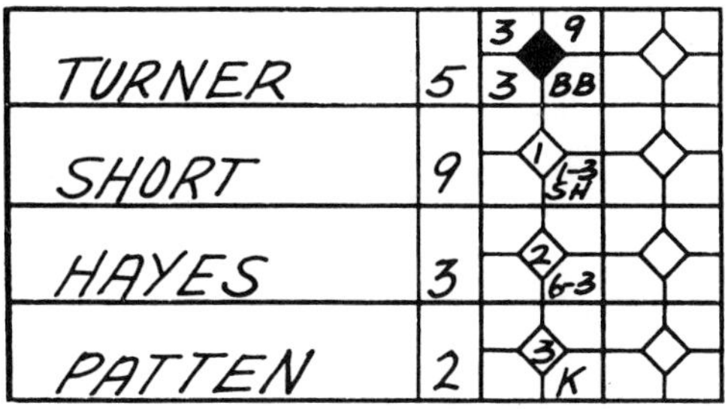

figure **71**

a runner, he should rush into the diamond toward the plate as soon as he receives the ball from an infielder, in order to keep the runner from scoring.

4. Patten up. Patten struck out (K).

Three outs.

One run, no hits, no errors. See bottom half of sixth inning (Figure 71).

THE SEVENTH INNING

The Visiting Team

1. O'Brien up. O'Brien, with a count of one and one, hit an inside pitch over the bag at third base for a two base hit (=7).

2. Hoyt up. Both the visiting team and the home team sent pitchers to the bullpen to warm up.

O'Brien, as well as the coaches, realized that he was the important runner and must get to third on the attempted sacrifice by Hoyt. The first

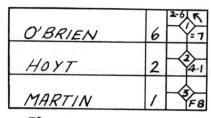

O'BRIEN	6	2-6 ↖ ① =7
HOYT	2	② 4-1
MARTIN	1	③ F8

figure **72**

ball pitched to Hoyt was directly through the middle of the plate. O'Brien, seeing the ball go toward the plate, could not see how a batter could possibly miss it. But Hoyt did miss the ball, and O'Brien, being off balance, was caught on a quick throw by Patten to Lowe (2-6).

One out.

All runners, especially the important runners, must be sure that a ball is actually bunted on the ground.

Hoyt was badly fooled on a curve ball and hit a twisting grounder toward right field. Hayes went for the ball but could not field it. Long, however, got the ball, and with a perfect throw to Lee covering first base, retired the runner (4-1).

Two out.

3. Martin up. Martin sent a fly to Day in center field (F-8).
Three out.

No runs, one hit, no errors. See top half of seventh inning (Figure 72).

The Home Team

1. Lee up. Lee hit a swinging bunt along the third base line on which Jones made a beautiful one hand pickup; but he was unable to set himself for his throw, which went wild over the first baseman's head. Lee went to second on the error and would have gone to third had not right fielder Collins made a quick back up of the play. Lee was credited with a hit (—5).

Jones, for his wild throw, was charged with an error (E-5).

2. Day up. What should the offensive team do? Bunt, because it had a lead of one run in the late innings and should by all means play for another run.

Day sacrificed and was out, Black to White, who was covering first. Lee went to third (SH 3-4).

One out.

3. Long up. How should the defensive team play? A run could not be given this late in the game; consequently, the infield played close.

Long, who had been hitting the ball hard during the whole game, was badly advised by someone who told him to make the squeeze play. He did so unsuccessfully on the first ball pitched, bunting a pop fly to first baseman Black (P-3).

Two out.

4. Lowe up. Lowe hit a long fly to Collins in right field.
Three out (F-9).

No runs, one hit, one error. See bottom half of seventh inning (Figure 73).

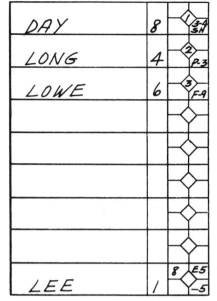

figure **73**

THE EIGHTH INNING

The Visiting Team

1. White up. White, with a count of one strike and one ball, swung at a curve ball, which he hit with the end of the bat for a weak fly to right field. It was just out of reach of Long and went for a base hit (—9).

2. Jones up. Would it be advisable to have this batter sacrifice the tying run to second base when, as a batter, he had been hitting the ball very hard during the game?

Jones properly bluffed a bunt on the first ball pitched, hoping that he might get the hole advantage. The first ball went high and was called a ball. Jones thought the second ball pitched ought to be a strike, and if it were, he would hit straightaway. It was a good ball and Jones hit it, but Long made a great play on the ground ball and threw Jones out at first. White advanced to second (4-3).

One out.

3. Smith up. With two balls and one strike, Smith made a base hit to right field (—9). White scored. For some unknown reason, Short threw the ball toward the plate after fielding it. He did not see a cut-off man within the diamond.

With men on base after fielding a ball in the outfield, there should always be a cut-off man for the outfielder to throw to within the diamond. Again it would have been correct defensively to have allowed the run to score in order to keep the runner from getting into position to score the winning run. The winning runner was allowed to go to second base, the scoring position. Smith's advance to second is scored as a fielder's choice (FC).

4. Collins up. Lee was taken from the box and pitcher Clark substituted. Collins singled to right field (—9). Short made a throw toward the plate in an attempt to cut off the winning run, but Hayes cut off a perfect throw on which the runner would probably have been retired. Catcher Patten shouted "Let it go!", but Hayes did not listen. This mistake allowed the winning run to cross the plate. Hayes knew that he had made a great error in judgment and went back toward his fielding position with his head down. Collins, wide awake to the situation, noticed that neither Hayes or Clark was watching him and stole second before Clark woke up to the fact that there was a runner on first base who might steal (*SB*).

5. Black up. Black hit a short fly, on the first ball pitched, to Short in right field for the second out (*F-9*). Collins took a chance which never should be taken with none or two out; he attempted to reach third base after the catch. He was an easy out, Short to Turner, who was covering the bag and who was properly backed up by the pitcher and the left fielder (*9-5*).

Three out.

Two runs, three hits, no errors. See top half of eighth inning (Figure 74).

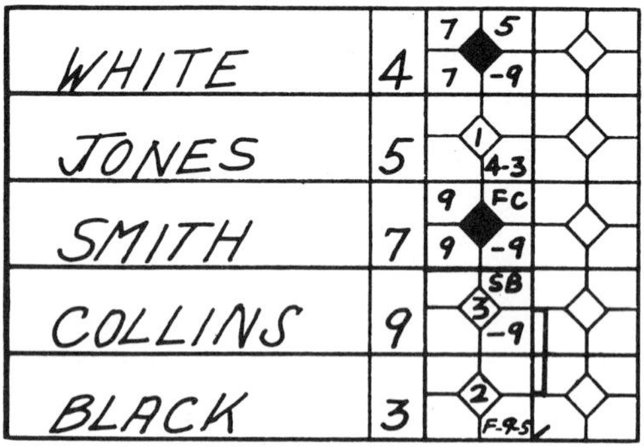

figure **74**

WHITE	4	7 5 / 7 -9	
JONES	5	1 / 4-3	
SMITH	7	9 FC / 9 -9	
COLLINS	9	SB / 3 -9	
BLACK	3	2 / F-9-5	

The Home Team

1. Thomas up. Thomas hit a ground ball to second baseman White, who fumbled and threw the ball to first too late for the putout (*E-4*). The coach at first base, while shouting sarcastic and unnecessary remarks at the second baseman for his error, failed to notice that first baseman Black had not thrown the ball to the pitcher. Thomas had his head down, and before locating the ball, stepped off the bag and was tagged out by Black. This was an unassisted putout by Black, the first baseman (*3U*).

One out.

The coach's business on the lines, at first and at third base, is not to hurl remarks at his opponents, but to keep his mind on the game and to watch the ball at all times, so that the runner knows where the ball is before stepping off the base. The runner should never step off the base until he knows exactly where the ball is.

2. Turner up. Turner received his third base on balls (*BB*).

3. Short up. Short hit a hard grounder to O'Brien at short, forcing Turner at second base (*6-4*). White, in attempting to make a relay throw from second to first, was hit by Turner as he made his slide into the bag. As a result, White made a wild throw to Black, on which Short went to second (E-4). Catcher Hoyt again failed to back up a throw at first base. Short reached first on a fielder's choice (FC).

Two out.

The catcher should always back up a throw to first base when a runner is not in a scoring position.

4. Hayes up. Hayes walked on four pitched balls (BB). Pitcher Martin's control was bad. A substitution was about to take place, when the visiting captain and the coach noticed that a new batter was coming into the game for Patten. Rather than substitute another pitcher before the incoming batter was announced, the coach waited. As soon as Jackson, a left-handed batter, was announced as hitting for Patten, a left-handed pitcher, Cronin, was sent to the rubber for the visitors. The home team took Jackson out of the game when the left-handed pitcher was substituted and sent in a right-handed hitter, Baker. (Note substitution procedure in Figure 75.)

5. Baker up. Baker hit a ball which bounded over the pitcher's head. The umpire, standing behind Cronin, could not get out of the way in time. The batted ball hit him and bounded into right field. Short crossed the plate, apparently with the tying run, and Hayes went to third base. An argument started, the home team contending that the run could score, but the umpire-in-chief ruled correctly that bases could not be run because there was no force situation. Short was sent back to third, Hayes to second, and Baker was safe at first. This is scored (−1) because the umpire was closer to the pitcher than any other position when he was hit by the batted ball.

The captain of the home team was somewhat confused on the rule pertaining to a batted ball, and also on the rule about a thrown ball.

According to Rule 5.09 (f): "The ball becomes dead and runners return, or advance to their bases without jeopardy or liability to be put out when—a fair hit ball touches a runner or an umpire before it touches an infielder including the pitcher, or touches an umpire before it has passed an infielder other than the pitcher." Accordingly, no bases can be run unless necessitated by the batter becoming a base runner; in addition, no run can score unless all of the bases are occupied.

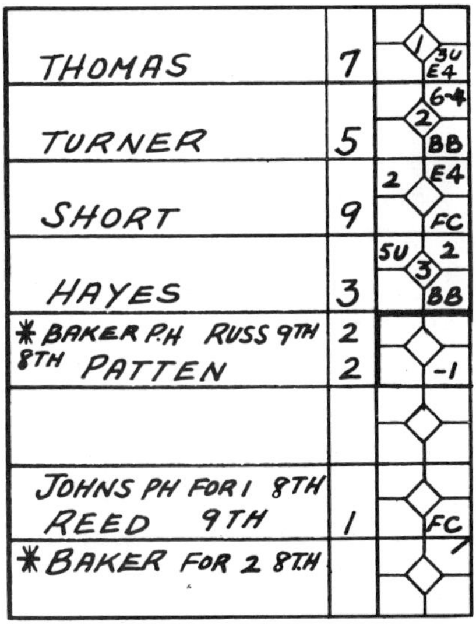

figure **75**

Rule 5.08 states that: "If a thrown ball accidentally strikes a coach or a pitched or thrown ball strikes an umpire, the ball is alive and in play." Thus the base runner or runners shall be entitled to all bases they can make.

6. Johns up. Johns came into the game as a pinch hitter for pitcher Clark (note substitution in Figure 75). The infield played deep of course. Cronin, an observant pitcher, began to pitch low curve balls to Johns, hoping that he would hit a ground ball to one of the infielders. Johns did. His hit was fielded by third baseman Jones, who had but to step on the bag at third for a force play on Hayes and the final putout of the inning (5U). Batter reaches first on a fielder's choice (FC).

Three out.

No runs, one hit, two errors. See bottom half of eighth inning (Figure 75).

THE NINTH INNING

The Visiting Team

The home team sent in a new battery, Reed to pitch and Russ to catch (note substitutions in Figure 76).

1. Buck up. Buck foolishly hit the first ball pitched and was out, Turner to Hayes (5-3).

One out.

Whenever a new pitcher comes into the game, it is well to make him pitch so that not only the batter but also the other members of the offensive team may have an opportunity to study his particular style of delivery.

2. O'Brien up. O'Brien worked Reed for a base on balls (BB).

3. Hoyt up. Hoyt, with two balls and no strikes, gave the signal for the hit-and-run play to the base runner. He hit a slow bounding ball back at pitcher Reed, who, without a chance of getting the runner at second, made that throw. Both men were safe (FC).

A hard hit ball gives an opportunity for a force play, but a slow hit ball should always be thrown to first, unless the catcher gives a different order.

4. Cronin up. Cronin swung at the first ball pitched. Russ tried to catch Hoyt off first base, but the play was not successful. O'Brien, playing "heads up" baseball, stole third on the play (SB).

Such a throw is a very dangerous play for any catcher to make.

How should the defensive infield play with a weak hitter at bat and a run on third base which cannot be given?

The infield at first played moderately deep but, on second thought, came in close, which was the correct thing to do in the last inning with one run behind. With Cronin, a weak hitter, at bat, the offensive team tried the double steal. Catcher Russ, seeing the batter was a weak hitter,

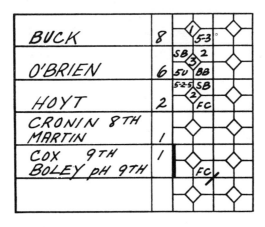

BUCK	8	5-3°	◇	◇
O'BRIEN	6	SB 2 ③ 5U BB	◇	◇
HOYT	2	5-2-5 SB ② FC	◇	◇
CRONIN 8TH MARTIN	1	◇	◇	
COX 9TH BOLEY pH 9TH	1	FC	◇	◇
		◇	◇	

figure **76**

made a bluff throw to catch the runner going to second base and threw to third in an attempt to get O'Brien. Both runners were safe (*SB*). The visiting team then took Cronin out of the game and sent in Boley to hit for him (note substitution in Figure 76). Boley hit to Turner at third base. O'Brien attempted to score but saw that he was caught and stopped for the run-down play which followed. The play ended with both O'Brien and Hoyt on the bag at third base. Turner tagged both men while they stood on the bag, automatically retiring Hoyt (*5-2-5*). He then said to O'Brien, "You are out." O'Brien stepped off the bag and was immediately touched with the ball for the completion of the double play (*5U*).

Three out.

With two runners occupying a base at the same time, the player originally entitled to the base is legally entitled to that base and is not out until he has released that right, either by putout or by legally touching the next base.

No runs, no hits, no errors. See top half of ninth inning (Figure 76).

The Home Team

Cox went in to pitch for the visiting team (note substitution in Figure 77).

1. Day up. Day, after one strike and one ball, hit a high fly behind third base. O'Brien and Jones went for the ball. O'Brien used good judgment in calling for the catch, as he was going toward the fly. Jones would have had to make the catch over his shoulder (*P-6*).

One out.

2. Long up. Long hit to right field for two bases (=9).

3. Lowe up. With a count of two balls and no strikes, Lowe hit, since he had pitcher Cox in a hole. He swung hard but raised a high foul fly which Hoyt, urged by both the pitcher and the first baseman, caught near the visitor's bench (*FO-2*). Long, seeing the catch, started for third

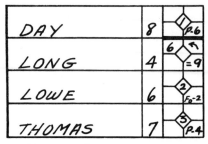

DAY	8	P-6
LONG	4	=9
LOWE	6	2
THOMAS	7	P-4

figure **77**

base but stopped half way between the bases. Hoyt failed to throw the ball to third baseman Jones. He was undecided what to do, and allowed the runner to run to third and slide safely into the bag.

As soon as Hoyt saw the runner stop between the bags, he should either have thrown to third base or have run straight at Hoyt and, if possible, have made the putout at the base the runner had left.

4. Thomas up. Thomas, doing his utmost to get pitcher Cox in a hole, made him pitch to a two ball and one strike situation. He then hit a slow curve ball high in the air. Second baseman White caught it for the final out of the game (P-4).

Three outs.

No runs, one hit, no errors. See bottom half of ninth inning (Figure 77).

The complete score sheet, as shown below (Figure 78 a, b), is a complete summary of the game in which individual records are totaled.

statistics

The scorebook is an invaluable reference for the coach. Statistics can be and often are very deceiving and the scorebook is helpful in determining the true value of a player. Some players have low averages but are tough in close games. Others, with higher averages, may not play as well with the chips down.

We keep the following statistics on our pitchers: innings pitched, hits, runs, earned runs, strike outs, walks, and earned run average. A good pitcher usually allows fewer hits than the number of innings pitched, strikes out more batters than he walks, and has an earned run average of 3.00 or less. The pitcher who allows many hits and walks must naturally strike out more players to be successful. Conversely, pitchers who allow fewer hits and walks do not have to strike out as many batters to be winners.

Our batting statistics include at-bats, hits, runs, batting average, runs batted in, total bases, sacrifice hits, stolen bases, strike outs (both taken and swinging), walks, hit batters, doubles, triples, and home runs. We also keep fielding averages, which include putouts, assists, and errors.

These figures, in conjunction with his own evaluations, help the coach select a line-up and determine which players need help and in what phases of the game. By adding hits, walks, and hit batters and dividing by

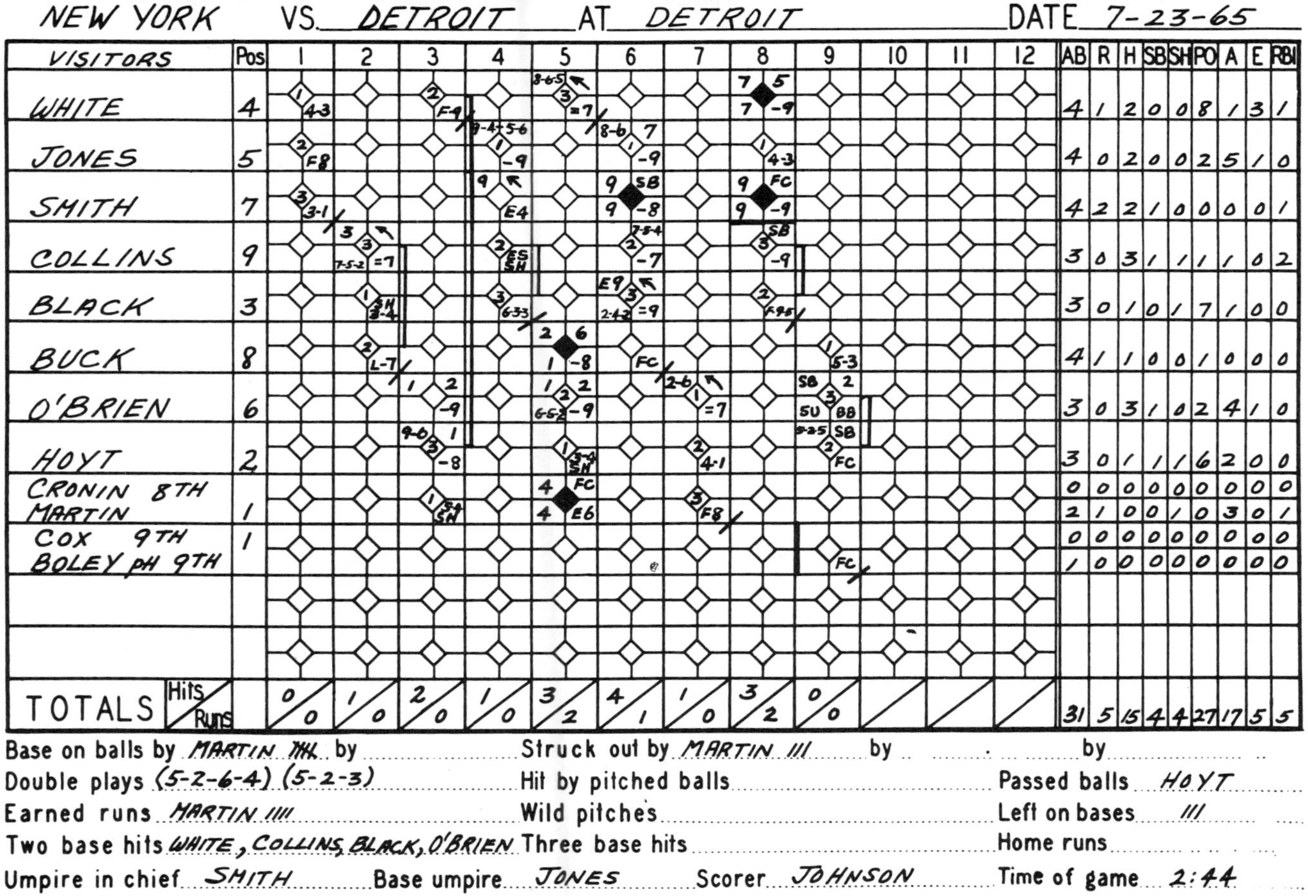

NEW YORK VS. DETROIT AT DETROIT   DATE 7-23-65

VISITORS	Pos	1	2	3	4	5	6	7	8	9	10	11	12	AB	R	H	SB	SH	PO	A	E	RBI
WHITE	4													4	1	2	0	0	8	1	3	1
JONES	5													4	0	2	0	0	2	5	1	0
SMITH	7													4	2	2	1	0	0	0	0	1
COLLINS	9													3	0	3	1	1	1	0	2	
BLACK	3													3	0	1	0	1	7	0	0	
BUCK	8													4	1	1	0	0	1	0	0	
O'BRIEN	6													3	0	3	1	0	2	4	1	0
HOYT	2													3	0	1	1	1	6	2	0	0
CRONIN 8TH														0	0	0	0	0	0	0	0	0
MARTIN	1													2	1	0	0	1	0	3	0	1
COX 9TH	1													0	0	0	0	0	0	0	0	0
BOLEY PH 9TH														1	0	0	0	0	0	0	0	0
TOTALS Hits		0	0	0	0	2	3	0	3	2	0			31	5	15	4	4	27	15	5	
Runs		0	1	0	0	3	4	1	0	2	0											

Base on balls by MARTIN, IHL. by
Double plays (5-2-6-4), (5-2-3)
Earned runs MARTIN, IIII
Two base hits WHITE, COLLINS, BLACK, O'BRIEN Three base hits
Umpire in chief SMITH Base umpire JONES Scorer JOHNSON

Struck out by MARTIN, III by
Hit by pitched balls
Wild pitches
Passed balls HOYT
Left on bases III
Home runs
Time of game 2:44

figure 78a

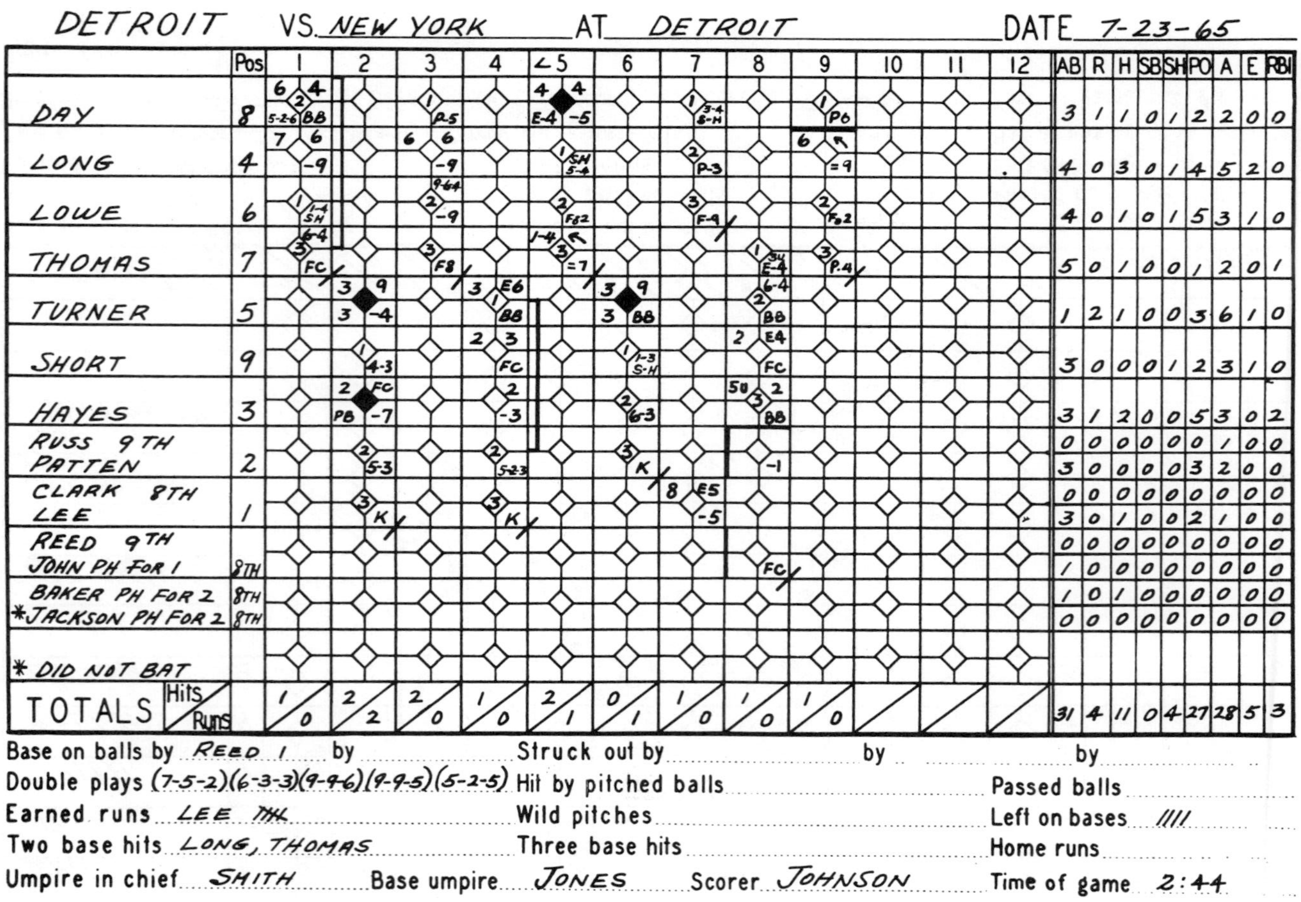

DETROIT VS. NEW YORK AT DETROIT   DATE 7-23-65

	Pos	1	2	3	4	5	6	7	8	9	10	11	12	AB	R	H	SB	SH	PO	A	E	RBI
DAY	8													3	1	1	0	1	2	2	0	0
LONG	4													4	0	3	0	1	4	5	2	0
LOWE	6													4	0	1	0	1	5	3	1	0
THOMAS	7													5	0	1	0	0	1	2	0	1
TURNER	5													1	2	1	0	0	3	6	1	0
SHORT	9													3	0	0	0	1	2	3	1	0
HAYES	3													3	1	2	0	0	5	3	0	2
RUSS 9TH / PATTEN	2													3	0	0	0	0	3	2	0	0
CLARK 8TH / LEE	1													3	0	0	0	0	3	2	0	0
REED 9TH / JOHN PH FOR 1	9TH													3	0	1	0	0	0	2	0	0
BAKER PH FOR 2	8TH													1	0	0	0	0	0	0	0	0
*JACKSON PH FOR 2	8TH													1	0	1	0	0	0	0	0	0
														0	0	0	0	0	0	0	0	0
* DID NOT BAT																						
TOTALS — Hits		0	2	2	0	2	0	1	0	0				31	4	11	0	4	27	28	5	3
TOTALS — Runs		0	2	2	0	2	0	1	0	0												

Base on balls by REED 1, by ....   Struck out by .... by ....
Double plays (7-5-2)(6-3-3)(9-9-6)(9-9-5)(5-2-5)   Hit by pitched balls ....
Earned runs LEE 1 MK ....   Wild pitches ....
Two base hits LONG, THOMAS ....   Three base hits ....
Umpire in chief SMITH .... Base umpire JONES .... Scorer JOHNSON ....

by ....   Passed balls ....
Left on bases ////
Home runs ....
Time of game 2:44

figure 78b

the number of at-bats, the coach arrives at an on base average. Obviously a fast man with a high on base average would be an ideal lead-off man. A right-handed hitter who does not strike out often and can hit to opposite fields could fill the bill for a second place hitter. A left-handed pull hitter also makes a good second batter. This type of batter can hit through the opening left by the first baseman when there is a runner on first. Players with high averages and power make good number three, four, and five hitters.

Strike outs are a vital factor in a baseball team's success or failure. We try to keep our strike outs down to one in eight or more times at bat. It is impossible to get a hit without hitting the ball. A team that hits the ball often enough will have a decided advantage in the percentage of base hits and the number of base runners over a team of strike out artists. To illustrate: a batter who strikes out once in four at-bats and gets one hit is batting .333 for the times he hit the ball, but is actually hitting only .250. Strike outs have cost him .083 points on his average. When you consider .083 points on a team average, the strike out takes on added importance. Every ball hit may not be a base hit, but it could result in an error for the defensive team, and thus another base runner and a potential run for the offensive team.

Fielding averages can be deceiving. Outfielders, pitchers, catchers, and first basemen normally have higher averages because the balls they handle are usually easier to play. The shortstop normally has the lowest average because of the difficult plays and long throws which he must make. It must also be kept in mind that some players with lower averages are very quick and aggressive and make errors on plays that other players would not be able to reach. This is where the coach's evaluation can be combined with statistics to make a sound judgment of his players.

proving the box score

The principal duty of the scorer is to KNOW what the score is, and proving the box score is the most important element in scoring. Each box score must be checked at the end of the game in order that the scorer may know whether it is accurate.

Never give out a box score to wire services, newspapers, or to official headquarters without first checking each detail carefully. The formula for the end-of-the-game check is:

Your at-bats plus bases given on interference plus bases on balls given you plus your hit batters plus your sacrifices equal opponents' putouts plus your runs plus your left-on-bases.

If a scorer has not memorized this formula, it should be written down in the score book and kept there for handy reference at all times.

how to put proof to work

Two men out. Batter hits into a force out at second. Batter is left on first base. It is difficult to prove to some laymen that the batter ever got to first base. However, since the scorer must account for the batter in some manner on paper, the scorer puts him on first base by a fielder's choice. All men who come to bat either score, are put out, or are left on base. If

general instructions 15

the scorer, after he has made the proof-check according to the formula outlined above, finds that the two totals are not equal, he knows that there must be an off in the box score. Perhaps the total of runs made or the total of men left on bases is incorrect. The scorer checks back and finds where the error is—he uses the proof-check to verify the score. Verifying the score is the scorer's most important job, and thus he uses the proof-check to complete a well done job.

knowing the score

Knowing the score is more important than distinguishing between hits and errors. Perhaps knowing the score appears an easy job, and it usually is, but when a problem arises and some question is raised pertaining to the score, it is the scorer's first duty to KNOW what the score is. The only way he can be sure of the score is to proof-check each inning as the game progresses.

Be sure to place a dot in the run column, opposite the scoring player's name, as soon as each run is made. After each inning, obtain the total number of runs scored during that inning. Adding the totals for each inning and comparing the result with the number of dots in the run column gives a simple method of cross-checking. Most scorers use such a system inasmuch as a scorer must provide a score check at any point in the game.

The score check alone, however, is not enough to assure accuracy, particularly at the end of the game or at the end of an inning during which a team bats around. Then the box score proof-check must be used.

Suppose, in a rapid bat-around rally, the action is recorded in the book as indicated below. (Fractions represent outs; dots stand for runs; X signifies a hit; and L indicates players left on base.) Notice that two columns are needed to record all the plays in the inning. Notice also that each column has two rows of entries.

How many runs were scored? By counting the dots in the *first* rows of both columns, we discover that 8 runs were scored. Still using the entries in the *first* rows of both columns, we proof-check as follows: 8 runs plus 2 men left on base plus 3 putouts—or a total of 13.

However, in the second rows of both columns we find that 14 men were "at bat." The totals of the two rows are not equal: they are "off" balance; therefore, the score cannot be correct.

Jones	LF	$\frac{1}{2\text{-}3}$	•X
Smith	RF	•X	•X
Green	1B	•X	LX
Crane	2B	2/8	LX
Lowe	SS	•X	$\frac{3}{5\text{-}3}$
Fox	C	X	
Dean	3B	•X	
Lucky	CF	•X	
Pelty	P	•X	

The scorer knows that the number of men left on bases is correct. Checking back to see what became of each batter, the scorer discovers that Fox has vanished in thin air. The X next to Fox's name indicates that he has hit, but despite the fact that seven players following Fox also hit, there is no dot after Fox's name to indicate that he had scored. This oversight, when corrected, shows that 9 hits were made during the inning. A new tally of totals for both rows in the columns gives 14 for each row— a balanced score.

consulting the umpire

Know when to consult the umpire and do consult him. The umpire decides whether runs count, and the scorer's job is to record the number of runs scored.

There is one out with runners upon first and third bases; the batter hits a fly ball to the outfield, which is caught for the putout. Runner on third tags up and goes home after the catch, but runner on first does not tag up. The ball is thrown to the first baseman who retires the runner on first before he can get back to the bag. Does the run count?

The run does count if it is scored before the third out was made; the run does not count if it crossed the plate after the third out was made. The play at first base was not a forced play except where the batter was involved. The batter was out when his fly ball was caught; therefore, he could not be involved in further play. What followed had to do with the acts of the base runner, not with the batter.

Score a double play, regardless of whether the run counts, with an assist for each fielder handling the ball. Also, if the run counts, be sure to credit the batter with a RBI (run batted in). Whether the run counts on such a play is entirely up to the umpire-in-chief. Inasmuch as the scorer must know when a force play has occurred, and inasmuch as a force play involves a time element on which the umpire's ruling is final, the scorer must get a decision on a play from the umpire immediately upon completion of the play. Remember no runs count on a play in which the third out is a play retiring the batter at first, or if a runner is forced at any base because the batter became a base runner.

The umpire should be asked whether certain plays are force plays. Suppose a runner, forced to go to third base, overslides the bag and is tagged out while oversliding. Such a play is considered a force-out and would relieve the infielder of an error, assuming an error has been made. If the scorer is in doubt as to how such a play was ruled, he should consult the umpire.

All scorers are bound by the umpire's decision that only one out was made even if they believe that, under the rules, two men are out. Scorers are bound by the umpire's ruling even to the extent of a close play at first base when the umpire signals "out" and then, after the first baseman drops the ball, changes his ruling to "safe." Such a play, involving a dropped ball, cannot be considered as beating out a hit because the batter obviously would have been ruled "out" had the play been perfect.

Note: If the teams change sides after the second out is made, it is the duty of the scorer to inform the umpire that only two men are out.

Tie games that are called after playing the required five innings should be reported in full. The records for such a game should be included in the averages of all players participating.

called games

The problem of scoring a called game is important and is sometimes very confusing. Called games also require the umpire's decision, but the scorer should be acquainted with the following examples, which cover the field.

		1	2	3	4	5	6	
1.	Baltimore	1	1	1	1	0		----------4
	Toronto	1	1	1	0	1		----------4

(Toronto, 1 run, 1 out in 5th)

		1	2	3	4	5	6	
2.	Baltimore	1	1	1	1	0	0	----------4
	Toronto	1	1	1	0	0	1	----------4

(Toronto, 1 run, 1 out in 6th)

		1	2	3	4	5	6	
3.	Baltimore	1	1	1	0	0	4	----------3
	Toronto	1	1	1	1	0		----------4

(Toronto, no run, 1 out; score reverts to the end of the 5th inning, the same as if the game were called while the teams changed sides in the middle of the 6th; or while Baltimore has 4 runs, 1 out.)

		1	2	3	4	5	6	
4.	Baltimore	1	1	1	0	0	1	----------4
	Toronto	1	1	1	1	1		----------5

(Toronto, no run, 2 out in 6th)

The point to remember is that after five innings, the score reverts to the last equal inning; the score remains as is at the time, however, if the (1) home club is ahead, or (2) the home club is at bat and the score is tied.

Visiting team, behind one run, makes two runs in the first of the ninth inning; rain ends the game at that point; the score reverts to the end of the eighth inning (see third example above). Do records made in the first half of the ninth inning count in the averages? No. Anything that happened after the end of the eighth inning should not be recorded in the box score because that was when the game ended. Those ninth inning plays do not count any more than do plays made in the first three innings when rain stops play at the end of three innings.

entitled to records

Here is a situation far different from the above. The first half of the seventh inning has been completed, with the home team leading by a 3-2 score. In the home half of the seventh, the home club scores 5 more runs, but the game is rained out before the inning is completed. In this case, it is not necessary to revert to even innings; the home team was in the lead, and the home players are entitled to all the records made during the last half of the incomplete seventh.

making proper decisions

Don't be a "homer." Be fair at all times and be very accurate. Set as a standard a total lack of partiality "by giving batters of the visiting club the same consideration on hit-error decisions" as the batters of the home club.

Don't let anyone tell you that by giving the batter a hit on a doubtful play the scorer is helping the batter and hurting no one. Scoring a doubtful play as a hit may be unjustly charging a pitcher with an earned run, and that does not add up to the pitcher's credit.

One of the best practical methods of calling plays involves four points:

1. When a ball is batted, don't try to identify the batter before calling the play a hit or an error. Leave out all personalities. Call the decision on the ball, as it is hit and played, nothing more. Use the same yardstick for home and visiting players.

2. When in doubt about a hit-error decision, analyze the play. If the fielder had retired his man, would it have been a great play, bringing the fans to their feet in appreciation? If so, the scorer should not penalize a defensive player with an error simply because he had failed to come up with a sensational play. A batted ball that can be caught only by miraculous skill should be scored as a hit.

3. Whenever possible, sit in the press box with fair-minded people. If it will help, take along as an assistant a fair-minded person who appreciates and understands the goal of fairness at which all unprejudiced citizens are shooting. There are those who enjoy sitting in the press box and call a "hit" before the scorer does. Then, after the scorer calls the play "error," these people make such remarks as, "Aw, give him a hit!" Don't

be persuaded by such hecklers to change your decision. No businessman would allow such a pest to sit in his office and criticize his work; neither should a scorer allow such a person to be in his office—the press box. If anyone insists on being a nuisance, he is interfering with an important part of the game—the scoring.

4. Make decisions promptly. Never change a decision later in the game. Such changes invite an endless string of arguments, and cause a scorer to second guess himself, to worry and to be less careful about making his first decision. Also, changed decisions often necessitate changes in newspaper and radio reports, and frequently place the scorer in a ridiculous position. Be very careful to score the first hit by each team with this thought in mind: "If this turns out to be the only hit, I am willing to stand by my decision of its being a hit clean enough to prevent the pitcher from getting a no-hit game."

facts and rule interpretations

Be accurate and be sure to score perfectly the points of fact and of rule interpretation. A later change of a ruling is justified on these points, but the sooner the change is made the better. A messenger can be sent upon the field to ask the proper authorities for such necessary information as follows:

1. On a close play at first base, the baseman drops the ball. If the scorer is in doubt, he should ask the umpire whether the runner beat the ball to the base or whether the runner was safe because the baseman dropped the ball. (If the umpire first called the runner out and then reversed his decision because the baseman had dropped the ball, an error is charged against the baseman because the umpire had already called the play.)

2. When neither the shortstop nor the second baseman covers the catcher's throw to second base on an attempted steal by a runner from first, and the runner goes to third, always check with the manager or coach as to which player was supposed to have protected the bag on that play. One can never be sure of scoring accurately unless this is done. The belief held by many people that the second baseman *always* covers second base when a right-handed hitter is at bat, the shortstop, when a left-handed hitter is at bat, is erroneous.

3. In case a scorer fails to note which defensive players made assists on a play—who took the cut-off, who handed the ball to the player, who pulled the hidden ball trick, and so forth—ask the men who know: the manager, the coach, or even the players. Find out, for it is important to be accurate.

get it right

If a scorer finds that a particular play is scored in violation of the rules, corrections should be made as soon as possible. A scorer does not want to be a party to a compilation of erroneous history, but that is precisely what happens when a player's record is kept inaccurately.

double checking for mechanical accuracy

From the mechanical side of scoring, a system of cross-checking as the game progresses enables a scorer to keep a close tab on the accuracy of the record in the score book. This method of cross-checking consists of recording each play in two or three places before the next play occurs.

For instance, record a hit in the inning square opposite the name of the player who hit. Also mark the hit in that player's hit column. At the end of the inning, total the hits for the inning. Such a method of keeping score provides two totals that can be checked against each other at any time. The total runs should be kept in the same manner.

It is helpful to record by an entry in the inning square the name or the number of the player who batted the run in; if the run was not batted in, record the error, or stolen base, or other method by which the run was scored. List these various ways in which runs are made at the bottom of the inning column, or in the run column beside each run mark. Thus, the scorer can easily make certain that every run is accounted for in some way. If such entries are made before the next play begins, subsequent checking will be simplified.

If "at bat" space is large enough, place in it, in addition to dots for times at bat, *SH* for sacrifice, *BB* for base on balls, or *HP* for hit by pitched ball.

Record at the bottom of each inning total any of the following: a stolen base, error, wild pitch, passed ball, balk, or double play. This helps in checking against such records in another part of the score book. Similarly, circles around hit dots in the hit column to denote extra base hits provide a cross-check, as do circles around catcher's putouts for strike outs.

Keeping an up-to-the-minute check enables a scorer to total a player's score the moment he leaves the game. Records of replacing players must be kept in separate spaces. Similarly, on change of pitchers, the hit-and-run cross-checks, the encircled strike outs, putouts, and *BB* in the "at bat" column speed up scorekeeping.

Here is one situation that is very important to record correctly because of its bearing on earned runs. A runner is on first base; the batter hits a ground ball to the second baseman, who throws wild to the shortstop covering the bag at second base. The throw, had it been accurate, would have retired the runner at second. Do not score the batter as having reached first base on an error and do not advance the player to second base. Rather, score the batter as having reached first base on a fielder's choice and record the error in the second base corner of the square (opposite the runner who would have been out at second base). So far as earned runs are concerned, the runner at second was out, not the batter.

Use a mark to distinguish clearly between errors of this type and errors that do not prevent putouts but that simply give the runner an extra base. These "extra base errors" do not necessarily prevent the runner's subsequent run from being earned. Record, of course, when a change in pitchers is made. Also, make clear by lines, arrows, or any way that is clearest, when a foul, a foul-fly error, wild pitch, or balk occurs, so that when a change in pitchers is made, the score book will show which pitcher was on the mound at the time. Likewise, in order to obtain a correct sequence of plays, record at what time stolen bases and passed balls occurred.

Use some system to show when and by the aid of which player or in what manner each runner reached each base. There is no set system for recording such plays. Scorer should use the code that appears clearest to him. By all means, use some system and keep a *complete* running account of the game.

picking up a protested game

If a game is protested (if scoring for a league game) and ordered replayed from an exact point in the middle of an inning, it is the duty of the scorer to provide each official with correct information as to the exact situation when the protest was made and the exact point at which the game shall continue, as: Smith was on third, Jones on first; two were out; one run had scored. A scorer cannot guess at this important position; he must know how to mark it and he *must mark* it.

box-score lines for pinch hitters

At the bottom of the box score, preceding the summary, the lines to designate a pinch hitter should be informative. Instead of using "X——batted for Smith in the 9th," it would be better to use:

X——Fanned for Smith in the 9th
or
X——Singled for Smith in the 9th
or
X——Flied out for Smith in the 9th

FIGURING AVERAGES. THE STANDARD FORM FOR FIGURING ALL AVERAGES FOR BATTING, FIELDING, AND PITCHING IS LIKE THE EXAMPLES GIVEN HEREWITH:

CLUB BATTING

	G	AB	R	OR	H	TB	2B	3B	HR	RBI	SH	SF	SB	CS	LOB	Pct.
Club.........G																
Boston..........162	5678	747	628	1540	2287	231	66	128	697	85	37	77	42	1189	.271

INDIVIDUAL BATTING

Name and Club......BATS	G	AB	R	H	TB	2B	3B	HR	RBI	SH	SF	SB	CS	Pct.
Doe, John, New York......R	161	631	121	201	370	29	4	44	130	0	5	31	5	.319
Marr, Joe Boston........L	67	119	9	28	45	6	4	1	12	1	1	0	2	.235

CLUB FIELDING

	G	PO	A	E	TC	DP	PB	TP	Pct.
Club.........G									
Detroit........163	4416	1848	129	6393	161	15	0	.980

INDIVIDUAL FIELDING – FIRST BASEMAN

Name and Club.........	G	PO	A	E	DP	Pct.
Carr, John, Chicago..........	119	884	45	5	74	.995
Bell, John, Boston........	37	335	30	2	36	.995

PITCHERS' RECORDS

Name and Club......Thrs	G	GS	CG	GF	ShO	W	L	Pct.	IP	H	R	ER	HR	SH	SF	BFP	Tot.	Int.	HB	SO	WP	BK	ERA
																	BB	BB					
Doak, Billy, Detroit...R	26	8	2	5	0	3	4	.429	83	67	31	27	11	3	4	336	33	5	1	69	1	0	2.93
Smith, Tom, Boston....L	39	35	11	3	5	18	8	.692	250	202	97	83	24	7	3	1041	90	4	4	145	13	1	2.99

ABBREVIATIONS EXPLAINED

A	Assists	E	Errors	L	Games Lost	SH	Sacrifice Hits
AB	At Bat	ER	Earned Runs	LOB	Left On Base	SO	Struck Out
BB Int.	Intentional Base on balls	ERA	Earned Run Average	OR	Opponents' Runs	ShO	Shut Outs
BB Tot.	Total Base on Balls	G	Games	PB	Pass Balls	TB	Total Bases
BFP	Batters Faced Pitcher	GF	Games Finished	Pct	Percentage	TC	Total Chances
BK	Balks	GS	Games Started	PO	Put Outs	3B	Three Base Hits
CG	Complete Games	H	Hits	R	Runs	2B	Two Base Hits
CS	Caught Stealing	HB	Hit Batter	RBI	Runs Batted In	TP	Triple Plays
DP	Double Plays	HR	Home Runs	SB	Stolen Bases	W	Games Won
		IP	Innings Pitched	SF	Sacrifice Flies	WP	Wild Pitches

This procedure is much more informative and no more trouble than the indefinite line after the X, which simply indicates that the batter went into the game for another player and does not tell what the batter did in the game. Of course, if such a pinch hitter remains in the game, the scorer would not use the footnote to designate what the pinch hitter did on each successive time at bat. The footnote is merely to show what the player did in the pinch.

desires of statisticians

Amateur players and a large number of our college baseball squads do not have occasion to satisfy the wishes of a statistician. However, the sports department of newspapers printing the box score should be ready to provide statistical facts. First, require the statistician to enumerate in detail the information he wants, and then give him this information. A scorer appointed Official Scorer for some professional baseball league should follow all instructions minutely. Those instructions should supply the Official Scorer with all the detailed information the statistician must have for his averages—individual and composite.

FOUR
official scorers

The official rules for one group of players differ, in some cases, from the rules for others. This is true of the various age groups such as Cub League, Little League, Babe Ruth League, American Legion, high school, Junior College, NAIA Colleges, NCAA Colleges, Sand lot, and professional baseball. It is impossible, therefore, to explain one method of scoring to cover all groups. Basically, however, many elements of scoring are the same for all groups: for example, figuring averages, identifying players by number, and the abbreviations used to denote what happens in a game. The real problem is the interpretation of the rules themselves.

It is our suggestion that each coach obtain a copy of the rules governing play in his league, and discuss these rules thoroughly with the players.

For the purpose of explaining scoring procedure and rules of scoring, we have used the rules of professional baseball. This chapter will discuss implications of various rules which we feel need further explanations, so that the scorer will be able to credit each player properly.

figuring averages

The following instructions are outlined as a guide for those scorers who are required to conform to the provisions of the official rules of scoring. The purpose of these rules is to promote uniformity of recording championship games—amateur, college and professional.

official rules of scoring

DETERMINING PERCENTAGE RECORDS

10.21 To compute

(a) Percentage of games won and lost, divide the number of games won by the total games won and lost;

(b) Batting average, divide the total number of safe hits (not the total bases on hits) by the total times at bat, as defined in 10.02 (a);

(c) Slugging percentage, divide the total bases of all safe hits by the total times at bat, as defined in 10.02 (a);

(d) Fielding average, divide the total putouts and assists by the total of putouts, assists and errors;

(e) Pitcher's earned-run average, multiply the total earned runs charged against his pitching by 9, and divide the result by the total number of innings he pitched.

10.22 To assure uniformity in establishing the batting, pitching and fielding championships of professional leagues, such champions shall meet the following minimum performance standards:

(a) The individual batting champion shall be the player with the highest batting average, provided he is credited with as many or more total appearances at the plate in league championship games as the number of games scheduled for each club in his league that season, multiplied by 3.1. EXAMPLE: If a league schedules 162 games for each club, 502 plate appearances qualify (162 times 3.1 equals 502). If a league schedules 154 games, 477 plate appearances qualify (154 times 3.1 equals 477). If a league schedules 140 games, 434 plate appearances qualify (140 times 3.1 equals 434).

Total appearances at the plate shall include official times at bat, plus bases on balls, times hit by pitcher, sacrifice hits, sacrifice flies, and times awarded first base because of interference or obstruction.

(b) The individual pitching champion shall be the pitcher with the lowest earned-run average, provided that he has pitched at least as many innings as the number of games scheduled for each club in his league that season.

(c) The individual fielding champions shall be the fielders with the highest fielding average at each position, provided:

    (1) A catcher must have participated as a catcher in at least one-half the number of games scheduled for each club in his league that season;

    (2) An infielder or outfielder must have participated at his position in at least two-thirds of the number of games scheduled for each club in his league that season;

194   *official scorers*

(3) A pitcher must have pitched at least as many innings as the number of games scheduled for each club in his league that season.

EXCEPTION: If another pitcher has a fielding average as high or higher, and has handled more total chances in a lesser number of innings, he shall be the fielding champion.

batting out of order

When a player bats out of turn, it is the scorer's duty to keep silent and not advise either team or the umpire that such a thing is taking place. For the Official Scorer to call attention to a player's batting out of turn would be to destroy the premium for alertness on the part of the opposing team.

When a team discovers that the other team has a player batting out of turn, or when the umpire discovers it as the result of an appeal, it is strictly the umpire's business to straighten out the matter.

The scorer, however, should know how to handle certain phases of batting out of turn. If discovery of a man batting out of turn is made *before* a pitch to the next batter, the proper batter is called out for not batting in turn. The next batter shall be the batter whose name follows that of the proper batter thus called out. Charge that as a time at bat and as an out to the man who should have been at bat in the first place, according to the correct batting order. Credit the putout to the catcher. If discovery of man batting out of turn is made *after* a pitch to the next batter, man batting out of turn is *not* out, and the *batting order continues from there,* with the man who normally follows the batter out of turn then batting.

What to do with the player or players who have thus lost turns at bat. They lost their times at bat by not coming into the batter's position. Leave a blank for them on the score sheet.

players taken from the game while at bat

When the batter goes out of the game with two strikes on him and a substitute batter misses the third strike, charge strike outs against the first batter. In all other cases, charge or credit the second, the substitute batter.

RUNS BATTED IN

10.04 (a) Credit the batter with a run batted in for every run which reaches home base because of the batter's safe hit, sacrifice bunt, sacrifice fly, infield out or fielder's choice; or which is forced over the plate by reason of the batter becoming a runner with the bases full (on a base on balls, or an award of first base for being touched by a pitched ball, or for interference or obstruction).

>   (1) Credit a run batted in for the run scored by the batter who hits a home run. Credit a run batted in for each runner who is on base when the home run is hit and who scores ahead of the batter who hits the home run.

>   (2) Credit a run batted in for the run scored when, before two are out, an error is made on a play on which a runner from third base ordinarily would score.

>   (b) Do not credit a run batted in when the batter grounds into a force double play or a reverse force double play.

>   (c) Do not credit a run batted in when a fielder is charged with an error because he muffs a throw at first base which would have completed a force double play.

>   (d) Scorer's judgment must determine whether a run batted in shall be credited for a run which scores when a fielder holds the ball, or throws to a wrong base. Ordinarily, if the runner keeps going, credit a run batted in; if the runner stops and takes off again when he notices the misplay, credit the run as scored on a fielder's choice.

when to award an rbi

RBI on infield error. Do not rob a batter of a run batted in on an infield error simply because there is an error; the batter gets his run batted in, unless the scorer thinks that had the fielder not erred, the runner would have been out at the plate or an out that would have retired the side would have been made elsewhere. This point seems to confuse some scorers. For instance, with one man out and a runner on third, the infield decides to play deep. The batter hits a ground ball to an infielder who bobbles it. The runner on third, off to a good start, scores. The way the infielder plays the ball makes it obvious that he was going to make a play for the batter because first base is the only base to which the infielder has a play. This is a run batted in.

No RBI on steal of home. A runner stealing home is not credited with a run batted in. A run batted in means a run scored by the action of the batter.

RBI on walk or hit batter. A batter is credited with a run batted in when he forces home a runner with a base on balls or by being hit by a pitched ball.

Certain double plays erase RBI. On all force infield double plays, there is no run batted in, even if the first baseman drops the ball and commits an error.

RBI on score after a catch (sacrifice fly). When a batter hits a fly ball which enables a runner to score after the catch, the batter is not charged with a time at bat and is credited with a run batted in. Even if the fly is dropped for an error, but would have permitted a run to score after the catch, a run batted in is to be credited and no time at bat is charged to the batter. If a runner advances but does not score, the batter is charged with a time at bat.

RBI for score on sacrifice. A sacrifice bunt that scores a runner accounts for a run batted in.

relation of rbi to earned runs

Runner (on third owing to an error by the third baseman on a previous play when he dropped a perfectly thrown ball) scores when the batter hits to the second baseman, who fumbles the grounder. Batter reaches first base. This is not an earned run because no runner can score an earned run if his stay on the bases has been prolonged by errors. However, it can be a run batted in (if less than two are out) if, in the opinion of the scorer, the runner could not have been thrown out at the plate. Scoring of earned runs and runs batted in follow in parallel lines in many instances, but this is an exception and a very logical one.

accounting for runs batted in

In order for a scorer to check himself on runs batted in, he should account for every run, marking each run in the scorebook at the time the run is scored. Thus, at the end of the game in which a team makes 15 runs and the scorer has only 12 runs batted in, he can glance back to see whether there were 3 runs that were not batted in. If the scorer finds that 1 run scored on an error, 1 was stolen, and 1 came in on a passed ball, he can check himself as correct in the listing of the runs batted in.

Accounting for runs scored. Here are the ways in which runs can be accounted for:

1. Batted in.
2. Stolen.
3. Interference.
4. Fielder holding the ball falls down or "goes to sleep."
5. Wild pitch.
6. Passed ball.
7. Balk.

8. Misplay which enables runner to score.

9. Attempting run-down of scoring runner.

10. During run-down of another runner on an unsuccessful steal or during run-down of another runner trapped off base.

11. Double play which is an infield force play or on which first baseman touches first base after picking up ground ball and throws to second for tag of runner who was on first base.

puzzlers for reference

Error or RBI? Here is a play in which the scorer must make a hairline decision between an error and a run batted in. Watch it very closely and use the best possible judgment. Runner on second base; the batter hits to deep short, shortstop throwing slightly wide to the first baseman's right. Batter apparently had the throw beaten, even if it had been accurate, for a base hit. The runner who was on second went to third, kept on running, and scored.

The scorer must decide whether the batter is entitled to a run batted in on the basis of the runner's speed and fine base running, or whether the simple fact that the throw, which was a bit wide, accounted for the run, making it an error for the shortstop. A *pitcher,* not the batter, gets the benefit of doubt on this error or run batted in play. In the Official Rules on earned runs, it is stated, "The pitcher shall be given the benefit whenever fielding errors are made and in determining the base to which a runner should have been held with perfect support on the part of his fielders."

Run scores and no error can be charged. A scorer will run into puzzling scoring plays where no error can be charged to account for the run. On such plays, in case of doubt, score run batted in. "The batter is entitled to the benefit of the doubt" in getting a run batted in because an error is not involved.

If the scorer thinks that the batter should not have a run batted in, account for the run scored "while the defense player went to sleep, fell down," and so forth. Best guiding points are: batter is entitled to benefit of other runner's heads-up running and speed; if runner stops at third and then starts running again, do not score run batted in.

Examples: 1. Runner on second base who goes to third when the batter hits a ground ball to an infielder. The batter would have been out at first but for a misplay on the throw. Pitcher, with ball in his hands, stands back from first and begins to argue with the umpire. Runner then starts from third and scores during the argument. This is not a run batted in.

2. Fast runner on first base; batter singles to center field on the hit-and-run play; the runner who was on first goes to third and the coach at third keeps the runner going for the plate, while the center fielder, not noticing the runner going for home, lobs the ball into the second baseman. The second baseman is not fast in turning around or throwing the ball to the plate. When the second baseman does see what is happening, or when other players yell at him as to what the runner is doing, it is too late. If the runner beats the throw to the plate, this is a run batted in. If the runner would have been retired, except for an error, do not score a run batted in.

3. Runners on first and second bases; the batter hits to the shortstop who flips the ball to the second baseman for a force out. Runner, who was on first, slides into second base and bowls over the second baseman, knocking him off balance. Runner, who was on second rounded third and goes home to score before the second baseman can collect himself and throw the ball to the plate. If the runner from second had already come around third, rounded the base, and did not slow up in his running stride, score a run batted in. Otherwise, score "while defense player fell down."

BASE HITS

10.05 A base hit shall be scored in the following cases:

(a) When a batter reaches first base (or any succeeding base) safely on a fair ball which settles on the ground or touches a fence before being touched by a fielder, or which clears a fence;

(b) When a batter reaches first base safely on a fair ball hit with such force, or so slowly, that any fielder attempting to make a play with it has no opportunity to do so;

> NOTE: A hit shall be scored if the fielder attempting to handle the ball cannot make a play, even if such fielder deflects the ball from or cuts off another fielder who could have put out a runner.

(c) When a batter reaches first base safely on a fair ball which takes an unnatural bounce so that a fielder cannot handle it with ordinary effort, or which touches the pitcher's plate or any base, (including home plate) before being touched by a fielder and bounces so that a fielder cannot handle it with ordinary effort;

(d) When a batter reaches first base safely on a fair ball which has not been touched by a fielder and which is in fair territory when it reaches the outfield unless in the scorer's judgment it could have been handled with ordinary effort;

(e) When a fair ball which has not been touched by a fielder touches a runner or an umpire. EXCEPTION: Do not score a hit when a runner is called out for having been touched by an Infield Fly;

(f) When a fielder unsuccessfully attempts to put out a preceding runner, and in the scorer's judgment the batter-runner would not have been put out at first base by perfect fielding.

> NOTE: In applying the above rules, always give the batter the benefit of the doubt. A safe course to follow is to score a hit when exceptionally good fielding of a ball fails to result in a putout.

DEFINITION OF FAIR BALL

2.00 A fair ball is a batted ball that settles on fair ground between home first base, or between home and third base, or that is on or over fair territory when bounding to the outfield past first or third base, or that touches first, second or third base, or that first falls on fair territory on or beyond first base or third base, or that, while on or over fair territory, touches the person of an umpire or player, or that, while over fair territory, passes out of the playing field in flight.

> NOTE: A fair fly shall be judged according to the relative position of the ball and the foul line, including the foul pole, and not as to whether the fielder is on fair or foul territory at the time he touches the ball.

Fair territory is that part of the playing field within, and including the first base and third base lines, from home base to the bottom of the playing field fence and perpendicularly upwards. All foul lines are in fair territory.

scoring hits

Failing to touch first base. It is *not a hit* if the batter hits to the outfield for two bases, fails to touch first, the ball is thrown to first, and he is called out. The batter did not reach first base safely. The play should be recorded as an out.

Fielders must have a fair chance. When a fair ball is partially or wholly stopped by a fielder who is in motion, but such player cannot recover himself in time to field the ball to first before the batter reaches that base, or to some other base in time to force out another runner, a base hit is scored.

If there is doubt about a ball hit with such force to an infielder or pitcher that he cannot handle it in time to put out the batter or force out a base runner—except when the ball is recovered by another fielder in time to retire the batter or force out a base runner—a base hit should be scored and the fielder exempted from the charge of an error.

Deflected drive. On a hard drive that the pitcher deflects, say to the shortstop, the scorer must be more lenient toward the shortstop than he would be on a drive hit straight at him. The player who is hustling is very likely to make an off balance play on a hard deflected drive, and that should be taken into consideration. It is better to score a hit rather than penalize an infielder on an almost impossible play.

Slow hit ball. When a ball is hit so slowly toward a fielder that he cannot handle it in time to put out the batter or force out a base runner, a base hit is scored.

Fielder touching the ball. No rule exists that states that a hit must be scored if a fielder fails to touch a ball, just as mere touching the ball is not an automatic error. An easy chance that trickles through a fielder's legs untouched is nothing but an error. The mere technicality that he did not touch it is not sufficient to credit the batter with a hit. On balls hit to the right or left of the fielder, the fielder must, of course, have time to move over and have a fair chance to make the play. The scorer's judgment will spot such cases.

Batted ball hits umpire or base runner. Rule 10.05 Section (e) states —A base hit shall be scored:

When a fair ball which has not been touched by a fielder touches a runner or an umpire. EXCEPTION: Do not score a hit when a runner is called out for having been touched by an Infield Fly;

Special notice should be given to Rule 7.09 (g) pertaining to a base runner who intentionally lets a batted ball hit him or interferes with the fielder.

If, in the judgment of the umpire, a base runner wilfully and deliberately interferes with a batted ball or a fielder in the act of fielding a batted ball with the obvious intent to break up a double play, the ball is dead. The umpire shall call the runner out for interference and also call out the batter-runner because of the action of his teammate. In no event may bases be run or runs scored because of such action by a runner.

Force out kills base hit. *In no case shall a base hit be scored when a base runner is forced out by a play.*

When a grounder to the outfield or a dropped fly results in a force out, the batter cannot be given a hit. The player dropping the fly is relieved of an error.

Runner on first base; batter hits for three bases; but the runner originally on first base misses second base and the ball is played there, thereby putting him out. Such a play is, in reality, a force out at second base, and the batter must not be credited with a base hit. However, if the runner from first had touched second, and then missed third base, the hit is credited as a triple because the runner was not actually forced to go to third.

Passing a runner. Bases full; two out; batter hits a ground ball into right field; runner on third stumbles and falls to the ground; runner from second passes the fallen player and is thus called out. Did the runner force the batter out of a base hit? No. This was not a force play; the batter is credited with a base hit.

Fielder's choice. When a fielder, after handling a batted or bunted ball, elects to try to retire a base runner instead of the batter, the play is known as a "fielder's choice." In case the runner is retired, or would be retired but for an error, the batter shall be charged with a time at bat, but no hit. If no one is retired on the play and there are no errors on the play, and in the judgment of the scorer the batter could not have been retired at first base by perfect fielding, the batter shall be credited with a base hit.

Oversliding bases. In the event of a batter oversliding second or third bases and being tagged by the opposing fielder (when the batter is attempting to stretch a single into a two base hit or to stretch a two base hit into a three bagger), the play should be scored the same as when a base runner attempts to steal, overslides the base, and is tagged out. In other words, the batter who overslides second base and is tagged out shall be credited with only a single, whereas the batter who overslides third base and is tagged out shall be credited with a two base hit.

Interference by base runner. Runner from second interferes with the third baseman fielding a batted ball; umpire calls him out. Such a play is not scored similarly to the play on which a batted ball hits a base runner for a base hit. Such a play is strictly a fielder's choice, except that (as on an ordinary ground ball that the fielder handles and attempts to retire a runner other than the batter and fails to do so) scorers can call a hit if they think the batter could not have been retired at first, or a runner forced. If there is an error on this attempted tag, no hit is credited.

Advancing on throw in. The fact that a batter makes second base on a continuous run while an outfielder, after fielding a hit, throws to third or home, does not make the hit a two base hit. The hit is scored as a single and the batter goes to second base on the throw in. If the scorer thinks that the batter could not have been thrown out at second base by a direct throw to that base, he should score it as a two base hit. But the batter should not be given a two base hit when, obviously, he is not entitled to it, but reaches second base merely because of the throw to another base.

Do not score on presumptions. Batter hits between third and short; the shortstop is in position to make the play and to retire the runner at first, but the third baseman comes over in front of him and the ball bounds off his glove. Had the third baseman completed the play, it would have been spectacular. In scoring this play, does the scorer take into consideration the fact that the shortstop would have had a fairly easy play had not the third baseman crossed over? No. What the shortstop might have done does not enter into such a case. The scorer can be guided only by what the third baseman did do. The play *appears* to be a hit, and must be scored as seen.

Analyze doubtful hit-error decisions. It is often very helpful to analyze a play backwards when the scorer is in doubt as to scoring a base hit or an error. Look at it this way: if the fielder had retired the batter, would it have been a great or a very unusual play? If so, do not penalize the fielder with an error because he failed to make a play that would have been sensational. A moment's thought on that angle of a play will often give the final decision in a flash. But be careful. This rule will not work on the next case, where two players are involved.

Pitcher covering first base. Watch throws closely at first base. Be sure that the scorer sits where he can see this particular play. For instance, the batter hits to the first baseman's right, who runs for it and gets the ball with a remarkable stop. The pitcher runs to the bag and crosses it just as a perfect throw gets there, but the pitcher drops the ball as the batter crosses the bag.

Did the throw beat the runner? The scorer may think that the runner got there first, in which case it is a hit, but if the scorer thinks that the throw got to the bag first, it is an error for the pitcher, and no hit. There is a great temptation in such cases, at times, to figure the batter deserves a hit because the first baseman made such a remarkable play. And if the first baseman had to throw while off balance, and consequently, made a poor or a late throw, the scorer could score a hit. However, if the throw was right there at the bag and beat the runner, it cannot be a hit. It is tough on the batter, but the fact is that he was robbed by the first baseman, and the latter is entitled to and should receive credit for an assist. The pitcher cannot be relieved of an out-and-out error by reasoning that the first baseman had to make a great play and did get the ball to the pitcher in time and in the right place. The first baseman performed his duty perfectly, and the batter is not entitled to a hit simply because another player failed to perform his duty.

The above is a case where the scorer cannot go back and decide some credit is due the batter because the first baseman made a great play. The fact that the first baseman made the play well enough to retire the batter, eliminates the hit angle. The throw to first, being covered by the pitcher, either does or does not beat the runner. That is as far back as the scorer has any license to go.

DETERMINING VALUE OF BASE HITS

10.07 Whether a safe hit shall be scored as a one-base hit, two-base hit, three-base hit or home run when no error or putout results shall be determined as follows:

(a) Subject to the provisions of 10.07 (b) and (c), it is a one-base hit if the batter stops at first base; it is a two-base hit if the batter stops at second base; it is a three-base hit if the batter stops at third base; it is a home run if the batter touches all bases and scores.

(b) When, with one or more runners on base, the batter advances more than one base on a safe hit and the defensive team makes an attempt to put out a preceding runner, the scorer shall determine whether the batter made a legitimate two-base hit or three-base hit, or whether he advanced beyond first base on the fielder's choice.

> NOTE: Do not credit the batter with a three-base hit when a preceding runner is put out at the plate, or would have been out but for an error. Do not credit the batter with a two-base hit when a preceding runner trying to advance from first base is put out at third base, or would have been out but for an error. However, with the exception of the above, do not determine the value of base-hits by the number of bases advanced by a preceding runner. A batter may deserve a two-base hit even though a preceding runner advances one or no bases; he may deserve only a one-base hit even though he reaches second base and a preceding runner advances two bases.
> EXAMPLES: (1) Runner on first, batter hits to right fielder, who throws to third base in unsuccessful attempt to put out runner. Batter takes second base. Credit batter with one-base hit. (2) Runner on second. Batter hits fair fly ball. Runner holds up to determine if ball is caught, and advances only to third base, while batter takes second. Credit batter with two-base hit. (3) Runner on third. Batter hits high fair fly. Runner takes lead, then runs back to tag up, thinking ball will be caught. Ball falls safe, but runner cannot score, although batter has reached second. Credit batter with two-base hit.

(c) When the batter attempts to make a two-base hit or a three-base hit by sliding, he must hold the last base to which he advances. If he overslides and is tagged out before getting back to the base safely, he shall be credited with only as many bases as he attained safely. If he overslides second base and is tagged out, he shall be credited with a one-base hit; if he overslides third base and is tagged out, he shall be credited with a two-base hit.

> NOTE: If the batter over-runs second or third base and is tagged out trying to return, he shall be credited with the last base he touched. If he runs past second base after reaching that base on his feet, attempts to return and is tagged out, he shall be credited with a two-base hit. If he runs past third base after reaching that base on his feet, attempts to return and is tagged out, he shall be credited with a three-base hit.

(d) When the batter, after making a safe hit, is called out for having failed to touch a base, the last base he reached safely shall determine if he shall be credited with a one-base hit, a two-base hit or a three-base hit. If he is called out after missing home base, he shall be credited with a three-base hit. If he is called out for missing third base, he shall be credited with a two-base hit. If he is called out for missing second base, he shall be credited with a one-base hit. If he is called out for missing first base, he shall be charged with a time at bat, but no hit.

(e) When the batter-runner is awarded two bases, three bases or a home run under the provisions of Playing Rules 7.05 or 7.06 (a), he shall be credited with a two-base hit, a three-base hit or a home run, as the case may be.

touching bases for credit

GAME-ENDING HITS

(f) Subject to the provisions of 10.07 (g), when the batter ends a game with a safe hit which drives in as many runs as are necessary to put his team in the lead, he shall be credited with only as many bases on his hit as are advanced by the runner who scores the winning run, and then only if the batter runs out his hit for as many bases as are advanced by the runner who scores the winning run.

> NOTE: Apply this rule even when the batter is theoretically entitled to more bases because of being awarded an "automatic" extra-base hit under various provisions of Playing Rules 6.09 and 7.05.

(g) When the batter ends a game with a home run hit out of the playing field, he and any runners on base are entitled to score.

The exception to this as indicated in rule 6.09 (h) pertaining to deflected balls.

Any fair fly ball is deflected by the fielder into the stands, or over the fence into foul territory, in which case the batter shall be entitled to advance to second base; but if deflected into the stands or over the fence in fair territory, the batter shall be entitled to a home run. However, should such fair fly be deflected at a point less than 250 feet from home plate, the batter shall be entitled to two bases only.

SACRIFICES

10.09 (a) Score a sacrifice bunt when, before two are out, the batter advances one or more runners with a bunt and is put out at first base, or would have been put out except for a fielding error.

(b) Score a sacrifice bunt when, before two are out, the fielders handle a bunted ball without error in an unsuccessful attempt to put out a preceding runner advancing one base. EXCEPTION: When an attempt to turn a bunt into a putout of a preceding runner fails, and in the scorer's judgment perfect play would not have put out the batter at first base, the batter shall be credited with a one-base hit and not a sacrifice.

(c) Do not score a sacrifice bunt when any runner is put out attempting to advance one base on a bunt. Charge the batter with a time at bat.

(d) Score a sacrifice fly when, before two are out, the batter hits a fly ball which

(1) is caught, and a runner scores after the catch, or

(2) is dropped, and a runner scores, if in the scorer's judgment the runner could have scored after the catch had the fly been caught.

> NOTE: Score a sacrifice fly in accordance with 10.09 (d) (2) even though another runner is forced out by reason of the batter becoming a runner.

If a runner scores after a fly ball has been caught, credit the batter with a run batted in but no time at bat.

The sacrifice rule does not mean that a sacrifice can be scored only when play is attempted at first base. "If a runner is not retired and no error is made, the batter . . . shall be credited with a sacrifice base hit or fielder's choice, provided he bunted the ball."

Although the sacrifice rule provides simply that a runner is advanced, it is obvious that where the front runner of two or three runners is not advanced and another runner does advance, no sacrifice should be scored, as indicated in rule 10.09 (c) above.

logic of sacrifice

Scoring logic is nicely applied to sacrifices, since the latter often are confusing. The batter must do two things in order to get a sacrifice:

1. He must intentionally bunt the ball—a half swing is not a bunt, and a tap in dodging a pitched ball carries no intention to bunt.

2. The bunt must be such that it advances a runner or runners to benefit the offensive team if (a) it is handled without an error, or (b) there is an error, but the runner would have advanced on errorless play.

Examples: Runner upon first base; no one out; batter bunts to pitcher:

1. Pitcher (a) fumbles or (b) throws to second where an error is made. If the runner would have been safe at second despite the error, sacrifice and fielder's choice; or if there would have been an out with perfect play, the play is not a sacrifice. If neither runner could have been retired, score a hit.

2. Pitcher throws to second and the runner there is safe, no error being made. Score *sacrifice* and fielder's choice, except if the batter could not have been retired, in which case score a hit. The way the ball was played proves that the batter deserves a sacrifice, at least.

3. Pitcher throws to first, the first baseman dropped the ball. Score a sacrifice, except that if the batter would have been safe despite the error, score a hit. The fact that the pitcher did not attempt a throw to second is evidence that it was a sacrifice. Do not rob the batter of a sacrifice because the first baseman drops the ball. The batter has accomplished his purpose in advancing the runner without the aid of an error, since the

error was not on the runner but on the batter. A batter should not and cannot be penalized for doing that which he intended to do.

Always remember that errors do not rob the batter of a deserved sacrifice. If the bunt is so good that neither the batter nor a force runner is, or could have been, retired, score a hit.

fielding records

PUTOUTS

10.10 A putout shall be credited to each fielder who (1) catches a fly ball or a line drive, whether fair or foul; (2) catches a thrown ball which puts out a batter or runner, or (3) tags a runner when the runner is off the base to which he legally is entitled.

(a) Automatic putouts shall be credited to the catcher as follows:

(1) When the batter is called out for an illegally batted ball;

(2) When the batter is called out for bunting foul for his third strike; (Note exception in 10.17 (a) (4)).

(3) When the batter is called out for being touched by his own batted ball;

(4) When the batter is called out for interfering with the catcher;

(5) When the batter is called out for failing to bat in his proper turn; (See 10.03 (d)).

(6) When the batter is called out for refusing to touch first base after receiving a base on balls;

(7) When a runner is called out for refusing to advance from third base to home with the winning run.

(b) Other automatic putouts shall be credited as follows (Credit no assists on these plays except as specified):

(1) When the batter is called out on an Infield Fly which is not caught, credit the putout to the fielder who the scorer believes could have made the catch;

(2) When a runner is called out for being touched by a fair ball (including an Infield Fly), credit the putout to the fielder nearest the ball;

(3) When a runner is called out for running out of line to avoid being tagged, credit the putout to the fielder whom the runner avoided;

(4) When a runner is called out for passing another runner, credit the putout to the fielder nearest the point of passing;

(5) When a runner is called out for running the bases in reverse order,

credit the putout to the fielder covering the base he left in starting his reverse run;

(6) When a runner is called out for having interfered with a fielder, credit the putout to the fielder with whom the runner interfered, unless the fielder was in the act of throwing the ball when the interference occurred, in which case credit the putout to the fielder for whom the throw was intended, and credit an assist to the fielder whose throw was interfered with;

(7) When the batter-runner is called out because of interference by a preceding runner, as provided in Playing Rule 6.05 (m), credit the putout to the first baseman. If the fielder interfered with was in the act of throwing the ball, credit him with an assist, but credit only one assist on any one play under the provisions of 10.10 (b) (6) and (7).

crediting putouts

The number of opponents, if any, put out by each player shall be set down in the (PO) column. When the batter is called out by the umpire for an illegally batted ball, for a foul third strike bunt, for being hit by his own batted ball, for interference with the catcher, or for failing to bat in proper turn, the putout shall be credited to the catcher. When a base runner is declared out on an infield fly, the putout shall be credited to the player who would have made the play except for the action of the runner or the announcement of the umpire. When a base runner is declared out because of being hit by a batted ball, the putout should be credited to the fielder nearest to the ball at the time of the occurrence.

Running out of base line or interfering. When a base runner is declared out for running out of the base line or interfering with a fielder, credit the putout to the player who would have made the play except for the action of the runner or the announcement of the umpire.

Runner hit by infield fly. When a runner, standing off the base, is hit by an infield fly, both the runner and the batter are to be declared out. Credit putouts to the fielder nearest the play who normally would have caught the fly. If the runner is hit by the infield fly while he is standing on his base, only the batter is called out, and the putout would be credited to the nearest fielder as stated.

ASSISTS

10.11 An assist shall be credited to each fielder who throws or deflects a batted or thrown ball in such a way that a putout results, or would have resulted except for a subsequent error by any fielder. Only one assist and no more shall be credited to each fielder who throws or deflects the ball in a run-down play which results in a putout, or would have resulted in a putout, except for a subsequent error.

> NOTE: Mere ineffective contact with the ball shall not be considered an assist. "Deflect" shall mean to slow down or change the direction of the ball and thereby effectively assist in putting out a batter or runner.

(a) Credit an assist to each fielder who throws or deflects the ball during a play which results in a runner being called out for interference, or for running out of line.

(b) Do not credit an assist to the pitcher on a strikeout. EXCEPTION: Credit an assist if the pitcher fields an uncaught third strike and makes a throw which results in a putout.

(c) Do not credit an assist to the pitcher when, as the result of a legal pitch received by the catcher, a runner is put out, as when the catcher picks a runner off base, throws out a runner trying to steal, or tags a runner trying to score.

(d) Do not credit an assist to a fielder whose wild throw permits a runner to advance, even though the runner subsequently is put out as a result of continuous play. A play which follows a misplay (whether or not it is an error) is a new play, and the fielder making any misplay shall not be credited with an assist unless he takes part in the new play.

crediting assists

The number of times, if any, each player assists in putting out an opponent shall be set down in the (A) column. One assist and no more shall be given to each player who handles the ball in aiding in a run-down play or any other play of the kind, even though he completes the play by making the putout. Credit an assist to each player who handles and throws the ball in such a way that a putout would have resulted except for the error of a teammate.

Dropped third strike. Batter strikes out and the catcher drops the ball; catcher recovers the ball and throws the batter out at first. Give the catcher an assist; also credit the pitcher with a strike out. The first baseman gets a putout.

Error does not erase assist. Be sure to credit an assist if a grounder is hit to an infielder who makes a good throw to first, the batter being safe because the first baseman drops the ball. Do not fail to give the infielder credit for his assist because of the other player's misplay. If a ground ball is hit into the outfield, the batter attempts to make second, and is safe there because the baseman drops the ball despite a good throw by the outfielder, do not fail to give an assist to the outfielder making the throw.

Assist on deflected ball. Credit an assist to a player who, by deflecting a batted ball with his glove or any part of his body, aids in retiring the batter or another base runner.

Example: Fly ball deflects from one fielder's glove; another fielder catches it before it strikes the ground. Give an assist to the first fielder touching the ball.

No assist on bad throw. Do not credit an assist to a fielder who makes a bad throw, even when the runner trying to advance on it is subsequently retired. A play that follows an error is a new play, and the player making it is not entitled to an assist unless he takes part in the new play.

However, when such a play occurs on the second out of an attempted double play, credit assist to the overthrower because it is a double play. It is a continuous play, since *continuous* means *not interrupted by an error*.

Example: Batter strikes out; catcher overthrows second base attempting to get the base stealer; center fielder recovers the ball and throws out the runner at third base.

Another Example: Runner on first base; batter hits a ground ball to the shortstop, who relays it to the second baseman for the attempted double play. The first out is made at second base, but the second baseman overthrows the first baseman. The catcher, backing up the throw at first, recovers the ball and retires the runner who hit the ball as the latter attempted to reach second base on the wild throw but had to return to first base. Score double play, with assists for the shortstop, second baseman, and the catcher.

No assist on steal of home. Do not credit an assist to the pitcher when, in legally delivering the ball to the batter, he helps to retire a runner attempting to steal home.

No assist on strike out. The pitcher is not credited with an assist in striking out the batter.

Interference and "out of line." Assists should be credited to every player who handles the ball in the play that results in a base runner being called "out" for interference or for running out of the base line.

DOUBLE PLAYS—TRIPLE PLAYS

10.12 Credit participation in the double play or triple play to each fielder who earns a putout or an assist when two or three players are put out between the time a pitch is delivered and the time the ball next becomes dead or is next in possession of the pitcher in pitching position, unless an error intervenes between putouts.

> NOTE: Credit the double play or triple play also if an appeal play after the ball is in possession of the pitcher results in an additional putout.

double play

A double play shall mean two continuous putouts that take place between the time the ball leaves the pitcher's hand and it is returned to him while he is standing in the pitcher's box.

Continuous means *not interrupted by an error.*

Examples: Runner on first base; none out; the batter hits a pop fly to the first baseman and the pitcher runs over to cover first base. The first baseman makes the catch and then tosses the ball to the pitcher, who starts back to the pitching mound with it. The runner makes a break for second base and is thrown out by the pitcher.

This is a double play, and is similar to the one in which a runner tags up at second and starts for third after a fly ball is caught, but is thrown out by an outfielder. They are double plays because two outs were made without the ball being returned to the pitcher, *standing in the pitcher's box*, with no error interrupting the continuity.

ERRORS

10.13 An error shall be charged for each misplay (fumble, muff or wild throw) which prolongs the time at bat of a batter or which prolongs the life of a runner, or which permits a runner to advance one or more bases.

> NOTE: (1) Slow handling of the ball which does not involve mechanical misplay shall not be construed as an error.
> NOTE: (2) It is not necessary that the fielder touch the ball to be charged with an error. If a ground ball goes through a fielder's legs or a pop fly falls untouched and in the scorer's judgment the fielder could have handled the ball with ordinary effort, an error shall be charged.

(a) An error shall be charged against any fielder when he muffs a foul fly, to prolong the time at bat of a batter, whether the batter subsequently reaches first base or is put out.

(b) An error shall be charged against any fielder when he catches a thrown ball or a ground ball in time to put out the batter-runner and fails to tag first base or the batter-runner.

(c) An error shall be charged against any fielder when he catches a thrown ball or a ground ball in time to put out any runner on a force play and fails to tag the base or the runner.

(d) (1) An error shall be charged against any fielder whose wild throw permits a runner to reach a base safely, when in the scorer's judgment a good throw would have put out the runner. EXCEPTION: No error shall be charged under this section if the wild throw is made attempting to prevent a stolen base.

(2) An error shall be charged against any fielder whose wild throw in attempting to prevent a runner's advance permits that runner or any other runner to advance one or more bases beyond the base he would have reached had the throw not been wild.

(3) An error shall be charged against any fielder whose throw takes an unnatural bounce, or touches a base or the pitcher's plate, or touches a runner, a fielder or an umpire, thereby permitting any runner to advance.

NOTE: Apply this rule even when it appears to be an injustice to a fielder whose throw was accurate. Every base advanced by a runner must be accounted for.

(4) Charge only one error on any wild throw, regardless of the number of bases advanced by one or more runners.

(e) An error shall be charged against any fielder whose failure to stop, or try to stop, an accurately thrown ball permits a runner to advance, providing there was occasion for the throw. If such throw be made to second base, the scorer shall determine whether it was the duty of the second baseman or the shortstop to stop the ball, and an error shall be charged to the negligent player.

NOTE: If in the scorer's judgment there was no occasion for the throw, an error shall be charged to the fielder who threw the ball.

(f) When an umpire awards the batter or any runner or runners one or more bases because of interference or obstruction, charge the fielder who committed the interference or obstruction with one error, no matter how many bases the batter, or runner or runners, may be advanced.

scoring errors

Dropped foul fly is an error. One of the more common mistakes of scoring is the failure to charge an error against a player who drops an easy-to-catch foul fly. The opinion prevails that the error is not to be charged unless the batter subsequently reaches first base. Nothing could be more erroneous. Anything which prolongs the time at bat of the batter is to be charged as an error. Certainly an easy foul fly that is dropped prolongs the time of a batter at bat. The scorer who fails to charge such an error, regardless of what the batter does, falls short in the requirements of a scorer's job.

Intentionally dropping fly. With runner on third base, the left-fielder gets under a high foul fly and apparently, realizing at the last moment that a catch would permit the runner to score, drops the ball. This is not an error if the scorer thinks that the left fielder deliberately dropped the ball.

Prolonging life of base runner. Runner on first base starts to steal second on the pitch; catcher throws to the shortstop covering second base, but the runner checks himself and starts back to first; shortstop drops the ball and the runner gets back to first safely.

If the scorer is very certain that a throw by the shortstop would have retired the runner at first base, an error can be charged to the shortstop for thus prolonging the life of the base runner. However, this is a *presumption* play in which the scorer is called on to assume that the first baseman would have caught the ball and tagged the runner. Authorities agree that to charge the shortstop with an error is unwise unless it appears to be a very flagrant misplay. This is one of those plays that must *be seen to be scored,* and the scorer must use good judgment in handling it.

Wild throw by catcher. An error shall not be charged against the catcher for a wild throw in an attempt to prevent a stolen base, unless the base runner advances an extra base.

Completing double play. An error shall not be scored against the catcher or an infielder who attempts to complete a double play, unless the throw is so wild that an additional base is gained. This, however, does not exempt from an error a player who drops a thrown ball when by holding it he would have completed a double play.

Second baseman trying to complete a double play throws wild to first, and although the runner there does not attempt to gain an extra base, a runner rounding third keeps on going, solely because of the wild throw, and scores. Error for the second baseman. The rule states, "unless the throw is so wild that an additional base is gained," but does not stipulate which runner gains an extra base.

Baseman at fault. In case a base runner advances a base through the failure of a baseman to stop, or try to stop, a ball accurately thrown to his base, the latter shall be charged with an error and not the player who made such throw, provided there was occasion for it. If such throw is made to second base, the scorer shall determine whether the second baseman or shortstop shall be charged with an error.

Exempt from error by "force out." In the event of a fielder dropping a fly but recovering the ball in time to force a runner at another base, he shall be exempted from an error, the play being scored as a "force out."

This rule applies generally to any defensive player who makes a misplay on a batted ball and then assists in getting the ball to a baseman in time for a force out or an out at first base. Even if he didn't assist in the recovery for the out, the error is eliminated.

Error on non-force play. The above rule does not necessarily apply where the fielder drops a fly, or fumbles a grounder, or the catcher drops a third strike but recovers in time to retire a runner on other than a force play (implied by the wording of the official rule). This calls for the judgment of the scorer as to whether or not the defensive team has lost an advantage as a result of the original misplay. (See explanation with examples under *Earned Runs*.)

Also, the rule does not necessarily apply to a player who mishandles a thrown ball, and yet retires another runner. He is not exempt from an error if he drops a thrown ball when, by holding it, he would have retired one man before another was retired.

Examples: Bases full; ground ball hit to the pitcher who has a possible play at every base and at home plate.

1. Pitcher fumbles the ball but recovers it in time to get the batter at first base or to force one of the other runners. No error, but if the baseman protecting the base drops the ball, losing the out, error for the baseman, assist for the pitcher.

2. Pitcher fumbles, throws to get a force out, the ball then being thrown on to first base, seconds late of a completed double play. No error.

3. Pitcher (whether he fumbles or not) tries for what would be a force out, except that he pulls baseman off bag, the latter throwing the ball to first for putout. Error for the pitcher. (If, however, there would have been no chance for the force, with no misplay by the pitcher, there is no error.) If the first baseman drops the ball, losing the out, error for the first baseman, assist for the thrower.

4. Pitcher (whether he fumbles or not) throws for what would be a force out, but the baseman juggles the ball, losing the putout, but throws the ball to first and gets putout there. Error for the baseman who juggles the ball (or fails to touch bag). Assist for baseman, too, and for the pitcher. If the first baseman juggles the ball, losing possible second putout, error for the first baseman and assists for the throwers.

Dropping a well-thrown ball when a mere holding of it would mean an out is an error because it is a clear case of prolonging the life of the base runner.

Error to player who had last chance. Always charge an error to the last player who had the chance to make the out.

Examples: Third baseman pulls the first baseman off the bag with a wide throw. The first baseman tags the runner and has him out, but drops the ball. Error for the first baseman, an assist for the third baseman.

First baseman fumbles a ground ball, recovers in time to make a good toss to the pitcher who is covering first base. The pitcher drops the ball, losing the out. Error for the pitcher only; assist for the first baseman.

Passed ball instead of error. A passed ball, but not an error, shall be charged to the catcher if he drops or misses a third strike, thereby allowing the batter to reach first base. Credit the pitcher with a strike out.

Failing to touch base. An error shall be charged to the first baseman (or pitcher or second baseman when either is covering first base) if, on receiving a throw in ample time to retire the batter, he does not touch first base as required by rule. The same rule shall be followed with respect to any fielder covering any base on a force play.

Guide to confusing infield plays. (To show the relationship between errors, earned runs, and runs batted in, it is to be considered that in each of these plays, there are runners on first and third, two men out, and perfect play has preceded in this inning.) In each of these plays there is an opportunity for a putout, yet none is made.

Error

(Unearned run; no run batted in. Note that it could be a run batted in if there were less than two out and there was no chance to get the runner at home.)

a. Ground ball sticks in the glove of a fielder in judgment of scorer; also, fielder, for some reason, holds the ball instead of throwing it.

b. Fielder throws to a base where no runner is going or no play is taking place; this is considered as if the ball were thrown wild to right base.

c. Baseman fails to try to catch an accurate throw, provided there was reason for it. Thrower's error if there was no reason for it.

d. Baseman has throw in ample time for force play but does not touch the base.

No Error

(Earned run, run batted in)

a. Fielder fields ground ball cleanly, falls down. Score a hit.

b. Fielder fields ground ball cleanly, throws to base other than first, and runner there is safe without an error being made. Score fielder's choice if batter could have been retired; score hit if batter could not have been retired or a runner forced.

c. Fielder fields ground ball cleanly, fakes throw or looks at base in anticipation of throwing, but sees that he has no play there. He turns to throw to another base and sees that he has lost the play there which he had in the first place. Score fielder's choice or hit, as in (b); if on a bunt, it can be a sacrifice, as well as a fielder's choice.

d. Failure to try to tag runner on a non-force play, when baseman has ample time to do so. Score fielder's choice or hit, as in (b).

e. Two defensive men go after a ground ball. One gets it and has time to throw a runner out, but in the confusion a base where there was a play is left open. Score hit.

Throw hitting base runner. The thrower is charged with an error whenever his throw hits the base runner, if an accurate throw would have retired the runner, *or* if the base runner advances an extra base as the result of being hit by the throw.

Error for extra base. Runners on first and second bases; batter hits to the shortstop who fields ball cleanly and throws perfectly to second base, but the runner from first beats the throw, filling the bases. Second baseman loses his temper over the umpire's decision and hurls the ball to the ground angrily. As the ball rolls off, the runner on third dashes for the plate to score. Error for the second baseman.

Throwing to coach. Coach at third base causes the pitcher to fall for the old "sucker" trick or gag of shouting "throw that ball here and let me see it." Coach then jumps out of the way when the ball is thrown, runners advancing as a result. Error for the pitcher.

Catcher hits batter. Catcher, attempting to pick a runner off a base, hits the batter, or the bat, and ball rolls away, runners advancing. Error for catcher.

Losing control of ball. Many pitchers have the habit of tossing the ball in the air several feet between pitches. With runners on bases, one of these tosses hits the pitcher's body and rolls away, runners advancing. Error for pitcher.

For other information on errors, see *Scoring of Base Hits.*

STOLEN BASES

10.08 A stolen base shall be credited to a runner whenever he advances one base unaided by a hit, a putout, an error, a force-out, a fielder's choice, a passed ball, a wild pitch or a balk, subject to the following:

(a) When a runner starts for the next base before the pitcher delivers the ball and the pitch results in what ordinarily is scored a wild pitch or passed ball, credit the runner with a stolen base and do not charge the misplay. EXCEPTION: If, as a result of the misplay, the stealing runner advances an extra base, or another runner also advances, score the wild pitch or passed ball as well as the stolen base.

(b) When a runner is attempting to steal, and the catcher, after receiving the pitch, makes a wild throw trying to prevent the stolen base, credit a stolen base. Do not charge an error unless the wild throw permits the stealing runner to advance one or more extra bases, or permits another runner to advance, in which case credit the stolen base and charge one error to the catcher.

(c) When a runner, attempting to steal, evades being put out in a run-down play and advances to the next base without the aid of an error, credit the runner with a stolen base. If another runner also advances on the play, credit both runners with stolen bases. If a runner advances while another runner, attempting to steal, evades being put out in a run-down play and returns safely, without the aid of an error, to the base he originally occupied, credit a stolen base to the runner who advances.

(d) When a double or triple steal is attempted and one runner is thrown out before reaching and holding the base he is attempting to steal, no other runner shall be credited with a stolen base.

(e) When a runner is tagged out after oversliding a base, while attempting either to return to that base or to advance to the next base, he shall not be credited with a stolen base.

(f) When in the scorer's judgment a runner attempting to steal is safe because of a muffed throw, do not credit a stolen base. Credit an assist to the fielder who made the throw; charge an error to the fielder who muffed the throw, and charge the runner with "caught stealing."

(g) No stolen base shall be scored when a runner advances solely because of the defensive team's indifference to his advance. Score as a fielder's choice.

scoring stolen bases

Double steal play. Runners on first and third. Runner on first runs to second, apparently beating the catcher's throw, but the second baseman takes the throw and quickly throws home without making any effort to tag the runner at second. Runner, trying to score from third base, is out at the plate. Is it a stolen base for the runner who beat the throw to second? No. It is a double steal play, and if one runner is thrown out, other runners cannot be credited with a stolen base.

Stolen base on catcher's overthrow. The rule on the *Double-Steal Play* applies in case one runner would have been out but for an obvious muff, but credit stolen base to a runner trying to steal when the catcher overthrows base, even if the catcher had a cinch play at the base. Catcher is exempt from an error on a wild throw in trying to prevent a stolen base, unless additional base is gained (Official Rules, under *Errors*).

Muff erases stolen base. In the event of an obvious muff of a ball thrown by the catcher, when, in the judgment of the scorer, the base runner would have been out if the ball had been held, the infielder making the muff shall be charged with an error and the base runner shall not be credited with a stolen base.

Indifference erases stolen base. No stolen base shall be credited whose advancing results from the opposing team's indifference thereto.

Faking is not indifference.

Example: Runners on first and third bases. Runner on first breaks for second, the catcher fakes a throw to second but holds the ball, or quickly makes a throw to third or to the pitcher. Runner going to second arrives safely. Stolen base? Yes. The fake throw or quick throw back is construed as an effort to stop the runners (and to prevent the runner from third base scoring) rather than indifference thereto.

Earning stolen base with big lead. The runner gets such a big lead off base on the pitcher's wind-up that no effort is made to throw him out stealing. This is a stolen base. There was no use to make a throw, where there was no possible play. This cannot be construed as indifference.

Stolen base on run-down play. Runner on first base takes his lead, and when the pitcher throws to first, the runner starts for second and is caught in a run-down between the bases. Finally, by beating the last throw, and with no error being made, the runner slides into second base safely. This is a stolen base.

Delayed double steal. On delayed double steal attempt, the catcher throws to the third baseman, who throws to the second baseman, who throws back to the catcher, retiring no one. This is a double steal regardless of any delay involved by getting either runner or both in a run-down play (that is *chase, hot-box, pickle,* etc.), provided runners beat the throws to reach bases safely and no error occurs.

WILD PITCHES—PASSED BALLS

10.15 (a) A wild pitch shall be charged when a legally delivered ball is so high, or so wide, or so low that the catcher does not stop and control the ball by ordinary effort, thereby permitting a runner or runners to advance.

> (1) A wild pitch shall be charged when a legally delivered ball touches the ground before reaching home plate and is not handled by the catcher, permitting a runner or runners to advance.

> (b) A catcher shall be charged with a passed ball when he fails to hold or to control a legally pitched ball which should have been held or controlled with ordinary effort, thereby permitting a runner or runners to advance.

A wild pitch, not an error, shall be charged against the pitcher if the batter reaches first base on such a pitched ball being delivered wildly to the plate.

Any pitched ball that strikes the ground before reaching home plate and passes the catcher, allowing runners to advance, shall be scored as a wild pitch.

Reaching first on wild pitch. Two strikes on the batter. Next pitch is a low curve at which the batter swings and misses for the third strike. Ball breaks into the dirt; the catcher is unable to hold it and the batter reaches first base. In such a case, of course, the play is scored as a wild pitch for the pitcher, rather than an error. Credit the pitcher with a strike out.

BASES ON BALLS

10.16 A base on balls shall be scored whenever a batter is awarded first base because of four balls having been pitched outside the strike zone, but when the fourth such ball touches the batter it shall be scored as a "hit batter." (See 10.18 (h) for procedure when more than one pitcher is involved in giving a base on balls.)

> (1) If a batter awarded a base on balls is called out for refusing to advance to first base, do not credit the base on balls. Charge a time at bat.

STRIKEOUTS

10.17 (a) A strikeout shall be scored whenever

> (1) A batter is put out by a third strike caught by the catcher;
>
> (2) A batter is put out by a third strike not caught when there is a runner on first before two are out;
>
> (3) A batter becomes a runner because a third strike is not caught;
>
> (4) A batter bunts foul on third strike. EXCEPTION: If such bunt on third strike results in a foul fly caught by any fielder, do not score a strikeout. Credit the fielder who catches such foul fly with a put-out.

(b) When the batter leaves the game with two strikes against him, and the substitute batter completes a strikeout, charge the strikeout and the time at bat to the first batter. If the substitute batter completes the turn at bat in any other manner, score the action as having been that of the substitute batter.

Strike out on foul third strike bunt. The pitcher should receive credit for a strike out if the batter is called out for bunting foul the third strike. The catcher is credited with a putout.

Strike out on error by catcher or pitcher. The pitcher shall receive credit for a strike out even though the batter swings at a wild pitch and reaches first base or swings at the third strike which is muffed by the catcher.

EARNED RUNS

10.18 An earned run is a run for which the pitcher is held accountable.

(a) An earned run shall be charged every time a runner reaches home base by the aid of safe hits, sacrifice bunts, a sacrifice fly, stolen bases, put-outs, fielder's choices, bases on balls, hit batters, balks or wild pitches (including a wild pitch on third strike which permits a batter to reach first base) before fielding chances have been offered to put out the offensive team. For the purpose of this rule, a defensive interference penalty shall be construed as a fielding chance.

(1) A wild pitch is solely the pitcher's fault, and contributes to an earned run just as a base on balls or a balk.

(b) No run shall be earned when scored by a runner who reaches first base (1) on a hit or otherwise after his time at bat is prolonged by a muffed foul fly; (2) because of interference or obstruction, or (3) because of any fielding error.

(c) No run shall be earned when scored by a runner whose life is prolonged by an error, if such runner would have been put out by errorless play.

(d) No run shall be earned when the runner's advance is aided by an error, a passed ball, or defensive interference or obstruction, if the scorer judges that the run would not have scored without the aid of such misplay.

(e) An error by a pitcher is treated exactly the same as an error by any other fielder in computing earned runs.

(f) Whenever a fielding error occurs, the pitcher shall be given the benefit of the doubt in determining to which bases any runners would have advanced had the fielding of the defensive team been errorless.

(g) When pitchers are changed during an inning, the relief pitcher shall not be charged with any run (earned or unearned) scored by a runner who was on base at the time he entered the game, nor for runs scored by any runner who reaches base on a fielder's choice which puts out a runner left on base by the preceding pitcher.

> NOTE: It is the intent of this rule to charge each pitcher with the number of runners he put on base, rather than with the individual runners. When a pitcher puts runners on base, and is relieved, he shall be charged with all runs subsequently scored up to and including the number of runners he left on base when he left the game, unless such runners are put out without action by the batter, i.e., caught stealing, picked off base, or called out for interference when a batter-runner does not reach first base on the play.

scoring earned runs

Definition of "fielding chances." Fielding chances to retire the side are three occasions on which an out is made, or would have been made with perfect support. However, when an error is made on a so-called double play ball, this can be considered only one fielding chance, not two, for an out.

Dropping foul fly. Batter's foul is dropped for an error. He walks and scores a run. That is an unearned run, just as if he had hit a grounder to first for an apparently easy out, and the first baseman had fumbled the ball.

One of the most useful ways to remember that a foul fly that is dropped is an error, regardless of what the batter does later, is to keep a picture of this play in mind. Runner on third, two out, batter hits a foul fly which a defensive player drops for an error. A chance has been offered to retire the side and no earned runs can be scored after that play. On the next pitched ball, the runner steals home. It is an unearned run, because if the foul fly had been caught, the runner would not have had an opportunity to make his steal of home base.

Direct error kills earned run. A run which scores directly on an error is always an unearned run, regardless of what happens later, provided there had been an opportunity to retire the runner with perfect play.

Example: Throw is made to pick a runner off base, or to catch a runner sliding in attempting to stretch a bit. On an error, the throw gets away, runner scoring. Run is unearned, but that is only a part of scoring the play. These points, too, must be considered.

a. If an errorless play would not have retired the runner, but would merely have held him at that base, the play is not to be construed as an opportunity to retire the runner.

b. If, however, errorless play would have retired the runner, this is an opportunity to retire the runner, and a run scored by such a runner cannot, under any circumstances, be earned.

Example: Brown, the first batter in an inning, leads off with a three base hit. The ball is thrown wildly to third with no chance to retire Brown there, but Brown scores on the bad throw. The next batter hits a home run. Under such conditions, Brown's run, as well as that of the batter who hit the homer, is not unearned. There was no chance to retire Brown at third base even had the throw been perfect. Brown would have been held at third and would have scored an earned run on the next batter's homer. In this case, there had been no chance to retire Brown even with perfect play. Therefore, Brown's run is earned.

Decisions must await events. In case of runs actually scoring on errors, base the earned run designation on what actually did happen. When

official rules of scoring   **221**

other advances occur on an error, and a run does not score, the scorer must wait to see what happens before calling a run earned or unearned.

Example: Pitcher attempts to pick a runner off first base, and the runner goes to second base on pitcher's wild throw. Runner would not have been out had not the error occurred. Batter at bat hits a three base hit, scoring the runner who had gone to second base. That run is earned, provided, of course, an opportunity for retiring the side had not been presented before the play. This type of play often requires the scorer to judge whether a runner scoring from third base on a single could have scored from second base on the same hit ball. If such considerations appear artificial, the scorer should remember that the purpose is to charge a pitcher with a run on an error that merely advances a runner a base (unless it is to home) and at the same time be fair with the pitcher.

Give pitcher benefit of doubt. The pitcher shall be given the benefit of doubt whenever fielding errors are made and in determining the base to which a runner should have held with perfect support on the part of fielders. A fielding error made by the pitcher shall be considered the same as any other fielding error. No run can be earned that scores as a result of batter having reached first base on catcher's interference, a fielding error, or a passed ball; nor can any run be earned after the fielding side has failed to accept chances offered to retire the side.

Catcher's interference with batter. The catcher's interference with the batter is neither a time at bat nor an error for the catcher. Simply carry two asterisks (*) and an extra line in the box score, thus:
* Smith, lf ....
* Awarded first base on catcher's interference.

Definition of "perfect support." Perfect support means play unmarred by:
1. Passed ball
2. Catcher's interference with batter
3. Error
4. Non-error misplay resulting in a run, which occurs when a defensive player misses a clear play at the plate (or runner would have been held at third but for misplay), but exempts himself from an error by recovering to get the batter at first base or to retire a runner by a force out.

Note: There is something to be said in favor of scoring such a play as an error, but it is not the custom to do this.

Note the direct parallel between earned runs and runs batted in on this type of misplay. Note also that all plays other than those listed in 1, 2, 3, and 4 are perfect support, including poor judgment by the defensive player. (It may be good defensive judgment as this example shows: Defensive team five runs ahead; runners on first and second base; batter singles to the outfield; outfielder fields the ball cleanly, throws to second base, and run scores. This is scored as an earned run and run batted in. The outfielder used good judgment in his attempt to keep another runner from reaching second base, which would probably have happened if he had thrown the ball to the plate.)

Relation of runs to misplay when recovery excuses error. It will readily be seen that on some plays the scorer's guiding principle is that the purpose of the offense is to score runs, and that of the defense, to prevent runs being made. This has been shown in the instructions on *Scoring Sacrifices*. This principle is illustrated also in scoring special plays on ordinary batted balls and on third strike battery errors.

1. *Misplay, then defense player recovers to retire the batter at first base or a runner on a force out.*

Examples: a. Third baseman fumbles a ground ball with an obvious play at plate, but recovers the ball and retires the batter at first base for the first or second out. No error; no run batted in; not an earned run. If the batter beats the throw to first base, the scoring is the same except that an error is charged against the third baseman for failure to retire the runner at the plate.

b. Third baseman or outfielder muffs a fly ball with runner on third base. Runner holds third until the muff is made because he has no chance to score on the fly ball. Then, as the third baseman or outfielder recovers and throws out batter at first or forces a runner at another base, runner on third scores. Scoring is exactly the same as in (a), charging of the error being dependent on whether the batter beats the throw to first base. Note, however, that if this is a line drive instead of a pop-up, the drive may be too hot to handle and be a hit, earned run, run batted in, and no error.

2. *Misplay, the defensive player recovers to retire a runner other than the batter at first or other than runner on force out.*

a. Batter gets a fielder's choice.

b. If the defensive team ends up on the play in a more advantageous position than before the play started, do not score an error; if run results directly from the misplay, charge an error; here, the scorer falls back on the rule: "The pitcher shall be given the benefit of the doubt whenever fielding errors are made, and so forth."

Examples: a. Runners on second and third bases; one out; batter hits to short either a ground ball on which the fielder has a play at the plate or a fly ball on which the runner on third would attempt to score. Shortstop fumbles the ball, picks it up and tags the runner coming across from second, the runner who was on third scoring. Scoring is as for two different plays; error for the run scoring, then a putout. (If the runner held third or if it was a ground ball on which the shortstop had no play at the plate, there is no error.)

b. Runners on second and third bases; two out; batter hits an easy pop-up to shortstop or a ground ball on which the fielder has a play at first base. Shortstop fumbles the ball, tags the runner coming from second. If the tag is made before the runner from third crosses the plate, score no error; if the tag is made after the run crosses the plate, it is an error. (The umpire, of course, rules whether the run scores.)

Note that the following play is not governed by the two guides cited above: Runner on first base; second baseman fumbles a ground ball, losing a play at first base on the batter. However, the second baseman recovers the ball, throws to the shortstop, who tags the runner as the latter carelessly overruns that base. This must be scored as two plays; error for the runner reaching second (and batter reaching first), then an assist and a putout.

3. *Battery misplay on strike out.* This must be considered separately from misplays on batted balls. The play comes up with runners at any or all bases trying to advance on the third strike that gets by the catcher.

Example: Runner on second base; two strikes on the batter; one out. The pitcher throws wild or the catcher fails to stop pitcher's good pitch on the third strike.

a. Catcher throws out the batter at first base; runner on second going to third; no error, but a wild pitch or passed ball, depending on which battery man was at fault. However, if the runner who was on second started to steal with the pitch, the play is a stolen base and should not be scored as a wild pitch or passed ball.

b. Catcher recovers and holds the ball to prevent a runner on second from going to third. This is a wild pitch or passed ball for either the pitcher or the catcher, depending on which player was at fault, because the batter reaches first.

c. Catcher recovers and throws to third base, retiring the runner going to that base, batter reaching first. No error; no battery error charged. It is a fielder's choice.

d. Runner on first; one out; ball gets by the catcher on the third strike. The catcher throws to first; the runner who was on first base going to second. Score wild pitch or passed ball and credit putout to the catcher, not to the first baseman. *"A batter is out when—a third strike is not caught by the catcher; provided there is a runner on first base and not more than one is out."*

e. Runners on second and third bases; the ball gets away from the catcher. Runner on third scores; runner on second is thrown out at third base, the batter reaches first. By the principle cited above, a misplay must be charged for the run scoring. It is a wild pitch or passed ball, rather than an error.

WINNING AND LOSING PITCHER

10.19 (a) Credit the starting pitcher with a game won only if he has pitched at least five complete innings and his team not only is in the lead when he is replaced but remains in the lead the remainder of the game.

(b) The "must pitch five complete innings" rule in respect to the starting pitcher shall be in effect for all games of six or more innings. In a five-inning game, credit the starting pitcher with a game won only if he has pitched at least four complete innings and his team not only is in the lead when he is replaced but remains in the lead the remainder of the game.

(c) When the starting pitcher cannot be credited with the victory because of the provisions of 10.19 (a) or (b) and more than one relief pitcher is used, the victory shall be awarded on the following basis:

(1) When, during the tenure of the starting pitcher, the winning team assumes the lead and maintains it to the finish of the game, credit the victory to the relief pitcher judged by the scorer to have been most effective;

(2) Whenever the score is tied the game becomes a new contest insofar as the winning and losing pitcher is concerned;

(3) Once the opposing team assumes the lead all pitchers who have pitched up to that point are excluded from being credited with the victory except that if the pitcher against whose pitching the opposing team gained the lead continues to pitch until his team regains the lead, which it holds to the finish of the game, that pitcher shall be the winning pitcher;

(4) Normally, the winning relief pitcher shall be the one who is the pitcher of record when his team assumes the lead and maintains it to the finish of the game.

EXCEPTION: Do not credit a victory to a relief pitcher who pitches briefly or ineffectively if a succeeding relief pitcher pitches effectively in helping to maintain his team in the lead. In such case, credit the succeeding relief pitcher with the victory.

(d) When a pitcher is removed for a substitute batter or substitute runner, all runs scored by his team during the inning in which he is removed shall be credited to his benefit in determining the pitcher of record when his team assumes the lead.

(e) Regardless of how many innings the first pitcher has pitched, he shall be charged with the loss of the game if he is replaced when his team is behind in the score, or falls behind because of runs charged to him after he is replaced, and his team thereafter fails either to tie the score or gain the lead.

(f) No pitcher shall be credited with pitching a shutout unless he pitches the complete game, or unless he enters the game with none out before the opposing team has scored in the first inning, puts out the side without a run scoring and pitches all the rest of the game. When two or more pitchers combine to pitch a shutout a notation to that effect should be included in the league's official pitching records.

(g) In some non-championship games (such as the Major League All-Star Game) it is provided in advance that each pitcher shall work a stated number of innings, usually two or three. In such games, it is customary to credit the victory to the pitcher of record, whether starter or reliever, when the winning team takes a lead which it maintains to the end of the game, unless such pitcher is knocked out after the winning team has a commanding lead, and the scorer believes a subsequent pitcher is entitled to credit for the victory.

Determining winning and losing pitcher. It is not possible to make a hard-and-fast rule for determining which pitcher should be credited with a victory or charged with a defeat when two or more pitchers are employed in a game. However, the following rules are guides to help in arriving at a decision:

1. When one pitcher is relieved by another with runners on bases, charge all such runners, if they score, to the first pitcher (and be sure to see that the runs are properly charged in making out any Official Blank). Here is one exception to this rule:

Pitcher B relieves pitcher A, who has left a runner on first base. On the next play, runner on first is forced at second. That leaves pitcher B's batter on first, and if the batter scores, he should be charged against A since he was on base only because of the fact that pitcher A did leave a runner on. But, if, in the opinion of the scorer, that batter could not have been retired at first base with a perfect play, then charge the batter to pitcher B if he scores. In other words, in such rare cases, pitcher B is in reality helped by the fact that there was a runner on first when he went into the game. Such help enabled him to retire a runner by force at second, when a play at first would have been impossible with no one on base. The first batter to face pitcher B is on base by the virtue of his own accomplishment in hitting the ball on which he could not have been retired at first base. In reality, the first batter to face B earned his way to first base off pitcher B, and should be charged to him.

2. The relieving pitcher coming into the game possibly *cold,* not fully *warmed up,* and in the midst of a batting rally, should not be charged with the first batter reaching first base, if such batter had an advantage because of the poor pitching of the preceding pitcher.

With the count two or three balls and one of no strikes, or three balls and two strikes, charge preceding pitcher if the batter reaches first base, but credit relieving pitcher if batter is retired.

With the count one or two balls and two strikes, charge the relieving pitcher if the batter reaches first base and credit him if the batter is retired.

3. Where the relieving pitcher goes into the game with the score tied or with even innings, he must win or lose the game regardless of the number of innings or how effectively the first pitcher may have pitched.

If the pitcher is relieved with the score in his favor and later the score is tied up off the relieving pitcher, then the latter wins or loses. A tie game at any stage (with no runners on base) must be considered to all intents and purposes as the start of a new game for the relieving pitcher.

4. When the first pitcher is retired after pitching, say, seven innings, he is entitled to the benefit of all runs scored by his side in an equal number of innings. For instance, Brown, of the home team, has pitched even innings with the score 2 to 0 against him. He is taken out of the game when his turn to bat comes around in the seventh inning, and before the close of that inning, his team scored two runs. Brown retires with the score a tie and the next pitcher is responsible for the outcome.

5. Do not always give the first pitcher credit for a game won, even if the score is in his favor, unless he has pitched at least five innings.

Of course, the scorer must use his own good judgment in interpreting this rule when a game is terminated in less than the regulation number of innings for any reason whatsoever. Also, in case the starting pitcher leaves the game before five innings and his team is ahead and remains ahead to win, if the relief pitcher, too, retires before the game is completed, the scorer should credit victory (as between first and second pitchers) to the one who did the best work.

6. Regardless of how many innings the first pitcher may have pitched, he is charged with the loss of the game if he is retired with the score against him, and his team is unable thereafter to either tie or overcome that lead.

7. If the pitcher retired from the game at the end of eight innings with the score against him, but his team comes first to bat in the ninth and scores enough runs to win, give the win to the retiring pitcher and not to the one who pitched out the last half of the ninth inning. Where such a condition arises prior to the final innings, award the game to the pitcher who did the best work. If in doubt about this, give it to the man who pitched the most innings.

It is very important that the scorer get the distinction between Sections 4 and 7. Section 4 concerns the case where the retiring pitcher finishes the first half of an inning, it being provided that runs made by his team in the last half of the inning are marked up to his benefit. Section 7 concerns cases where the retiring pitcher finishes the last half of an inning, and provides that runs made in the first half of the next inning (if that inning be the last) also be marked up to his benefit. So far, the rule follows the general won-and-lost custom of the relief pitcher being given the benefit of no runs by his team until he enters the game. But when one runs into the exception of Section 7, where the runs in the last half of an inning (previous to the last) bring victory, award the victory to the pitcher who did the best work. If in doubt, award victory to the pitcher who pitched the most innings.

Note that in both of these cases, the retiring pitcher was not knocked out, but finished by retiring the side. Recognized authorities agree that when a pitcher is taken out of the game, with one or two men out, he loses all right to the benefit of run subsequently scored by his team.

8. It is important to give the number of runners on bases and the number of outs when one pitcher is relieved by another.

9. In giving a pitcher credit for the number of innings pitched, divide each inning into three parts; thus, if a pitcher is taken out of a game in the sixth inning after one is out, give him credit for 5 1/3 innings. If he is retired before an out is made, add a plus mark to the number of complete innings that he pitched, thus 5+.

No attempt has been made in the foregoing to cover all of the many situations that present themselves to the scorer in games where pitchers changed. In isolated cases, the application of these rules may work a hardship on one pitcher or the other; but on the season's play, applications of the rules usually even up and balance.

FIVE
practical problems

the captain

The captain is elected by his teammates or appointed by his coach or manager. He is a player of ability who knows the rules. He is a leader among his teammates both on and off the playing field—a man of high character with even temperament, courage, and clarity of mind. He is always eager to win, but he is never downcast in defeat. His sportsmanship is an inspiration to his teammates.

The really great captain plays clean baseball and never finds fault with any umpire's decision. The captain has no right to question the judgment of the umpire, and under no conditions whatsoever may he or any other member of the squad ridicule the opinion of an official. When a question arises over the interpretation of the rules, the captain is the only player permitted to address the umpire.

The captain or the coach gives the batting order of his team to the umpire, and informs the umpire of any substitution or change made as the game progresses.

The captain and/or the coach of the home team and the captain and/or coach of the visiting team meet with the umpire at the home plate for discussion of the ground rules just before the game starts. The home captain is required to make special ground rules to cover balls batted or thrown into the crowd, and such rules must be acceptable to the visiting captain and coach. If an agreement cannot be reached, the umpire makes the ground rules.

organization and management

Ground rules are the cause of much dispute among amateur players. They are especially important if the game is played on other than an enclosed playing field. It is advisable to fix the number of bases which a runner can take in case of an overthrow to first base or to third base.

Ground rules should state clearly that the award of bases shall be governed by the position of the runner or runners at the time the throw is made. It is best for the captains to agree that an overthrow is to be followed by a certain number of bases (either one or two) beyond the base which the runner held or had just left when the overthrow was made. For example, if a runner is on first base when a wild throw is made into the crowd either to first or to third base, he is given the agreed number of bases, without regard to any effort he may have made to reach second base before the ball was pitched.

If the batter hits safely to the outfield with a runner on first base, for example, and the ball is thrown wild by the outfielder, the runner is given the number of bases agreed on by the captains. If the runner is on or beyond second base when the throw was made, second base is considered the base from which the play originated. If he has not reached second before the throw, first base is considered the originating base.

When a wild pitch occurs, the base which the runner was entitled to occupy at the time the pitch was made is considered the base from which the play originated.

Not only must each captain have a thorough understanding of the ground rules, but he must also explain them to each of his fellow players, thereby avoiding unnecessary controversy and wrangling.

the student manager

Popular election. The election of a student manager by the student body is unsatisfactory because student politics often bring to that office an unqualified, incompetent man wholly on account of his popularity.

The selective merit system. The student manager should be selected by the athletic director on the recommendation of the coach, the captain, and the active student manager. At the beginning of the training period, members of the student body who for some reason are unable to compete for positions on the ball team go into active open competition for the senior managership of baseball. In some colleges and universities, each fraternity delegates a non-letter man to enter the competition. The work done by each of these men is recorded. Efficiency, promptness, character, and personality are noted, so that at the end of the playing season a complete record of each man's ability as a prospective manager is available for discussion.

Some colleges and universities allow freshmen to compete for managerial positions, while in others only second year men may compete. By elimination on a basis of merit, one of the group is selected for the senior manager. The merit system has been found satisfactory by every coach who has used it.

Duties of the student manager. The duties of the manager are many and varied. He, together with his assistants, is the coach's right-hand man, and he tries to anticipate the wishes and needs of the coach and players with regard to equipment. Every article necessary to the sport must be on the field. Here are a number of duties which the coach usually assigns to the student manager:

1. Listing all equipment needed for practice and for games and seeing that it is on the field at the proper time.

2. Keeping the equipment clean; seeing that the gloves, mitts, and shoes are oiled.

3. Courteously attending to the needs of the visiting team. This is one duty in which many athletic associations fail. The feeling among the student body and many athletic competitors is, "The game starts at 3:00 P.M. As long as the visitors are there, ready to start the game on time, why worry about them?"

The attitude toward visitors at our larger universities is a good example of proper attention to competitors. It shows the real competitive spirit which should be the foundation of every college, preparatory school, and high school in our country. "You are strangers within our gates, our guests, and we are here to look after your needs." Any coach whose team competes against these universities will find two or three undergraduate managerial competitors at his service whenever he rises from his chair.

4. Making an inventory of all equipment at the end of the season, cleaning every article, and packing wool and cotton goods in moth balls.

5. Keeping a receipt book, never spending any money without obtaining the signature of the person paid.

6. Reporting each trip and attaching thereto the receipts for money spent.

7. Equalizing the work of the competitors in line to succeed the senior manager. Do not allow too many duties to be placed on any one individual. Keep a record of the work of each, and at the close of the season make proper recommendations for the future manager to your superiors. Also make suggestions for any improvements which might be made in the conduct of the sport.

the management of team travel

Many a coach will agree that to look after the details of transportation and hotel accommodations for a baseball squad is much like the service given to a wife by her husband. Each item for a trip, tickets for the party, and hotel lodgings must be worked out in advance. The schedule, with every minute detail, is submitted to each member of the team. A complete itinerary for a long trip is made up, and each player is given a copy. On a short trip a few hours away from school, it is enough to talk to the squad as a body a day or so before the scheduled contest, giving them full particulars about the trip.

All meals en route or at a hotel should be ordered beforehand. The desired menu should be submitted, accompanied by such information as the time of the meal, the number of men in the party, and the quality and sizes of portions desired.

The manager or coach pays the bills for the party and takes receipts for all the cash spent. Money for expenses should never be given to the players individually, because some athletes are tempted to spend all or part of the money foolishly and are apt to eat food that is not good for them. Also, it would be inconvenient to require separate receipts from every player: managers could not account in a businesslike way for the money expended.

It is desirable that the members of the student athletic squad miss as few classes as possible. They should be kept in familiar surroundings, because a change often may affect their performance. They rest better in their own homes and are accustomed to the food and water. Coaches avoid strange food and water as much as possible.

Most men in athletic authority insist that all short trips (of less than four or five hours) be made by bus. Often some loyal citizen will donate an automobile for the trip in order to reduce expenses. This donation sometimes must be accepted, but it is better to have the squad go as a group by bus. Such close, jovial associations increase team spirit. The coach should always go in the bus with his team. The older mind will oftentimes avoid various mishaps.

All members of the squad should stay together at the hotel and in the dressing rooms before the contest. If advantage is taken of donated automobiles in order to reduce the expense account, the players, although apart on the journey, should be together within a short time after reaching the city where the game is to be played. Many an athlete has unwittingly tired himself by unnecessarily walking around the streets of a city or on the campus of a college or school. This one thing, unconscious exercise, has caused coaches to increase the cost of team transportation, declining offers of motor cars by loyal followers. Keeping the squad together on the trip also gives coaches an opportunity to advise the players properly on arriving at their destination.

Athletes become very tired sitting around in strange surroundings. Long waits are tiresome, but an entire squad should be able to find many things to do to help pass away the time. If it is at all possible, the team should leave its school the day of the game and arrive at the place for the contest with plenty of time to dress and go onto the field for practice.

equipment

Purchase. The coach, or whoever is in charge of purchasing equipment, should make a study of prices and be able to recognize values, always with one consideration in mind: the economical use of funds. Equipment in hand should be checked to avoid overpurchase, and the equipment purchased must be suitable for the service for which it is intended.

Price, quality, and service are three important considerations in buying. Good equipment lasts longer, looks better, and, in fact, is better than cheap equipment. Buyers with experience insist upon quality and know what to pay for it. Unless the coach is a good judge of woolens, textiles, and leather goods, he should buy guaranteed materials from a reputable concern. It is not practical to allow players to pick their own equipment, because they are rarely good judges of materials. It is advisable, however, for each player to select his style of bat, and the weight should be to his own liking. The coach can recommend a light or heavy bat for a player, but he should not make a choice as to shape or style.

Early buying offers an advantage in that it gives the purchaser a chance to select his equipment and gives the firm from which the purchase is made ample time to deliver the goods.

Care of equipment. A good stockroom in which every sport may keep its equipment is a great asset to any athletic association. The room should have sufficient space for all uniforms and leather goods. It should be neatly shelved in such a way that all articles are easy to find. Above all, the room must be well ventilated, neither overheated nor damp. Overheat destroys the life of leather and dampness causes mold to collect and injure all other materials.

1. *Leather Goods.* Shoes can be kept soft and pliable with a waterproof oil. A good plan is to keep a pan of oil with several brushes in the locker room, so that the players can oil their shoes before going on the playing field each day. After a game on a rainy day, each player should see that his shoes are properly cleaned and oiled before placing them in his locker.

When the season is over, a good scheme is to have the shoes well oiled and to place the name of the wearer on a small tag attached to the shoes, if they are worth keeping, until the ball season opens again.

Each player should take care of his own glove or mitt. A can of saddle soap or petroleum jelly should be handy in the locker room so that the player can take a little and rub it on his glove on entering from the playing field. This will keep the leather soft and pliable.

2. *Woolens and Textile Goods.* Woolen and textile goods are cleaned periodically, because soiled garments worn next to the body can cause dangerous infections. Uniforms do not need cleaning as often as stockings

and underclothes, which must always be clean. In many small schools the players take their clothes home to be washed. No matter how it is done, *cleanliness is imperative.*

A few stitches taken with a needle and thread at the proper time may save many dollars worth of equipment. At the end of the playing season each uniform should be repaired, thoroughly cleaned, properly marked, and packed away in moth balls until the next season.

arrangement of the schedule

Two important things to be considered when the schedule of games is made are the money which can be spent for games and the scholastic ability of the players.

If there is little money in the treasury and there are few legitimate sources of revenue, ball games away from home should be curtailed. Sometimes, however, it is cheaper to play games away from home than at home, for the receipts at the gate on the home field are often insufficient to pay the umpires, buy baseballs, or furnish traveling expenses to the visiting team. The amount of available cash for equipment and other expenses must be carefully considered before a tentative schedule is made.

If the scholastic standing of the players is high, more games can be played than should possibly be considered if the classroom work is below the standards set by the school. Schedule makers should never jeopardize the scholarship of the players by arranging too many games. Amateur baseball should be a stimulus and an aid to education rather than merely a matter of playing the game itself.

A ball team with a well-balanced scheduled is not handicapped in early spring with too hard games. The coach is responsible for the work of the team, and he should be consulted by the schedule makers in regard to the games which his team must play. If the team is made up of players with little experience, the easiest games should be the first on the schedule. Competition in real games gives the players experience, which is necessary if the team is to have much success. The coach will have a better opportunity to develop his squad and team play if there is a big margin of victories early in the season. Early victories give inexperienced players confidence and team morale.

If the coach does not make the schedule himself, he advises the schedule makers as to the exact schedule he desires, but he cannot always expect to have his desires fulfilled. He must, of course, try to put through the schedule submitted, but there must be some give and take with the schedule makers of other schools. Certain dates may be refused by another school and other dates submitted. After all, arguments for each contest should be made so that the games will be as fair for one team as for the other. Certain dates are more satisfactory to one school than to another on account of local situations and conditions, and the schedule should be made accordingly. The fact must not be overlooked that the teams having natural rivalry should play near the close of the season, preferably at the very end. The schedule does not always give a team its best opportunity to win its championship games, but in the long run the average will be about even.

Two games a week, after a period of proper training, makes a satisfactory schedule for most schools. This makes about sixteen games in all. Rain may cause a few to be postponed. College teams should schedule more than that number because a smaller number of games does not provide enough competition for the full development of the game. College players are more mature than the preparatory school players and have reached the age when the finer strategic points of the game can be more clearly taught and emphasized. Even with a larger number of games, the schedule makers should distribute them throughout the playing season, unless the personnel of the pitching staff warrants closer dates. Games can very well be played on Friday and Saturday, but a Saturday game with a mid-week game will prove to be a much better distribution.

The week before the games against the rival school should have a series of contests that will not in any way leave the players handicapped by fatigue or mental distress. Easy games and a little rest before such important games will prove to be very beneficial to any squad of players.

The coach should be the only adviser to all members of his baseball squad when they are on the offensive. No offensive play should be made unless the coach has given orders for it. One of the reasons for this requirement is that a young lad without years of experience cannot carry in mind clearly the offensive strategy of baseball. A young player has enough to think about if he can play his part in the defensive game. He should not be burdened with responsibility for the offensive tactics. For example, a bunt or a hit-and-run situation should never be left to a lad's judgment. At times it is the duty of the coach also to tell his team just what to do on the defense, especially when there are tying or winning runners on the bases. He must never shirk his responsibility in such a case, and he should never "second guess" any of his players.

The first duty of a coach is to formulate his attack and defense. It is to be expected that young players in every ball game will make misplays and errors of judgment, and the coach must not then be tempted to make unjust criticism or sarcastic remarks. In fact, harsh criticism and sarcasm have no place in good coaching. Gentle words, though sometimes sternly spoken, do young players far more good than any verbal abuse. A player who knows that he has made a misplay or an error of judgment is sensitive enough about it. Each member of the squad has the game at heart and is doing his best. Knowing this, the coach should guard against cutting, stinging, and sarcastic remarks. It is the coach's and captain's job to keep his fellow players from displaying any rowdy tendencies. When the umpire says, "Play ball," he is in full charge of the game. From that moment

the coach 18

on, the coach should, with a clear mind and words of encouragement, urge his men on to win the game.

The good coach makes a close study of the personnel of his squad and gets to know each player's ability, his disposition, his likes and dislikes. In every way he tries to win each player's confidence. He is clean and above board in his dealings with every member of the team. His knowledge of each player's offensive strength is valuable, especially when a difficult offensive situation arises. There may be cause for the substitution of a player; if so, the coach must act according to the rules and must see that the opponents also follow the rule for substituting players. The wise coach makes all substitutions on his personal line up card or scorebook. It prevents batting out of order.

The coach makes sure that every member of his squad knows the rules governing the game. Every season he should review the rules carefully and demonstrate every essential point on the field. If the coach wants to make any play vivid to his players or any rule governing such a play clear to them, he must let them see the play actually executed and hear the proper interpretation of the rule covering it. It is to his advantage in working out plays with his team to arrange games between squads, thus providing his men with actual experience and opening many opportunities for the discussion of various points in the rules.

No favoritism or partiality can be shown in the selection of a squad. The substitute should be treated with as much consideration as any other member of the team, but ability and merit should win advancement, and the greatest care should be exercised in the selection of players for the different positions. Every coach should be fair, carefully weighing each man's ability before making his selection; but once the decision is made, there should be no retraction. No set rules can be given for the selection of a baseball squad, but any player who knows how to play the game and has some natural ability should be retained on the squad of any ball club.

The coach must have enough confidence in himself to inspire confidence in his players. Each player should be made to feel that the success of the team rests directly on him. We have found that a player does his best work when responsibility is placed upon him. Individual enthusiasm must be maintained during the whole season, because individual enthusiasm results in team morale and team spirit. These must be developed by the coach in his own way, adapting his system to fit the various personalities of the players.

The day after a game the coach discusses and criticizes any mistakes that were made. Those who made mental, not physical errors, should be criticized, but those who played "heads up" baseball should be given credit. *Give credit where credit is due.* Each mistake and each good play is pointed out and impressed upon the minds of the whole squad. The practice for the day after a game is so arranged that the mistakes, errors of omission and commission can be demonstrated.

signals

When should a base runner try to steal the base ahead? When does a batter bunt? When can the hit-and-run play be used as an offensive attack? When should the signal for a squeeze play be given? All of these offensive tactics are started by the coach by means of signals. Only experience in our national game and years of study will qualify a man to advise the team in such important maneuvers. It is thus very important for a coach to have a simple set of signals that really constitutes silent advice to his active players. A coach cannot expect the school or college player to master the defensive art of baseball together with every offensive tactic. The coach assumes this responsibility. His signals should be as simple as possible, and each member of his squad should know them perfectly.

An offensive attack can be governed by two signals only. Too many signs become confusing to a group of young players. A few conspicuous signs can be made by means of natural body movements. A few examples are given below. We do not, however, advise any coach to use them, as they may not coincide with or be suitable to his natural body movements. These signs are given from the bench:

1. *Steal signal:* clapsed hands over either knee. *Hit-and-run signal:* same as the steal, with both thumbs showing.

2. *Steal signal:* left leg crossed over right knee. *Hit-and-run signal:* same as the steal, with the right hand on the left shoe.

3. *Steal signal:* right leg over left knee. *Hit-and-run signal:* same as the steal with the left hand on the right shoe.

4. *Steal signal:* arms folded on the chest. *Hit-and-run signal:* same as the steal, with the hands showing on the biceps muscles of both arms.

5. *Steal signal:* a bat between the legs with one hand off. *Hit-and-run signal:* bat off the ground with one hand off.

Take the first set of signals and see how they would work in an offensive attack. The runner can be on any base. He glances at his coach as he returns to the bag from the position he assumed when the ball was pitched. He sees the hands of his coach clasped over the knee with the thumbs showing, and knows that he must try to steal the base ahead when the next ball is pitched. At the same time the batter glances at the coach and sees the same signal. This means that he must make an effort to hit the next pitched ball. Both the batter and the base runner know that the hit-and-run play is to be executed. If the base runner and the batter see only the clasped hands over the knee, both of them know that an attempt is to be made to steal the base ahead cleanly. The runner never attempts to steal unless he gets a good jump. The batter, if possible, helps the runner by swinging through the pitch to miss the ball.

The signal for a suicide squeeze play could be given in the same manner as for the hit-and-run play. The base runner would know that he must steal and the batter that he must bunt the ball. With a runner on third base, it is common knowledge that the squeeze play is the only offensive attack that could be made.

The bunt play for a sacrifice does not need any signal. The batter could be told just what he should do before he leaves the bench for the batter's box. If the steal or the hit-and-run play is not signed for by the coach, the base runner knows that the bunting game might be used. In other words, the base runner is always looking for the bunt play unless the steal or the hit-and-run signal is given by his coach.

Experience has taught us that the coach should give his own signals. The coach may want someone else to give the signals for offensive strategy because he is afraid that some opponent may catch on to his signals. But the following anecdote will show why we are against the practice of having anyone other than the coach give the signals.

Several years ago a varsity coach requested his freshman coach to use a very simple set of signals that could be given by some player on his squad who was not actively in the game. This young coach decided that a red-headed boy would be the proper fellow to flash the signals because he was easy to see. The coach decided that the red-head should take his cap off for the steal signal. His cap held in the left hand was the hit-and-run signal. These were conspicuous signs, very simple and very easily seen by all members of the squad.

As a spectator at an important freshman ball game which was being played on the home diamond against one of the school's great rivals, the varsity coach was eager to see how these simple signals would work. The game proved to be a pitcher's battle. The score in the sixth inning was two to two, when suddenly the most unorthodox offense began to be displayed. The first batter was hit by a pitched ball and went to first base. This runner stole second base, stole third base, and stole home plate on three successive pitched balls. The next batter singled to the outfield and was safe at first base. This runner stole second base on the first ball pitched, stole third on the second ball pitched, and scored on a long fly to the opposing left fielder. The fifth batter in this inning, after two men had been retired, was safe at first base on an infielder's error. This runner stole second base; then he stole third base as the umpire called the second ball on the man in the batter's box. The varsity coach was frantic and rushed immediately to the players' bench in order to find out why such offensive tactics were being used. The answer was that the red-headed boy had taken off his hat and forgot to place it back on his head.

adjustment of uniforms

All players should wear their uniform in the same manner and neatly. A well dressed team and ball player can play better baseball. They must have respect for their uniform.

Several years ago a short thesis was asked for as one of the requirements in a baseball course. The subject was, "How would you advise a young ball player to adjust his uniform and why?" The paper written by Grayson Brothers, Duke 1936, should be of interest to any coach.

The purpose of the baseball uniform is more than to be an ornament for a player; it is designed for protection. It can be assumed that anyone should know how to put clothing on, but there are several important considerations that may be overlooked in putting on a baseball uniform.

The greatest risk of injury in baseball comes from sliding. It is possible in the act of sliding to tear and to scrape the skin from the hips, the thighs, the knees, and the lower limbs. Injuries of this kind may result in infections of a permanent nature, although these are very rare. Everything should be done, however, to protect the body, because the harm done through improper protection may result in temporary lay-offs that decrease the efficiency of team play.

It is easy to understand the importance of care in the adjustment of a uniform when it is realized how easily an injury may be brought about. There is not too much flesh on the hip bone and on the bone just below the knee-joint on the outside of the leg. Naturally the skin and other body tissues over these bones are easily ruptured. Skin burns and ruptures should be avoid as much as possible; thus the proper protection should be given to these parts through hip pads and proper adjustment of the uniform. Too much stress cannot be placed on the necessity of extreme care in the way a player dresses for a baseball contest.

I would advise every coach to demonstrate to his squad on the first day of practice, the day the uniforms are given out, the proper manner in which uniforms should be adjusted to the body. As a coach I shall follow a definite procedure and shall make sure that each player understands the real reason for it.

I shall have one of my players dress as a model. I shall have him put on his undershirt, which should cover the upper part of the body and extend well below the hips. Then follows adjustment of his supporter over the bottom of the undershirt to prevent it working up above the belt during play; this position of the shirt offers additional padding for the hips. The top shirt should be put on next, and it should reach at least halfway between the hips and knees.

I shall now have the player sit down and put on his sanitary hose and his outer hose, bringing both well up over the knee-joints. Supplied garters, which should be wide enough to prevent cutting off the blood circulation, should then be drawn up over the knees. The pants or trousers should be turned inside out, and the bottoms of the pant legs should be pulled up to and over the knees. The garters are placed over the pants on the legs, low enough below the knees to make a base for a padding for the bones on the outside of each leg just below the knee joint. If the full length of the trouser legs is greater than is necessary to reach from the waist to the points where the garters are placed, the extra length should be rolled or folded together with the hose down over the knees. This forms a padding about two inches in width over the bones, which should be protected in sliding. There should be a pad just below the knee joint about one-half inch thick if the hose and extra length in the legs of the pants are folded properly.

I shall then have the model stand up and tie on his hip pads. These hip pads should be tied over both the inner and the outer shirt, and when adjusted properly should protect the body from the waist line almost to the knees. When the pads are tied around the waist line, the pants should be turned back to the right side by merely taking hold of the belt and pulling them up. The pads should then be placed inside the pants in proper position. After fastening the belt there is nothing left to do but put on the cap and the shoes and go to the field.

practice schedule

Every coach must get his baseball team partially conditioned indoors prior to outdoor practice. He must also organize his practice for game days.

Pre-season daily practice indoors. There are certain drills and fundamentals which cannot be executed indoors. The goal of indoor practice is to avoid these and work with drills and fundamentals which are adaptable for indoor performance, and are necessary for the development of the team. Thus, time will be saved for the drills and fundamentals which can only be done outdoors. It is advisable to have a watch or alarm clock to time activities. This will help the coach keep on schedule. Practice should never last over two hours.

One week prior to the first day of practice, the coach should call a meeting of all candidates for the team. At this time he explains the practice plans, training rules, prospects of the team, equipment necessary, and what he expects of the team in general.

Daily practice outdoors. If possible, a team should have at least two or three weeks of outdoor drills before the first game. If the team has been practicing indoors, the coach must be certain to cover the drills and fundamentals that could not be covered, such as actual ground balls in the dirt, sliding in the dirt or grass, fly balls and pop flies, long hard throws, cut-off and relay plays, the double play, base running, batting practice, and practice games.

The coach who is going outdoors for his first practice session can go along very well with some of the easier drills listed above. However, his players should have been running and throwing on their own time for at least two weeks prior to the first day of practice. The first day, weather permitting, should be a good, big practice session.

The second week of practice initiates practice game situations. A pitching rotation for the pitchers who will be pitching the regular season games should be started in the third week. The starting line up should be working and playing games together. Particular attention should be paid to starting pitchers, double play work, pop flies, base running, and the batting order.

organization for one diamond or practice area

It is of prime importance for a baseball coach to keep his players busy every minute of a practice session in order to impress upon them that they have to work before they can become a winning team.

It is necessary to have a set pattern for practice so the players will know what they are supposed to be doing every minute. The coach's mind must be flexible to take weather and last minute developments into consideration.

The coach must think in terms of the player and how to get the most out of him. When a player comes on the field, the first thing he wants to do is either throw or bat a ball, and he should be permitted to start his practice his way. Since these are the most important fundamentals of the game, they should be done first in practice.

Loosening up period—15 minutes. As soon as they come onto the field, the outfielders and infielders should begin organized pepper games. Pitchers and catchers should begin working together. They should all be doing some type of loosening up, running, throwing, or calisthenics.

Batting practice—60 minutes. Here is where a coach can get the most out of a practice. While the batters are taking their licks (no more than two on deck at a time), the extra pitchers and catchers should be assigned to infield and outfield fungoing. At first this practice may appear chaotic, but if it is properly arranged, the player who is hitting the fungos to the infield will learn to time his hits so they are made between pitches to the plate.

Meanwhile, the infielders are learning to field the ball off the bat at the plate, in addition to the fungos. It sharpens their wits and keeps them busy all the time.

Infielders, outfielders and catchers should alternate daily as to who hits first. Pitchers may be included in this practice by giving them the first ten minutes.

Fielding in position—10 minutes. After batting practice, the coaches, managers, and pitchers who hit good fungos should be assigned a position in the infield where they can hit the ball in rapid succession for about 10 minutes. During this time every fielder will receive individual attention from the coach, who can point out his fielding weaknesses and work with him to correct them.

While this part of the practice is going on, fungo hitters are assigned to hitting to the outfielders. The catchers are working along the sidelines on pop flies, blocking the ball, shifting to either side to handle wild pitches, and working on bunts.

Fundamentals of play—20 minutes. After fielding practice, everyone should be called and instructed to work on the general fundamentals of the game such as sliding, base running, actual bunt situations, pick offs, cut-off plays, run-down plays, the defense and offense of the delayed and double steals, and handling of pop-ups by the infield and outfield.

Considerable time should be spent on pop-ups. All the players should learn to distinguish each others' voice and should know who would be the one to make the catch. Many games are lost because of a mix-up on a seemingly easy pop fly.

Outfield-infield practice—10 minutes. The regular infield practice, with the outfielders making their throws to the bases and the infielders throwing around the horn, should be started.

The outfielders should throw in from the outfield first. The left fielder throws three or more throws to second base and the same to home. He can fake some throws to third and throw to second. The center fielder makes his throws to third and home, faking to third and throwing to second. The right fielder throws to third and home, faking to second and throwing to first. The third baseman cuts off the throws to home from the left fielder. The shortstop cuts off the throws to third base from the center fielder and right fielder. The first baseman cuts off throws to home from center and right field.

The outfielders can either run after they finish throwing or continue fielding fly balls. The infielders now take over with all the enthusiasm they can put forth. The coach should have a routine way of hitting infield grounders and of throwing the ball around. Use this same system prior to all games. It keeps a team from looking lost on the field.

Running—5 minutes. The five minutes running is used for the infielders. The outfielders will have run about ten minutes. The catchers run according to what work they have in infield practice. The pitchers have a 15 minute running session. This running session must be made as enjoyable as possible. No player likes to run just for the sake of running; he usually thinks of running as a pill he has to take with every practice.

Alternate practice sessions. Once the team is in shape to play, the above practice session should be used on alternate days, Monday, Wednesday, and Friday. Practice games or scrimmages should be held on Tuesday, Thursday, and Saturday. In case of rain the coach should decide which is needed most, practice games or practice of fundamentals.

pre-game practice

Pre-game practice must be carried out with real enthusiasm. Some games are won by scaring the other team in practice. A catcher, for instance, by showing his arm, can keep the opposition from stealing. Outfielders can keep them from tagging up and advancing on fly balls or scoring from second on a single.

The umpires should be advised to report to the field at least one-half hour before game time. This allows time for delays in transportation and prevents a late start. *Games must start on time!*

Pre-game batting practice. During batting practice, someone should hit fungos to the infielders and outfielders. Caution should be used in hitting to the infielders. Do not hit fungos at the same time pitched balls are hit. Hit fungos between pitches.

All extra men should take three swings at the beginning of batting practice. Following them, the starting lineup should start a round of one bunt and four swings each. If time permits, let them continue one bunt and four swings on a second round. If a few minutes are left, do some hit-and-run practice by giving each batter one pitch only. For faster batting practice use a pitcher who can throw perfect strikes.

Infield-outfield practice. While the home team is taking batting practice, the visiting team, which has finished its batting practice, starts warming up on the side. This is ten minutes before they take the field, which is thirty minutes before game time. As soon as the home team completes batting practice, the visitors charge to their positions. The coach, with four balls, assumes a position near the mound and hits to the outfielders, who make several throws to the following bases: The left fielder throws to second base and home; the center fielder and the right fielder throw to third and home. A fungo hitter then hits to the outfield for fly ball practice. This hitting should be done from a position just outside the foul lines beyond first and third bases. From these positions there is no danger to infielders, who are taking infield practice as the coach hits balls to them. While the visiting team is taking infield practice, the home team is loosening up for its practice, which is taken in the same manner. The home team practice stops ten minutes before game time, and the groundskeeper uses this time to prepare the field for the game.

Following is a sample time schedule of pre-game practice for a 3:30 P.M. game. Since the visitors are normally free earlier than the home team, the visitors should take their hitting practice first. However, if they have a late arrival time, they should notify the home team coach so he can reverse the order of hitting and fielding practice.

2:00—Visiting team batting
2:30—Home team batting

3:00—Visiting team infield and outfield practice

3:10—Home team infield and outfield practice

3:20—Groundskeeper prepares the field for the game

3:25—Umpires and coaches discuss ground rules. Home team coach presents his lineup card to plate umpire first, then the visiting team coach presents his lineup card.

3:30—Game time

Pitcher warm-up drill. Twenty minutes before game time have the pitcher do some type of loosening up exercise. Ten to fifteen minutes before game time, depending upon the weather and the individual, the pitcher should begin to throw. Starting easily, he should gradually increase his speed until he feels loose enough; he should work up a sweat, gauging his time so that he will not be warm too long before game time. He will need a few minutes rest prior to going out on the mound—long enough to wipe off the sweat and get a drink of water. Never rest longer than five minutes.

intra-squad games

A regular ball game between the first and second teams will be found beneficial. Such games give a coach an opportunity to criticize both the defensive and offensive play under actual playing conditions. If a player in these contests makes a mistake in his base running or errs on the defense, the coach can stop the game and give a full explanation in regard to the error. He can also offer words of encouragement and give commendations.

We do not, however, change nine players from the offense to the defense, or vice versa, after three men are out. Two or three full innings are completed before a change is made. As soon as three men have been retired by the defense team, a new inning begins. The only change made is the pitcher. We change the pitchers after three men are out. If there are runners on base, we leave them there. This sets up more game situations. The pitchers warm up on the sidelines prior to three outs to avoid waste of time in the change of pitchers.

training of players

In preparation for the baseball season, players should start preliminary work on their own about a month before practice sessions start. In order to be ready for the opening practice, time and effort must be expended to get into condition. Pre-practice work should be divided into four categories: Running, stretching, throwing, and weight work.

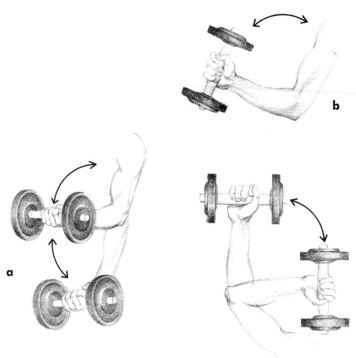

figure **79**

Running. Early conditioning requires plenty of running. The only way to get into shape, and to develop speed and stamina is to run, run, run. Good legs make good ball players. Running is hard work and demands initiative and self-sacrifice. This applies to all players, especially pitchers. Remember, it is possible to play with a sore arm, but practically impossible to play with a sore leg.

Stretching. All parts of the body need plenty of stretching. Stretching exercises will prevent muscle pulls in the legs and back. All players, especially pitchers, should stretch their arms. To stretch the arm, all one needs to do is to hang from a suspended bar, the top of a door, or any other available place that is above the head. This will also stretch the shoulder muscles. Just hang for a minute or so: *do not pull up*. Do this anytime, but particularly just before the daily workout. Two or three stretches of a minute or so will suffice; *Do not overdo it*. Stretching should be continued throughout the season. Make it a daily habit.

Throwing. After stretching, start throwing easily. Test and find out how much easier it is to throw after a good arm stretch. Throw everyday. Don't throw hard until the arm is warmed up.

Pitchers in early season practices should not throw hard for a week. Start spinning curves the first day. Don't try to break them off, just spin the ball to get the feel.

Weight work. This phase of training applies to pitchers. However, other players may use it after consultation with the coach or the trainer. Working with weights is not designed to develop bulging muscles, but to improve muscle tone. The following is a tenative program:

Get a barbell or any fifteen lb. weight that is easy to control. Standing, with the arm fully extended at the side, palm up, weight in hand, *bend* the arm *slowly* to complete flexion. Return to full extension. Do this ten times. This exercise strengthens the anterior arm muscles *above the elbow* (note Figure 79, *a*). Then, in the same basic position, but with the forearm in the midway position (thumb pointing up), repeat this exercise ten times. This variation of the exercise also strengthens arm muscles *above the elbow* (note Figure 79, *b*).

To strengthen muscles in the *back of the arm, above the elbow*: Raise the arm above the shoulder with elbow bent, and straighten the arm ten times (note Figure 79, *c*).

To strengthen muscles of the arm, *below the elbow*: Rest the elbow and lower arm on a table, with the wrist extending over the end of the table, weight in hand, palm up; flex the wrist ten times (note Figure 80, *a*). Next hold the weight with the thumb pointing up. Rotate it to the right and left ten times (Figure 80, *b*). This develops the muscles most important for wrist action in throwing the curve ball or any breaking pitch, the rotator muscles of the wrist and elbow. Turn the hand over so that it faces the floor, then return it to the starting position (ten times) (note Figure 80, *c*).

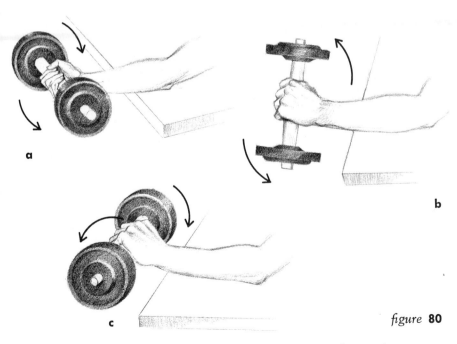

a

b

c

figure **80**

These exercises are to be done *only three times a week*. Add one repetition to each exercise per week. In other words, initially, each exercise is done ten times a day, three days a week. The next week, each exercise is done eleven times a day, three days a week, and so on until twenty repetitions a day are reached. At Michigan State, this program is instituted in the fall of the year. When the maximum of twenty repetitions is reached, the player is called in for evaluation and consultation.

We emphasize that these exercises are not designed to develop Charles Atlas muscles, but to tone and strengthen the important muscles used by a pitcher. For players other than pitchers twice the number of repetitions per day is recommended.

Special tips for pitchers. Pitchers should always do their running at the end of practice, just before going into the clubhouse. In this way, the pitcher will not be standing around in a damp sweatshirt—risking a sore arm. All pitchers should have at least two sweatshirts. Prior to a workout on a cold, windy day, it is advisable to put some oil on the arm, shoulder, and back. After a good workout, or after pitching a game, pitchers should get an alcohol massage on the arm, shoulder, and back muscles. This massage closes the pores and prevents arm soreness. It should be of short duration, only long enough to close the pores.

All players should play plenty of "pepper" games. These help to develop quick reflexes, and are good for stomach muscles and overall conditioning. Never use more than two fielders for each hitter.

Many pitchers develop a blister on the thumb side of the middle finger of the pitching hand. This is caused by the pressure exerted on the ball by this finger—especially when throwing the curve ball. The fingernail is always pointed in this area. When pressure is exerted on the ball, as in throwing the curve, the point of the nail projects into the skin, causing a blister to form. This condition can be eliminated by keeping this point of the nail filed down. Never use clippers on this nail. Use a nail file or emery board.

The following player progress chart can prove very valuable to the coach in finding the weaknesses of his players. It can give him a good evaluation of the player or team. From the chart, the coach can plan his drills for the correction of weaknesses in all phases of the game. Most players like to work constantly on their strength or the things they do best. A strong team constantly works on the things in which they are weak.

The chart can be used for individual players as a guide to plan their work. They can evaluate themselves.

Using the chart in the beginning of the season will aid the coach in his overall season planning. A check in the middle of the season will prepare him for the stretch drive. A check at the end of the season will give coach and team things to work on during the summer, winter, and the next year's early season practice.

PLAYER PROGRESS CHART

Grade:
A = Excellent;   B = Good;   C = Fair;   D = Poor.

Player's Progress:
(1) Beginning of Season; (2) Middle of Season; (3) End of Season

(1)   (2)   (3)

Pitching

_____ _____ _____   1. Control
_____ _____ _____   2. Holds fingers on ball properly
_____ _____ _____   3. Curve
_____ _____ _____   4. Change-up

player progress

(1)	(2)	(3)	
—	—	—	5. Backs bases properly
—	—	—	6. Covers first
—	—	—	7. Fields his position
—	—	—	8. Fields bunts
—	—	—	9. Throws to second on double play
—	—	—	10. Conceals pitches
—	—	—	11. Second base pick-off
—	—	—	12. (a) Rotation good on fast ball
—	—	—	(b) Rotation good on curve ball
—	—	—	13. Holds runners close to bag
—	—	—	14. Stands on mound properly
—	—	—	15. Keeps eye on target
—	—	—	16. Keeps eye on flag (wind)
—	—	—	17. Follows through
—	—	—	18. Striding foot lands properly
—	—	—	19. Checks position of infield and outfield before delivery
—	—	—	20. First base pick-off

Catching

(1)	(2)	(3)	
—	—	—	1. Shifts well
—	—	—	2. Does not take too long to get rid of ball
—	—	—	3. Steps to throw; no lost motion
—	—	—	4. Throws on double steal
—	—	—	5. Catches foul flies
—	—	—	6. Picks up bunts properly
—	—	—	7. Uses one hand only when necessary
—	—	—	8. Blocks home plate properly
—	—	—	9. Blocks all pitches properly
—	—	—	10. Removes mask properly
—	—	—	11. Relaxes whole body when catching ball
—	—	—	12. Hides signs; can switch signs
—	—	—	13. Is field general
—	—	—	14. Weight on balls of feet
—	—	—	15. Keeps eye on flag (wind)
—	—	—	16. Tags home properly on force play
—	—	—	17. Calls pitches
—	—	—	18. Uses voice
—	—	—	19. Checks defense before pitch
—	—	—	20. Backs up plays

Infield

(1)	(2)	(3)	
—	—	—	1. Anticipates what to do with ball
—	—	—	2. Spreads feet properly
—	—	—	3. Bends knees; tail low
—	—	—	4. Weight on balls of feet
—	—	—	5. Uses cross-over step when breaking to sides
—	—	—	6. Straightens up to throw only when necessary

_____ _____ _____ 7. Fields ball out in front of body
_____ _____ _____ 8. Charges the ball, does not let ball play him
_____ _____ _____ 9. Fields ball on side only when necessary
_____ _____ _____ 10. Can make double play shortstop or second
_____ _____ _____ 11. Tags correctly
_____ _____ _____ 12. (a) Can go to his right
_____ _____ _____   (b) Can go to his left
_____ _____ _____ 13. Gets rid of ball quickly
_____ _____ _____ 14. Uses crow hop or throws from position without step
_____ _____ _____ 15. Makes run-down play correctly
_____ _____ _____ 16. Uses voice to help teammates
_____ _____ _____ 17. No hitch before throwing
_____ _____ _____ 18. Makes relays properly
_____ _____ _____ 19. Keeps eye on flag (wind)
_____ _____ _____ 20. Relaxed wrists in fielding ball
_____ _____ _____ 21. Backs up plays

Outfield

_____ _____ _____ 1. Gets good jump on ball
_____ _____ _____ 2. Plays ground balls well
_____ _____ _____ 3. Knows how to shade sun
_____ _____ _____ 4. Knows how to get set to throw
_____ _____ _____ 5. Anticipates running speed of base runners or hitters
_____ _____ _____ 6. Throws low
_____ _____ _____ 7. Backs up bases
_____ _____ _____ 8. Runs on toes when fielding flies
_____ _____ _____ 9. Uses voice to help out on flies
_____ _____ _____ 10. Plays rebounds off fences well
_____ _____ _____ 11. Weight on balls of feet
_____ _____ _____ 12. Keeps eye on flag (wind)
_____ _____ _____ 13. Gets in position to throw
_____ _____ _____ 14. Throws to proper bases

Batting

_____ _____ _____ 1. Knows strike zone
_____ _____ _____ 2. Strides correctly
_____ _____ _____ 3. Hitches, yet hits well
_____ _____ _____ 4. Swings level
_____ _____ _____ 5. Keeps head and eyes on ball
_____ _____ _____ 6. Rolls wrists on swing
_____ _____ _____ 7. Has good follow-through
_____ _____ _____ 8. Never guesses
_____ _____ _____ 9. Steps toward pitch
_____ _____ _____ 10. Keeps elbows away from body
_____ _____ _____ 11. Can hit curve
_____ _____ _____ 12. Can hit change of speed
_____ _____ _____ 13. Can hit fast ball

(1)   (2)   (3)

——— ——— ——— 14. Can hit behind runner
——— ——— ——— 15. Not afraid of pitched ball
——— ——— ——— 16. Bends knees slightly
——— ——— ——— 17. Starts swing at proper time
——— ——— ——— 18. Has proper grip on bat
——— ——— ——— 19. Is relaxed at plate
——— ——— ——— 20. Weight on balls of feet
——— ——— ——— 21. Keeps both eyes on ball and level
——— ——— ——— 22. Takes signs easily

Bunting

——— ——— ——— 1. Bat parallel with ground
——— ——— ——— 2. Bunts in front end of batter's box
——— ——— ——— 3. Can bunt toward first
——— ——— ——— 4. Can bunt toward third
——— ——— ——— 5. Always bunts strikes
——— ——— ——— 6. Commits himself at start of pitchers stride
——— ——— ——— 7. Carries bat shoulder high
——— ——— ——— 8. Weight on balls of feet
——— ——— ——— 9. Bends knees
——— ——— ——— 10. Relaxes arms and grip
——— ——— ——— 11. Angle of bat is good

Base Running

——— ——— ——— 1. Crosses feet over on steal
——— ——— ——— 2. Rounds bases well
——— ——— ——— 3. Takes enough lead
——— ——— ——— 4. Is daring on base paths
——— ——— ——— 5. Slides correctly
——— ——— ——— 6. Slides early enough for proper slide
——— ——— ——— 7. Slides all ways
——— ——— ——— 8. Knows how to slide to break up a double play
——— ——— ——— 9. Uses good judgment
——— ——— ——— 10. Runs with head up
——— ——— ——— 11. Checks for position of all opposing players after each pitch
——— ——— ——— 12. Watches wind after each pitch
——— ——— ——— 13. Looks at coach when rounding second or third
——— ——— ——— 14. Knows number of outs
——— ——— ——— 15. Watches preceding runner on bases, hits, and stolen bases

APPENDIX

Lenox D. Baker, M.D.

Professor of Orthopaedic Surgery
Duke University School of Medicine

By proper preseason condition, those injuries which occur as the result of sore muscles and poor coordination can be avoided. Early training should consist of running, throwing, strenuous calisthenic exercises, and toughening of the hands and feet. The preseasonal work should be supplemented by lectures by the coach and by the trainer, since mental as well as physical conditioning is important. The individual who assumes the responsibility of coaching or training an athletic team must remember that the players look upon him as an authority on all phases of the sport. It is his responsibility to see that all injuries are recognized and are given proper treatment.

Every club should have a team physician, preferably one who is interested in sports and certainly one who is capable of handling athletic injuries. The team physician should see all injuries of serious or doubtful character; he should see all injuries which do not respond to treatment within a reasonable length of time; and he should serve as adviser to the trainer and coach. The manner of handling minor injuries by the coach or trainer should be outlined and supervised by the consulting physician. Clean showers, well-ventilated dressing rooms, and clean uniforms are absolute necessities of a well-organized team. Freshly laundered sweatshirts,

treatment of minor injuries
in baseball

athletic supporters, and sweat socks should be issued each day. In those institutions or clubs that cannot buy such services, the players should be taught to care for these items themselves.

Preventive measures for common injuries will be discussed under the respective headings. Any open wound may become infected, and the administration of tetanus antitoxin is necessary to avoid the danger of lockjaw. The usual precautions have been the administration of 1500 units of tetanus antitoxin, preferably combined with 1000 units of gas antitoxin; however, antitoxin frequently causes serum sickness and may force the player to miss as much as a week from practice. Tetanus toxoid can be used to produce an immunity which will last at least two years in 90 per cent or more of the individuals to whom it is administered. The coach or trainer should see that all members of his squad have been given tetanus toxoid. The immunization should be started two to three months before the season opens, and "booster doses" should be given several weeks before each season thereafter.

common baseball injuries

Sliding burns (Brush burns, Strawberries, or Abrasions). Such injuries in which the outer layer of skin is rubbed off down to a bleeding or oozing surface are frequently seen on the outer aspect of the thigh and buttocks as a result of sliding.

Prevention. Practice the art of sliding in a soft sliding pit made of sand or sawdust or in a grass area, with extra pants for padding and in stocking feet, until the timing is perfected. Once your mind is made up to slide into a base, complete the slide and meet any new situation that might have developed in the game after the slide has been completed. Protect the hip regions with properly adjusted, well-made, properly fitted, sliding pads.

Treatment. The best cleansing agent, and the one least likely to be harmful to the cells of the raw surface, is warm water and a mild soap. After the surface has been thoroughly cleansed with soap and water, it should be covered with a light coat of 5 per cent sulfathiazole in a vanishing cream base and sterile gauze dressing. Do not use paste prepared with petroleum jellies, and so forth, because these have no drying agent in them and keep the injured surface macerated. After application of the cream, or of some type of sterile dusting powder, such as bismuth formic iodine or zinc sterrate, the injury should be covered with a sterile gauze dressing. If the area does not become inflamed or infected and there is no evidence of pus, the first dressing may be left in place until the area is completely healed. Healing can be hurried by cleanliness and by protecting the wound from repeated injury.

Spike cuts. Spike cuts are sometimes unavoidable owing to the actions of the opponents. Such cuts are frequently deeper than they appear to be on the surface, and occasionally major blood vessels or tendons may be injured. All such wounds should be seen by the team physician.

Prevention. When on defense, fielders should remember to play their base in such a way that the bag protects their feet and legs from the oncoming runner, since most spike cuts occur as a result of the baseman's being exposed to the spikes of the opponent when he slides. To avoid, in so far as possible, complications from such wounds, clean sweat stockings should be worn at all times. These stockings are the long sanitary hose.

Treatment. Soap and water is the best cleansing agent. The player should be taken at once to a doctor and have the wound inspected and sutured, if stitches are indicated (and they usually are because they approximate the edges of the wound and allow for early healing). When such wounds occur, those players who have had tetanus toxoid should have a *booster* injection; those who have not had tetanus toxoid should have tetanus antitoxin administered because there is always the danger of lockjaw.

Blisters on the feet. There is no excuse for athletes collecting blisters on the feet.

Prevention. If the athlete will toughen his feet properly, break in his shoes during the preseason, and wear properly fitted hose, blisters will not occur. Blisters result from irritation of the skin by friction and are preventable. Occasionally, blisters occur in the palms of the hand as a result of gripping the bat. These, like blisters of the feet, can be prevented by toughening the hands during the preseason training program.

Treatment. Blisters, unless they become unduly large or become infected, should not be opened. They represent an accumulation of fluid beneath the outer layers of skin. This fluid acts as a cushion and protects the underlying tender inner layers. If the blister is going to be exposed to further trauma, it should be covered with adhesive or Scotch tape. If the outer layer can be kept intact for several days, new skin will grow underneath, and healing will take place in a relatively short time. If the blister opens itself and the outer layer of skin is destroyed, the wound should be treated as described under sliding burns.

Athlete's foot (Epidermiphytosis, Toe Itch, Ringworm). Athlete's foot is caused by a fungus infection in the skin and manifests itself usually in itching, redness between the toes, or by the presence of small blisters over the sole of the foot and heel. It is a common infection and one that can lead to disability if not controlled early.

Prevention. Training and shower rooms should be clean and well ventilated, and floors should be cleaned with strong solutions of lysol. The individual should dry his feet thoroughly after each shower and should apply a light dusting of Desenex or Sopronol powder to the feet once a day.

Treatment.[1] If there are signs of active athlete's foot, one of the above powders should be applied in the morning, and an ointment of Desenex or of Sopronol should be applied at night. If the Desenex powder is used in the morning, the Sopronol ointment should be used at night; if the Sopronol powder is used in the morning, the Desenex ointment should be used at night.

If the toes become raw and there appear signs of secondary infection (infection by other organisms, a mixed infection), potassium permanganate foot-soaks should be used once a day. A solution of 1 to 6000 is sufficient.

All the above treatments are safe and may be used without undue caution. Improved Whitfield's ointment,[2] Castellani's paint,[3] 2 per cent Dahlia (aqueous solution) and oil of Cade, and other drugs have been used in the treatment of athlete's foot. These drugs should be used with precaution and always under the supervision of a physician.

Jock itch or gym itch. Jock itch usually results from chafing in the groin between the legs and it may consist of nothing more than a simple chafing. Usually jock itch is the result of a fungus infection which has been transferred to the groin region by the jock strap.

Prevention. Thorough drying of the groin area, application of cornstarch dusting powder, the use of clean jock support, and protection of the skin from the elastic support by inserting soft pads (folded linen handkerchief makes an excellent pad) are good preventive measures. Never wear a damp support. If the feet are infected with athlete's itch, exercise precaution in putting on the athletic support to avoid contact with the feet. The best preventive we know of is the use of Cooper's jockey shorts, which go over the knee. They are form fitting and fit close to the skin. Put the underwear on first, then put on the supporter. The underwear protects the skin from the supporter and serves as sliding shorts. For cold weather, the shorts remain long. In warm weather, we cut them off just above the knees.

Treatment. If there is a simple chafing of the skin, thorough cleaning,

---

[1] Mr. Coombs wishes to express his appreciation to Dr. J. Lamarr Calloway, Professor of Medicine in Charge of Dermatology, for the outline of the treatment of athlete's foot.

[2] Whitfield Ointment Improved

Benzoic acid	4 gms.
Salicylic acid	2 gms.
Thymol iodide	0.3 gms.
Equal parts of Lanoline and Petrolatum sufficient to make	30 gms.

[3] Castellani's Paint

Saturated alcoholic solution basic fuchsin	10 cc.
5 per cent Phenol	100 cc.
Boric acid	1 gm.
Acetone	5 cc.
Resorcin	10 gms.

the application of cornstarch dusting powder, and the use of a clean pad between the athletic support and the skin will usually be all that is required. If there is a fungus infection, such as seen in athlete's foot, the treatment is the same as for athlete's foot.

Stone bruises (Heel Bruises, Policeman Heels). Injuries to the weight bearing surface of the heel area of the foot may be disabling for several weeks. The player should be taken off his feet and the foot should be elevated and surrounded with ice packs for 72 to 96 hours, after which walking may be allowed if pain is not severe. When weight bearing can be tolerated, the bruised heel should be protected with a sponge rubber heel pad, and the heel should not be subjected to reinjury until all pain and symptoms have subsided.

Muscle bruises (Charley Horses, Torn Muscles, Hemorrhage in the Muscles). So called Charley Horses, whether they be due to a direct blow on the muscle or to too sudden a strain put upon the muscle during exercise, are the result of hemorrhage (bleeding) in the muscle. Those caused by sudden, quick starts, slipping, and so forth, are usually the result of not having the muscles properly warmed or loosened, and of the athlete not being in proper condition.

Prevention. Always take a thorough and complete warm-up period before participating in actual play. To avoid bruises and similar injuries, be on the alert. Play the game as taught in order to avoid collision.

Treatment. Ice packs should be applied immediately to limit the bleeding and to relieve pain. If muscle spasm can be prevented, recovery will be much earlier. The player should be taken to the team physician immediately at the sight of the injury for procaine injection,[4] following which the injured part should be taken through light exercises. The application of ice, if symptoms warrant additional therapy, should be continued for 48 to 72 hours. Later, light massage, application of heat, and the use of the part should hasten recovery. Diathermy (special electrical machine) or moist heat is preferable to dry heat.

Such muscle injuries can be serious, particularly if there is hemorrhage into the muscle from bony regions, because calcification may take place in the muscle.

Sprained ankles. Sprained ankle is the most common serious injury seen in athletics. The treatment for sprained ankle depends on its severity. In many cases, tendons about the joint are torn and without X-ray it is difficult to differentiate between a sprained ankle and a fracture about the ankle. All such injuries should be seen by the team physician.

[4] Both local procaine injection into the exact site of acute tenderness and intravenous procaine therapy are of definite value in the treatment of these injuries. This therapy should be given by an experienced physician only. For local use of procaine, read the description of the technique of injection in the *Treatment* of sprained ankles.

Prevention. The coach, or the groundskeeper working under his direction, should see that the playing field and the territory surrounding the playing field are level and dry, and without loose rocks, roots, or soft spots. The athlete should wear well-fitted shoes and be alert to avoid awkward steps. He should maintain good balance at all times, and he should master the techniques of pivoting and sliding.

Treatment. The treatment of sprained ankles has been revolutionized by the use of the local injection of procain. Immediately after the accident occurs, the ankle should be surrounded with ice packs and the injured player should be taken to the team physician. All sprained ankles should have X-rays made in at least three views to rule out fracture.

Technique of procain injection (*to be done by a physician only*). As a precaution against procain shock, 60 to 90 milligrams of sodium phenobarbital should be given to the patient hypodermically. The injured ankle should be palpated slowly and thoroughly. All tender spots should be located and one of the commonly used dyes, such as gentian violet, should be used to spot each tender area.

It is most important that all areas of point tenderness be localized and that the procain injection be directly into the exact site of the local tenderness. After the tender areas have been located and marked with the dye, the foot and ankle region should be thoroughly cleaned with ether, alcohol, and iodine, and the skin of the marked areas should be infiltrated with a few drops of 1 per cent procain, using a hypodermic needle. A 21-gauge needle then should be attached to the syringe of procain, and with the assistance of the patient, the physician should probe for the exact site of the tenderness and inject a few cc.s. of procain. Each area of point tenderness should be so treated.

The treatment cannot be hurried, and the injection must be exact if the desired results are to be obtained. Promiscuous injection of wide areas about such injuries are of no benefit and are not to be tolerated. After the injection the patient should be allowed to walk.

The physician will have to decide as to the seriousness of the sprain and as to the necessity of strapping the ankle. If it is obvious that there has been a fairly severe sprain and that there is a tendency of the swelling to increase, strapping should be applied, and the patient should be put to bed with the foot elevated and surrounded by ice for a period of 24 to 48 hours.

Before applying the adhesive, always shave the leg. Strap the ankle in a position for weight-bearing, and support the foot in a direction opposite to the force that caused the injury. If the injury is on the inner side of the ankle joint, the foot should be turned in slightly for the strapping. The reverse is true if the injury is on the outer side of the ankle. If the patient is not to be under constant supervision, adhesive strapping must never be placed completely around the anterior surface of the ankle or over the top of the foot, since more swelling may occur, and circula-

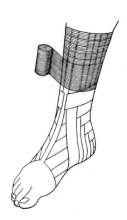

figure 81

Ankle strapping: This is a basket-weave type sometimes called "Gibney strapping." The adhesive strips
are about one inch in width. The longitudinal straps
are carried well up the leg while the cross-straps are
brought forward far enough to allow about one half
inch of skin surface to remain uncovered. This adhesive strapping is then fixed by the application of
a two-inch bandage around the whole ankle and foot.

tory disturbance in the toes may result. To avoid irritating the skin, trainers
often use a cotton knit sock covering under the tape prior to applying
the tape (see Figure 81 for Ankle Strapping).

The player who suffers a sprained ankle should be allowed to re-
sume practice as soon as the pain does not interfere with his activity. The
time element will vary, depending on the individual and on the extensiveness of the injury. When the player starts to play again, the ankle
should be supported with an adhesive strapping, which should be changed
daily or should be reinforced as needed and changed every two to three
days, depending on the condition of the skin and the need for support.

Sprained or twisted knee. The knee is a complicated joint with
intra-articular cartilages and is frequently injured in athletics.

Prevention. Same as for sprained ankle.

Treatment. If the knee is only sprained and there is only slight tenderness about the joint without swelling, the joint
may be treated with rest and application of cold
compresses. Participation in athletics may be re-
sumed as soon as symptoms allow. If the injury
results in extensive swelling of the joint (so-called
water on the knee), with inability to extend the
joint, the player should be seen by the team physician and X-rays should be made. Injuries to the
knee may result in a tearing of the capsule of the

figure 82

Knee strapping: One-inch adhesive strips are first applied in a criss-cross fashion from above down. These
are then covered by horizontal strips applied from
above down. Care is taken not to extend any of
these strips over the back part of the leg and joint.
This is then covered by a three- or four-inch circular
elastic bandage.

joint or the ligaments in the lateral aspects of the joint, or there may be a tear or derangement of one of the semilunar cartilages or cruciate ligaments of the joint. If the team physician is not a competent orthopaedic surgeon, he should refer such injuries to an orthopaedic surgeon for treatment, which may consist of traction, application of cold packs, application of a plaster shell, or adhesive strapping. Surgery may be necessary (see Figure 82 for Knee Strapping).

Injuries about the wrist. A sprained wrist is an uncommon injury. Usually, if there is any severe pain associated with an injured wrist, damage has been done to one of the small bones or possibly to one of the forearm bones. All such injuries should be seen by a competent physician and multiview X-rays made to rule out fractures.

Treatment. If the X-rays are negative for fracture, treatment should consist of adhesive straps for support (see Figure 83 for Wrist and Finger Strapping).

Sprained thumb and finger joints (Baseball Finger). Fingers are frequently subjected to injury when they are struck by a thrown ball. A simple strain of a joint of the fingers may be treated by the local application of ice or cold soaks. In those instances where the accident occurs in the distal joints of the fingers, the tendon which extends the finger may be torn from the bone (baseball finger) with the loss of the ability to extend the finger.

Prevention. Never wear any type of ring on the athletic field. Keep your eyes on the ball. Never hurry your throw until the ball has been caught. Keep the fingers of the ungloved hand closed or together with the side of your hand toward the approaching ball until the ball has been caught.

figure **83**
Wrist and finger strapping (below left): Alternate circular and longitudinal layers of one-inch adhesive strips are applied to the wrist, carried forward as far as the base of the thumb. The amount of support is in direct relation to the number of layers applied. The diagram shows three layers, but six or even more may be used. The sprained finger is strapped to an adjoining finger by circular one-inch adhesive strips.

figure **84**
Thumb strapping (below right): First one-inch adhesive strips are applied around the thumb, being carried well down around the wrist. Longitudinal strips are next applied, and then circular strips around the wrist to fix the first two layers in place.

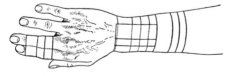

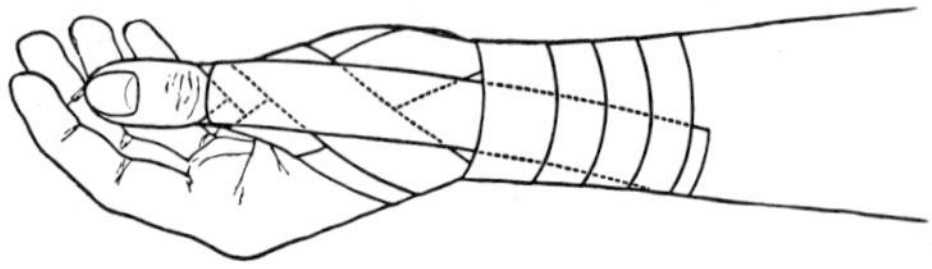

Treatment. Simple sprains can be treated with cold soaks and light exercise. True baseball finger should be seen by a doctor and treated with splints or by surgery. Immobilization of simple sprains is not recommended; neither should simple chip fractures about the middle joint of the fingers be immobilized since such treatment may result in a stiff, or partially stiff finger (see Figure 84 for Thumb Strapping).

Injuries to webspaces of hand and nailbeds. It is not uncommon for the skin or for the nailbed to be broken when the fingers are struck by a ball. The results of such injuries may be a split of the skin between the joints of the thumb, a split of the skin of the fold between the thumb and the first finger, or a split of the skin between two adjacent fingers. The split may be superficial, but it may be deep and require the attention of the team physician.

Prevention. Same as prevention under sprained thumb and finger joints. Long fingernails are usually the cause of nail injuries. Fingernails should be kept short and even. They should never be cut but should be sanded with an emery board or file. All corners should be rounded.

Treatment. Any tears of the skin should be repaired immediately after antiseptic clean up. Tetanus toxoid or tetanus antitoxin should be used as explained under *Spike Cuts*. The treatment of injuries of the nailbeds depends on the extent of the injury. If there is no break in the skin, no treatment other than the use of cold soaks to relieve pain is indicated. If the nailbed has been torn loose, the hand should be cleaned thoroughly with hot soapy water. Any loose parts of the nails should be cut away, but the remaining portion of the nail should not be disturbed, since it will protect the tender underlying tissues. Sterile dressings should be applied and the finger protected until healing has occurred.

final advice for treatment of the body

(1) Do not unduly prolong the exercise or work, for to do so will usually develop sore muscles.

(2) Protect the arm and shoulder muscles from wind and cold, and in rainy weather. Always have a sweater or heavy clothing handy to cover the arms and shoulders.

(3) Do not let anyone massage the muscles of the body unless certain tendons are sore. A massage will aid soreness, so let nature do her part without such artificial means. Overworked, tired, or strained muscles need complete rest. In small schools the coach is the trainer, and he must be careful as to his procedure for all ailments. Let the sore muscles rest, but if the strain is severe, cold or hot applications will prove to be as good an aid as anything. If the condition is very severe, get a doctor.

If the ailment is in the arms or shoulders, the player should keep up the exercise for his legs. If the ailment is in some other part of the body, the player should continue his exercise, provided the muscles of the injured part are not brought into play.

(4) Do not use strong liniments.

(5) In preliminary practice, start off gently, never violently. The body should be thoroughly warmed up before practice begins.

(6) Before going into a work out, toss a ball awhile so that the muscles of the body may come easily into proper coordination before they are required to do any strenuous work.

(7) If you are a pitcher, ten or fifteen minutes of work before you enter a ball game should be time enough to loosen up the shoulder, arm, and body muscles.

(8) Eye glasses on the field are an accepted piece of equipment today. Many players who need glasses have gone to contact lenses: they have proved to be excellent if fitted properly. Those who wear them do experience some difficulty on windy, dusty days and if their eyes are not used to them prior to the season. It is recommended that contact lenses be used at least two months prior to the baseball season.

To protect the eyes during windy, dusty days, motorcycle glasses with plain lenses can be used, especially for practice. Caution should be used to purchase shatter-proof glasses.

The final advice is never to wear a ring during an athletic contest. We have seen so many permanent injuries caused by athletes wearing jewelry on athletic fields that we have established this rule in our coaching work, that a player wearing any jewelry is not allowed on the playing field over which we have authority.

L. C. "Cap" Timm

Head Baseball Coach
Iowa State University

A few years ago, we were confronted with the problems of building a new diamond. In searching for written material, we were appalled by the lack of helpful information. There is a need for written material specifically describing the construction and maintenance of baseball fields.

Probably the first prerequisite to being a baseball coach or manager is to be a groundskeeper, agronomist, and an embryo engineer. The established purpose of this work is to set forth certain guide lines, knowledge, suggestions, and procedures, as a source of information and reference. It is our sincere hope that through the dissemination of this information benefits will be derived from the experiences of others.

Our investigations have left us with an even greater admiration and respect for the experts and specialists in the fields of agronomy, entomology and various phases of engineering. It is with a feeling of deep humility that we have endeavored to present this specialized knowledge in simplified version so that others may find it as useful as we did.

Baseball is always a good game. American boys have probably had more real fun from baseball than any other sport—even on vacant lots, pastures, or perhaps, the street. Our own initiation to the game, as youngsters, was on a side hill cow pasture. When a player was called upon to

construction and maintenance
of baseball facilities

21

slide on a close play, he first had to make a quick decision as to whether or not the object he was sliding into was actually the base.

However, all people connected with baseball will agree that the game is much more satisfactory to players, coaches, and spectators when the facilities are the best—or as good as possible. Players perform better on a good diamond, and the spectators watch with greater understanding and comfort when the facilities are well-planned.

The opposite side of the coin gives a reverse picture. All coaches have seen infielders play "scared" and become "gun-shy" on a rough field. When the players make snide remarks such as, "What a rock pile—sand pit—ploughed field—pavement—or obstacle course," it's a good bet that the playing will be second rate.

Many items contribute to the making of a good field, and each requires separate study. Each will have its own topographical and geographical problems. No single formula is applicable to every instance, and it will be necessary to make the appropriate adjustments to each particular local situation. Three major features are common to all fine playing areas: good construction, good soil structure, and top grade, dedicated maintenance. All these features must be present: no single item is insurance for a high class field. Constant maintenance without good construction and drainage cannot make a field playable. On the other hand, a well-constructed field with good drainage but without good maintenance is also inadequate. A field that has these three main features in combination has a reasonable chance of staying good regardless of the heavy traffic through a long schedule from April through September. A good facility can be available earlier in the spring and made playable sooner after rain.

The classification of the type of operation desired will have to be decided upon. This will run from the cow pasture variety, through different stages of mediocrity, to a first-class playing facility. The decision will depend upon funds available, local construction problems, "know-how," and the interest and desire to have a facility that can be looked upon with pride. A little extra planning and a little extra money will pay dividends in a satisfaction that both time and money were well spent.

The references used to compile this material are shown in parentheses, i.e.: (1) to (8) refer to bulletins and pamphlets; numbers (11) to (15) refer to information, drawings, or suggestions of individuals; numbers (20) to (33) refer to products and materials and companies who have them available. See these references at the end of the chapter.

general survey and preliminary study

In developing a new area, there are a number of factors that warrant consideration in the preliminary study. If there is a choice of several sites, the final selection of a location may well depend upon the evaluation of the following factors:

1. Availability of the area
2. Size of the area
3. Topography of existing terrain
   a. Natural drainage of the area
   b. Amount of grading and fill necessary
   c. Soil of the area: foundation sub-soil and surface topsoil
      (See Section on Top Soils—Soil Analysis)
   d. Vegetation of area: condition and value of existing turf.
4. Location of area: desirable aspects for players and spectators as to:
   a. Accessibility
   b. Practicability
   c. Convenience
   d. Transportation
   e. Parking
   f. Safety
   g. Adaptability: multiple purpose consideration
5. Funds available
   a. Initial cost of area
   b. Cost of development
   c. Cost of maintenance
6. Orientation of playing field: with special consideration for the safety of players and the comfort of spectators.
7. Availability of utilities
   a. Water
   b. Electricity
   c. Sewage
   d. Drainage outlets
8. Time allotted for development
9. Adaptability of facility for immediate plans
10. Future possibilities of development

orientation of area

A study of the playing field as oriented by the compass is a *must*. There have been installations which spoiled the game because they were haphazardly, and wrongly oriented. A poor orientation may force playing, of at least a portion of the game, when the angle of the sun's rays is at a precarious position. This makes playing difficult and very dangerous. When a thrown or batted ball is coming toward a player at a speed of from 80 to 120 miles per hour, he needs help, not handicaps. It is poor planning to think first about the location of a parking lot and then have the diamond oriented in relation to it.

In most instances, the dangerous time is from late afternoon until sunset. This is the time when the azimuth angles of the setting sun are low on the horizon and more in line with the flight of the ball. The blob of brightness is even worse because of the diffusion and deflection of light coming through a dust- and moisture-laden atmosphere. First considerations should be: the time of the day the games are to be played; the season of the year; and the location of the sun at specific hours in the middle of the season. We know the sun moves, or rather the earth turns, 15 degrees in each hour; so a reasonable idea of the sun's location, at a given time, for the duration of the season can be determined.

Late afternoon games create a certain orientation problem, especially in spring and late fall. Games scheduled exclusively at twilight present a different problem. In these instances the problem is low angle rays of the afternoon sun. Games scheduled in the early afternoon, especially with daylight savings time, will create still another problem because the altitude rays of the sun will be nearly straight up. With these conditions, if the diamond is located in the southwest, all infielders and outfielders will be forced to wear sun glasses.

Besides the time of day and season of the year, primary consideration regarding the low rays of the setting sun must be given to:

Players: The hitter, catcher, pitcher, and other players must be protected and should rate top priority in that order. Obviously these positions are the most hazardous because they are involved in the greatest amount of action. When a pitcher is throwing a ball in the direction of the hitter and the catcher at speeds of 75 to 95 miles per hour, they cannot protect themselves looking into a blinding sun. And if the hitter hits a screaming line drive directly back at the pitcher, he needs protection also. Infielders and outfielders have a little more time to react: they need protection according to their relationship to the sun and in proportion to the amount of play in their position. When protecting players from the hazardous low rays of the sun, a general rule of thumb is to orient so that these rays intersect the long axis of the diamond (which is a line drawn through home plate, pitcher's box, second base, and into center field) at right angles.

Spectators: Naturally, spectators will enjoy the game more if they are sitting with their backs to the sun. It is obvious that they need consideration. It is, however, impossible to orient so as to give equal protection to all players and spectators. The rule book recommends only one orientation, that is, with home plate located west of southwest, with the line from home plate through the pitcher's box, second base to center field, running east of northeast. This recommendation is primarily for the spectators.

Other considerations:

1. *Parking lot:* should be given consideration as to accessibility, economy, and convenience, but not to the extent that it forces the game to be played under adverse orientation.

2. *Neighboring environment:* batted balls flying into a line of heavy traffic or congested housing areas should warrant consideration.

3. *Obstacles or natural barriers* could have an effect.

4. *Background for hitters* might well be a consideration if, for example, a building, beyond straightaway center field, reflected a lot of light.

5. *Winds:* prevailing local or seasonal.

6. *Daylight savings time* is not sun time, and it can change the angle of the sun's rays on a field at a given time.

There will be some variations in the angle of the sun at a given time from the extreme north to the deep south and also in the wide belt of a time zone. For example, the Central Standard Time Zone extends from the Ohio line to western Nebraska. In the deep south or in the eastern end of a time zone, it would be better to move the orientation more to the south or more to the north.

In summary, for the best protection to key personnel, and with consideration for the comfort of spectators, it is recommended:

1. Avoid orienting the apex of home plate in the east, southeast, northeast, or west.

2. For late afternoon games orient the apex of home plate 20 degrees south of southwest *or* 20 degrees north of northwest—preferably the latter.

3. For twilight schedule, orient apex of home plate 20 degrees east of north.

4. For very early afternoon games, with daylight time, orient 20 degrees north of northwest.

5. For a fall schedule, orient 20 degrees north of northwest.

6. For best all-around orientation (with geographic variation) for late afternoon, twilight, fall schedule, and very early afternoon games, 20 degrees north of northwest.

recommended field dimensions

Various classifications	Base distance	Pitcher's distance	LF & RF line	Center field	Area size in acres *
Little League	60 ft.	46 ft.	180 ft.	200 ft.	1¼
Pony League	75 ft.	54 ft.	250 ft.	300 ft.	2
Babe Ruth *or* Senior Little League	90 ft.	60 ft., 6 in.	300 ft.	335 ft.	3
High School, Junior Legion *or* Connie Mack	90 ft.	60 ft., 6 in.	310 ft.	360 ft.	3½
College *or* Non Pro	90 ft.	60 ft., 6 in.	335 ft.	400 ft.	4
Professional **	90 ft.	60 ft., 6 in.	335 ft.	400 ft.	4

* This represents the minimum square area in acres (one acre equals 43,680 sq. ft.) for playing area and foul territory. This does not include space needed for stands, storage, parking, etc.

** Represents minimum dimensions of professional diamonds by 1958 rule.

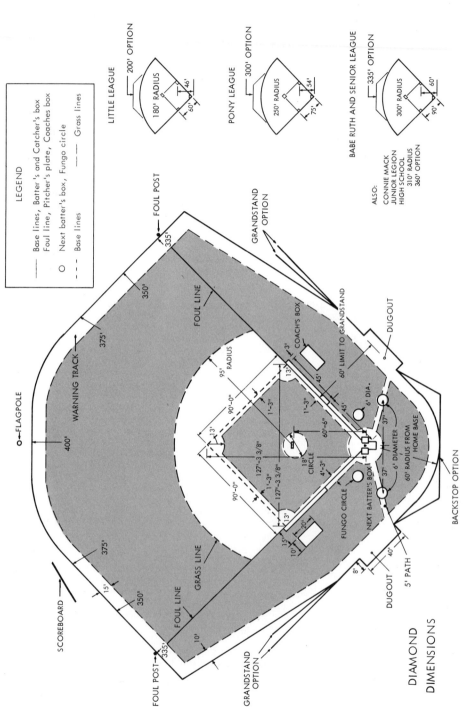

LEGEND

— Base lines, Batter's and Catcher's box
Foul line, Pitcher's plate, Coaches box

O Next batter's box, Fungo circle

— — — Base lines

——— Grass lines

LITTLE LEAGUE
200' OPTION
180' RADIUS
46'
60'

PONY LEAGUE
300' OPTION
250' RADIUS
54'
75'

BABE RUTH AND SENIOR LEAGUE
335' OPTION
300' RADIUS
60'
90'

ALSO:
CONNIE MACK
JUNIOR LEGION
HIGH SCHOOL
310' RADIUS
360' OPTION

FOUL POST
335'
350'
375'
400'
375'
350'
335'

FLAGPOLE

SCOREBOARD

WARNING TRACK

FOUL LINE

GRASS LINE

FOUL LINE

15'

10'

FOUL POST

GRANDSTAND OPTION

GRANDSTAND OPTION

60' LIMIT TO GRANDSTAND

COACH'S BOX

45'

45'

3'

13'

95' RADIUS

1'-3"

1'-3"

90'-0"

90'-0"

60'-6"

18" CIRCLE

6' DIA.

127'-3 3/8"

127'-3 3/8"

4'-3"

1'-3"

13'

6' DIAMETER

37'

37'

37'

6' RADIUS FROM HOME BASE

60' RADIUS FROM HOME BASE

FUNGO CIRCLE

NEXT BATTER'S BOX

15'

10'

20'

BACKSTOP OPTION

DUGOUT

DUGOUT

5' PATH

40'

8'

DIAMOND
DIMENSIONS

figure 85

A few additional dimensions for Little League (L.L.) and Pony League (P.L.):

	L.L.	P.L.
Mound elevation above home plate	6 in.	10 in.
Batter's box	3 ft. × 5½ ft.	4 ft. × 6 ft.
Coaches' box	4 ft. × 8 ft.	8 ft. × 16 ft.
	(6 ft. from base line)	(10 ft. from base line)
Distance from home plate to backstop	(20 ft. minimum)	(40 ft. minimum)

Little League, Pony League, Babe Ruth and Senior Little League list only one distance down the line with optional but preferred distances in straightaway center field. In a large, enclosed park, there will be fewer home runs; however, there will be more exciting doubles and triples with

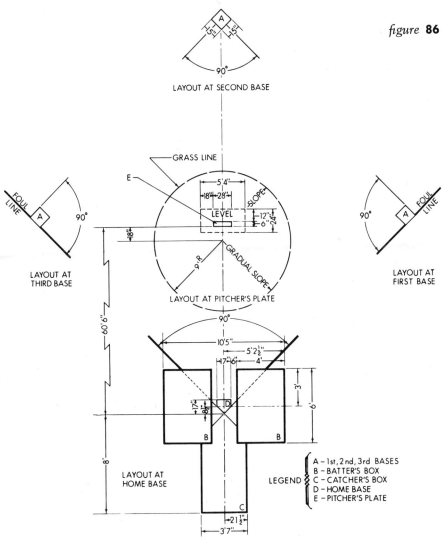

figure **86**

LAYOUT AT SECOND BASE

GRASS LINE

LAYOUT AT THIRD BASE

LAYOUT AT FIRST BASE

LAYOUT AT PITCHER'S PLATE

LAYOUT AT HOME BASE

LEGEND
A – 1st, 2nd, 3rd BASES
B – BATTER'S BOX
C – CATCHER'S BOX
D – HOME BASE
E – PITCHER'S PLATE

all players getting into the action. In a small park there are too many cheap "Chinese" home runs. They are not a true evaluation of skill or power, and defensive action is eliminated.

The sizes of the specific areas of a full sized playing field are approximately:

Infield grass area	7,000 sq. ft.
Skinned portion, including base paths, mound, and home plate area	8,500 sq. ft.
Outfield	95,000 sq. ft.
Total playing area in fair territory	112,000 sq. ft.
Sideline—foul territory	36,000 sq. ft.
Total playing area—fair and foul	146,000 sq. ft.

See Figure 85 for Diamond Dimensions; Figure 86 for Dimensions (legend of mound, bases, and home plate area).

safety precautions and suggestions

1. Proper orientation: protect players and spectators in hazardous positions from looking into the sun.

2. Playing area: obstruction free—level ground without gopher holes.

3. Soil: firm, but a loose top with enough give to prevent catching spikes when sliding.

4. Warning track or reverse slop to warn an outfielder of his approach to the fence.

5. Home plate with a beveled edge, flush with the ground.

6. Mound: flat top with gradual slope in all directions. Firm footing where the pitcher's stride hits the ground.

7. Water outlets in ground protected by flush board or covered with rubber or fiber mat.

8. Fences
    a. Fence posts anchored to fence on outside of playing area and below top of fence.
    b. Round smooth pipe on top of fence—no sharp ends of wire exposed. An 8 ft. high fence is recommended.
    c. Fence that will curl—stapled to creosoted board (2 ft. × 10 in.).
    d. Fences painted first with aluminum paint or rustoleum then dark green to avoid glare and reflection for players and spectators. (This applies especially to center field and the backstop for a better background.)

9. Dug-outs
    a. Four foot fence in front for player protection and to keep balls in play. This is not necessary but advisable.
    b. Heavy roofing material glued to concrete floor and steps.
    c. High enough to avoid bumping head.

10. Light towers, poles, foul line markers, score boards, and flag poles located outside of playing area.

11. Bull pens located preferably outside playing area, and, if possible, oriented in the same direction as the diamond.

12. Batting practice safety.
    a. Deep tunnel cage for protection and to save balls.
    b. Barricades in front of pitcher, first baseman, and back of second base for ball rustler.
    c. Fungo circles back of the front edge of tunnel cage to be out of line of batted balls.

13. Tarpaulins used over pitchers mound and home plate area will give insurance for good footing in these two hazardous positions.

14. Drinking fountain: curved outlet so water will come out in an arc for sanitation, and for tooth protection. Have a step-up to fountain for smaller children.

15. Bleachers
    a. Guard rail around top and at ends of sections.
    b. Written certification of inspection of bleacher construction from a qualified person as exoneration from gross negligence.

16. Blanket insurance against liability may be practical and/or necessary protection.

development of a low cost economy field

Many of the baseball diamonds in this country were laid out on any available plot and literally just "growed" from that beginning. Perhaps some who read this may be initiated into a problem similar to the following example:

The High School Superintendent calls in his baseball coach to inform him that the Board acquired a certain plot of ground. They want him to develop the best baseball diamond possible but to be mindful that the funds are definitely limited.

From the start, it will be obvious that it will not be possible to have a development as pretentious as a major league park. But let us hope that you might be lucky—that your newly acquired area has a well established turf, and that the area where you wish to orient the infield is the highest ground with natural drainage away from that area. This stroke of luck could make the job easier and at the same time allow staying within the limits of a narrow budget.

For this simple development, locate home plate, bases, fence lines, backstop with masons' cord, establish and lime-mark all grasslines, boxes, arcs and circles that divide grass from skinned portions of the infield baselines, home plate area, and mound. Sell the sod to a contractor and have him cut the sod within the confines of your lines. Roto-till the soil in these skinned areas and add the desired and necessary amendments plus enough fill soil to bring the soil up to the level of the sod. Cut all edges straight with an edge cutter. Remeasure the area and carefully locate home plate, pitcher's plate, base anchors and foul line markers. Build the mound with heavier soil (clay-loam), and contour it on a gradual slope to proper elevation. Put up the backstop, fences, scoreboard, and distance markers. Build the dug-outs or ground level shelter benches. You are now in business.

If the terrain and topography of an acquired site is rough uneven ground and is essentially a weed patch, you have a problem that is entirely different and definitely more complicated. Just marking out a diamond as in the over-simplified example described above, will never be satisfactory. There will naturally be problems that will require more planning, work, and money. Study the information in the rest of this chapter for assistance in selecting and adapting the improvements necessary to remedy the immediate situation and still stay within a limited budget.

drainage and grade elevations

Before getting into the details of laying out a field, it is necessary to have an appreciation of the importance of adequate drainage—both surface and sub-surface.

In baseball one must contend with the elements. It is desirable and necessary to have a field playable as soon as possible after a rain and also in the early spring. A field that is laid out on flat land and has heavy, impervious soil may be useless for days after an ordinary rainfall.

Good drainage should insure getting rid of rainwater hastily by surface run-off, percolating through the soil, or through sub-soil tiling. The ideal field should be a *crowned* or *turtlebacked* area that has a gradual slope of 1 per cent (one foot per 100 ft.) in every direction, from the edge of the grass circle around the pitcher's mound to the limits of the entire playing area (including foul territory).

The field should be constructed to withstand heavy traffic. Poor drainage means more compaction; more compaction means shallow roots and poor turf. Good drainage and good soil structure of the infield area (especially the skinned portion) is most important. A well established turf in the outfield, regardless of grade, will absorb a tremendous amount of water.

The rule book states, "The infield should be graded with a gradual slope from the baselines to the pitcher's plate, which shall be 15 in. above the base line level." (The intent of the rule is 15 in. elevation above home plate—not the baseline.) This gives a grade elevation of slightly under 3 per cent. According to agronomists and turf managers, 1 per cent grade is sufficient and 3 per cent is too much. The rapid run-off would make it difficult to maintain a good turf, and most of the water would run onto the skinned portion which is the most important area to keep dry. Furthermore, that much grade would make it difficult for a player to keep a well placed bunted ball from rolling foul.

Many baseball men have the mistaken belief that the skinned portion should be flat and have no grade. They probably get this idea because the rule book states that the "baselines and home plate area should be level." These are areas that need surface drainage the most. Because of the heavy use and blowage, the center of the base paths have a tendency to become "dished" and hold surface water. If the 1 per cent grade is carried through, there would be only a ½ in. drop on the baselines and a 1 in. drop behind home plate. No one can tell these minute differences, and surface drainage can be improved with this grade.

Actually our concern of infield grade is far from the edge of the grass circle around the mound to various points on the infield. However, to make the work easier for the grader, establish a point 59 ft. from the apex of home plate towards pitcher's mound and set a stake with an elevation mark of 7 in. above home plate. (This spot is 18 in. in front of the pitcher's plate and it is from here that the 9 ft. circle is scribed for the mound area. Be mindful also that 8 in. of soil will be added later to bring the mound up to regulation height.) From this 7 in. elevated point, start a gradual slope of 1 per cent grade in all directions to the limits of the playing area—including the sidelines to the dug-outs and the backstop. This grade should include the skinned portion (where the grade may be reduced a little), base lines and home plate area. The drop in elevation (from the future mound circle) to home plate will be 6 in.; to the first and third baseline, 4½ in.; to the second and third baseline, 5 in.; and to the edge of the outfield grass, 9-10 in. Some fields have been constructed with an additional 2 to 3 in. grade in the first 15 ft. outside of the baselines and back of the skinned portion of the infield. This should speed drainage from the diamond, including the run-off from the tarpaulin. However, some groundkeepers feel that this isn't necessary if the grade of 1 per cent is true and if there is not a pronounced ridge at the edge of the grass built up by blowage and overdrag.

The drop in elevation from the sidelines to the limits of the dug-out and the backstop will be 7 to 8 in.

If the grade of 1 per cent (some use 1 in. for every 10 ft. on outfield turf) was carried from the *edge of the grass behind the skinned area* to the perimeter of the outfield on a full sized field, there would be an additional drop in grade from 20 in. to 23 in. down the line and from 25 in. to 30 in. in deep center field. This sounds like quite a lot; however, it is barely discernible to the naked eye. Some outfields have used the 1 per cent grade to a point 25 ft. from the fences and then reversed the grade the last 25 ft. with a steeper 3 to 5 in. rise. This would require a fairly shallow tile system to carry off water from the trench created by this change of grade. This reverse slope does have a safety feature in that the outfielder will be forewarned when he is approaching the fence. It also gives opportunity to use excess soil that otherwise may need to be hauled away. (See Figure 87 on grading elevations and tiling.)

bid specifications (5)*

From the preliminary study and items listed in the following section, it is necessary to arrive at information and data to incorporate into bid specifications for contractual purposes.

Plot the area and record all data and specific information. With these findings, plus detailed information set forth in subsequent sections of this chapter, study, make estimates, draw plans and blueprints to include all the details of the project. These will include:

1. Materials: kind, type, size, variety, quality, rates, and amounts.
2. Methods of: procedure, handling, application, and installation.
3. Specification clauses regarding: appropriate time schedule, maintenance and repair, accepted standards guarantee, completion schedule, penalty clauses, and provisions for payment.

suggested order of planning and construction procedure

1. Survey the area. Secure the services of a qualified surveyor. (He has the necessary equipment to do a faster, more accurate, and professional job.) Decide where to orient home plate. This will be the point of reference directly or indirectly for all other measurements. Run distance hubs to establish location of bases, foul lines, fences, backstops, dug-outs, light towers, and any other appointments.

2. Run elevation and grade lines. This data should give information for fill soil requirements, irrigation, tiling and sewer systems. If a lot of grading and filling is necessary and the available top soil is usable, scoop it up and stockpile it on the side for later replacement. Top soil is at a premium the world over.

3. Have soil analysis made from fresh samples taken from different locations in the area.

4. Roto-till hard pan, sub-surface soil.

5. Install irrigation system and outlets.

6. Excavate and pour concrete footings for light towers, dug-outs, stands, and locker room.

7. Install the tile system—drain outlets, sewer lines.

* See references at end of chapter.

GRADE ELEVATIONS
AND
PRIMARY TILE SYSTEM

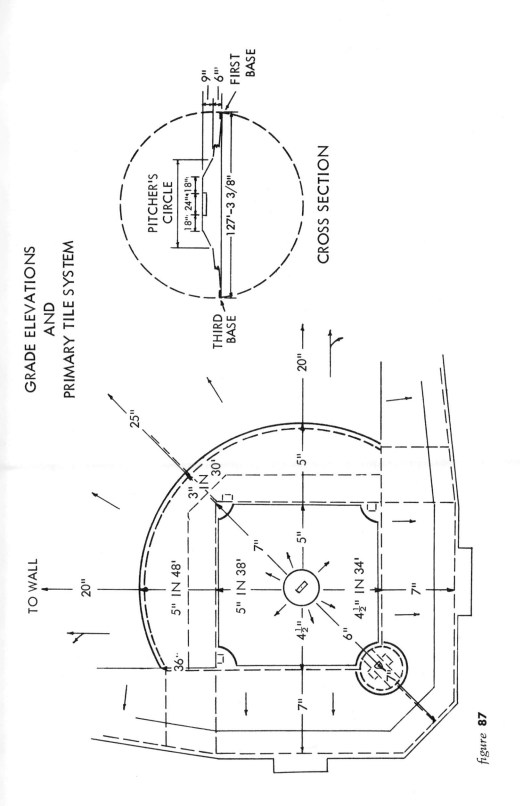

PITCHER'S CIRCLE

9″
6‴
FIRST BASE

8″ 24″ 18″

127′-3 3/8″

THIRD BASE

CROSS SECTION

TO WALL

20″

25″

3″ IN 30″

5″ IN 48′

5″ IN 38′

4½″ IN 34′

5″

5″

7″

4½″

6″

7″

7″

7″

20″

36″

figure 87

8. Install electric lines, cables, outlets to light towers, dug-outs, and stands.

9. Bring in rough fill (crushed rock or cinders) where necessary to meet grade.

10. Lay out stabilized areas—haul in aggregate for warning track, paths to home plate, in front of dug-outs, coaches' box, on deck, and fungo circles.

11. Replace and prepare top soil—from soil analysis formula, mix in soil structure amendments (sand, calcinated clay (21), peat moss, Aqua-Gro (25)), fertilizers, lime, and insecticides as needed.

12. Sterilize soil—to kill weed seeds, insects, and pests with herbicide (Sodium Arsenite)—if deemed necessary.

13. Roto-till the soil for uniform and thorough mixing. At the same time remove foreign material such as rocks, roots, etc.

14. Rework the area to grade elevations with a York Rake (33) or other acceptable grading equipment. Recheck grade elevations with surveyor's transit. Correct any faulty grade, pockets, or soft spots.

15. Roll area to firm the soil.

16. Install backstop, fences, scoreboard, flag pole, and foul line markers.

17. Build pitcher's mound, bull pen, catcher's and hitter's box with heavier clay-loam soil.

18. Broadcast starter fertilizer (Milorganite-processed sewage sludge) and shallow mix it into the soil to a depth of ½ to 1 in.

19. Finish grade using wooden tined rakes.

20. Remeasure diamond and recheck grade elevations carefully. Set home plate, pitcher's box, and base anchors. Mark all grasslines, circles, arcs, and boxes with chalk or lime to know exactly when and where not to plant.

21. Plant area (seed, vegetatively, or sod), roll lightly, mulch seed or top dress sod, and water regularly.

22. Finish construction and installation of dug-outs, light towers, stands, locker rooms, showers, toilets, storage space, concessions, and parking lots.

irrigation system

The first installation in a new area will be the irrigation system. It will require the deepest digging in that the pipelines must be laid below the frostline. The exact depth will vary with local environment. In central Iowa, five feet is the minimum depth. Be sure that the installation is adequate to supply plenty of water under the most severe heat and drought conditions. The capacity of the system will depend on a number of factors, such as pipe, size of main and secondary lines, water pressure, friction loss, and the water used in showers and rest rooms.

Main lines will be 3 to 6 in. cast iron for permanency. The tubing for auxiliary lead lines should be 1½ to 2 in.—preferably the latter. Copper pipe is being replaced by plastic tubing and a new product trade named "Transite" (31). Tubing made of these materials is cheaper in cost, less expensive to install, suffers less friction loss, and appears to be chemically resistant to all types of soil.

Outlets should be conveniently placed—usually around the perimeter of the area in back of first, third, home, and along the fence line. An outlet back of second and the pitcher's box is an added convenience. There will be other outlets to drinking fountains, showers, toilets, and concessions. Surface outlets should be equipped with frost-proof hydrants and sub-surface outlets equipped with stop and waste valves to prevent frost damage. Several square feet of coarse gravel should be placed below the drain valve at the base of the ditch.

The most common sprinkling system is hose with "rain bird" type sprinklers. At first glance this looks most economical. If, however, you must water extensively, it takes a lot of hose, time, and labor to soak an area of 145,000 sq. ft. Traveling sprinklers are used quite extensively especially in the outfield areas. Pop-up sprinklers have not proven satisfactory and are no longer recommended. The most costly system to install is an automatic system; however, it may be cheaper in the long run in labor saving and convenience. This system is installed with four lines set up to be independently operated by a timing device in a central control panel. Each line is activated electrically and has a separate cable that is trenched about 10 in. deep. Because of operating difficulties, the hydraulic type is not recommended. There are different sized sprinklers available which are interchangeable. The outlets should be rubber covered for safety.

tiling system

The purpose of tiling is to drain rain water from the playing field as quickly as possible. Anyone promoting the game is concerned about playing the contest at the scheduled time. It is obvious that tiling the area will cost some additional construction money, but when tiling is necessary, the money is well spent.

The need and extensiveness of the tiling will be dependent upon the nature of the soil (sub-surface and surface) and the funds available. If the sub-surface is heavy, impervious, and a plastic soil (such as northern clay), it will lack the permeability for natural drainage. This problem will be compounded if the surface soil is compacted and lacks porosity.

Tiling plans should be drawn in accordance with information gathered from: surveyor's elevation stakes, surface grading, and direction of natural water shed of area, including catch basins and sewer outlets to carry water away from the playing field in a manner conforming with the local condition. Plans have been drawn of some fancy tiling systems—parallel, circular, and very comprehensive square—all with herringbone laterals. However, these elaborate systems disregard some basic principles and some inadequacies of draining primary areas—the skinned portion and baselines of the infield in particular.

Primary system. This should be a tile system to expedite drainage of the skinned portion of the infield, the base paths, and the catcher's and hitter's box at the home plate area. A good infield and outfield turf will absorb and hold a great deal of water. If the area is at all playable, games are not held up because of the turf area but because of the wet and slippery skinned portions. A well-conceived tile system in the infield is money well spent. As a principle, the tile should be laid in shallow trenches (18 in.) from the surface), and the trench should be wider at such vital spots as the catcher's box, the hitter's box, and the side of each base that gets most play. Furthermore, the tile should be laid at right angles to the direction of flow from the surface grading.

The primary tile line should follow the base lines all around the infield and include the batter's and catcher's box. The lowest point of the infield will be at the edge of the outfield grass. This is the place where one often finds a wind blown ridge that prevents good surface drainage. This is a logical place for a shallow circular tile line. A 4 in. tile 18 in. deep will draw moisture from approximately 15 ft. The distance from the baseline tile to the edge of the outfield grass is roughly 50 ft. Therefore, a parallel line halfway between the baseline and edge of the outfield grass is needed. If the extremity of the outfield is graded with a reverse slope, a tile line through the formed water retaining trench would of necessity be a primary line (see Figure 87).

Secondary system. Could include in the following order:

1. A line at or near the low grade limits of the sidelines in foul territory past the backstop and connected with each dug-out, or at least connecting the dug-outs with the run-off mains from the infield.

2. A line approximately 20 ft. back of the skinned portion of the infield and parallel lines 20 ft. outside the first and third baselines. These lines could be of special help to handle the run-off from a water-laden tarpaulin.

3. Additional herringbone laterals in the infield, or sump drains.

4. Sump drains in the infield. The Boston Red Sox are reported to have many of these in their infield. They dug 200 holes (in a staggered pattern) 3 ft. deep and 8 in. in diameter with a mechanical post hole digger. These holes were filled with crushed rock, covered with untreated building paper, and then the top soil, which had been quite heavily amended with granulated calcinated clay, was replaced.

5. Additional lines in the outfield laid at right angles to the grade and about 40 ft. apart.

tiling details

1. Power machines for trench digging are faster, more efficient, and more economical than hand-dug trenches. Some machines are made with a hydraulic sighting device for holding to a specified grade.

2. Depth and grade direction of tile will depend upon soil percolation test, surveyor's elevation stakes, surrounding natural water shed, and sewer outlets. Some tiling men used to have a concern about tile depth and the frost line. This should be no problem if the trench has the proper grade elevation for complete drainage. Keep tile depth as shallow as possible.

3. The size of the tile will graduate from 4 in. laterals to 6-8 or 10 in. mains depending on how many laterals run into them. Large mains should be tight fitting, bell tile and should drain into catch basins, manholes, or sewer outlets. Catch basins are vitrified tile with a grating top and open gravel-filled bottom.

4. Elevation of tile should be on a grade. Water doesn't run uphill. As a rule of thumb the *minimum* grade should be 0.1 of 1 per cent (always referred to in tenths) or 1.2 inches drop in every 100 ft. A 4 in. tile with a 0.15 per cent grade will allow for a flowage velocity of 0.8 cu. ft. per second. Generally allowance should be made for slightly more grade with small tile if the soil is quite sandy.

two methods of laying tile

Conventional method: Clay drain tile was laid in the bottom of the trench with space between each joint. To prevent soil particles from clogging the tile system, each joint was covered with a piece of copper screen. The screen was cut in squares equal to one-half the circumference of the tile; for example, a 4 in. tile had a 6 in. square of screen, and for a 6 in. tile a 9 in. square was used. These squares of screen were secured by wiring around the tile so that the screen covered the joint and extended over the end of the next tile. It can readily be seen that this is slow, costly handwork. The trenches were then back-filled, around and above the tile, with pea gravel or crushed stone. (Caution: limestone should not be used because enough of it will dissolve and cause clogging.) The amount of backfill will depend on tile size—12 in. deep for a 4 in. tile, 14 in. deep for a 6 in. tile, and 16 in. deep for an 8 in. tile. The backfill is covered with a strip of untreated building paper cut to the width of the trench. This paper will rot out in a couple of years, but by that time, the soil will have settled and have enough natural compaction to prevent small particles of soil from filling in extensively around the backfill and tile joints.

New method: Very recently a method using more modern materials has been successful. Instead of short clay tile, long perforated plastic pipe is being used; instead of wiring on squares of copper screen by hand, the full length of the plastic pipe and the joints are being covered with fiberglass mesh (31) from a continuous roll of the material. The fiberglass mesh will allow moisture to go through, but filters out the silt. These materials are more expensive. However, time and labor saved may offset the extra cost. Backfill the trench with pea gravel or crushed rock and cover with untreated building paper as described in the first method. The tiling engineer consulted by the author had never substituted fiberglass mesh for untreated building paper to cover backfill, but he could see no reason why it wouldn't be an excellent cover if the width was the same as the trench.

sub-surface fill soil

Material for sub-surface fill in the low areas should be a coarse aggregate of crushed rock, crushed brick, cinders, steel mill slag, or similar material. This gives assurance of sub-surface drainage through this porous material. This coarse material, rolled in, could also give a good sub-surface base for warning track, coach's box, path to plate, and area in front of dug-outs. Use a finished aggregate of desired material for the top 2 or 3 inches.

top soil

Agronomists describe good top soil as a sandy loam that is fertile, friable (will crumble with finger pressure), of good granular structure, well-aerated, and with high infiltration qualities of porosity and permeability insuring easy drainage. They further explain that the structure of soil is made up of solids, liquids, and gases. There should be enough solid particles to guarantee a firm solid footing when a foot is jammed down at a sharp angle, and enough space in between the solid particles for air movement and water percolation and retention. Too many fine solid particles (clay and silt), especially when subjected to a lot of traffic, rain, and heavy equipment, become squeezed together (compacted) and thereby reduce movement of air and water through the soil. Too much sand, or other inert granular particles, produces a loose structure and does not have sufficient binding qualities for good footing.

It is unlikely that the local soil will measure up to the agronomists' definition of the ideal. It is gratifying to know, however, that even soil too heavy with clay or silt or too sandy and granular can be remedied and improved. Economy usually dictates that the existing local soil be used and "doctored" for suitability.

Soil analysis. The answer now rests with agronomists' soil analysis. They can test for granular structure, rate of water percolation, and retention ability, and study the compaction ratio. From these results they can, within limits, prescribe a formula of soil amendments for improvement of its structure.

In soil analysis they also test for nitrogen, potassium, phosphorus and lime. They can set forth an accurate formula for the necessary fertilization.

A number of years ago we collaborated with an agronomist from our university in making a mechanical aggregate analysis of soil being used in baseball diamonds. The reason for the study was the lack of specific information or recommendations on preferred soil structure. It was obvious that the usual soils were used by trial and error or "by guess and by gorry." The purpose then was to get a more scientific approach to the subject.

Soil samples were secured from the skinned portions of infields and the mounds of the recommended best diamonds in each of the eight NCAA geographical districts, and from the best major league diamonds as recommended by top players at that time. We received quite a variety of soils—from very sandy to varying kinds of clay, silt, and adobe. The analysis and evaluation were done by Dr. B. J. Firkins by using the Bouyoucas Hydrometer Method. We realized the study had its limitations: that not enough samples were analyzed, and no comparison was made between the soils of the "best" and the "worse" or "worst." However, we felt that we could draw some reasonably accurate conclusions. These are as follows:

1. It is impossible to determine an exact formula to fit different soils in all areas of the country. Dr. Firkins felt that the soil should be of a fertile, friable, loamy nature, and consist of approximately 65-75 per cent sand and 25-30 per cent combined silt and clay (of approximately even proportions).

2. Good soil structure is necessary for satisfactory results of drainage and maintenance.

3. "Know how" and constant good maintenance are vital. One major league infielder commented as follows on a certain field, "Two years ago it was the best in the majors; this year it is the worst." Surely the soil structure didn't change that much.

4. Suggested procedure to remedy overbalanced soil:
   a. Too much silt and heavy clay: compacts easily, doesn't drain well. Sand content can be raised and the composition lightened by approximately 10 per cent by adding 3 cu. yds. of washed mason's sand per 1000 sq. ft.
   b. If the existing soil is too sandy—too loose, blowy, has poor compaction and footing—the binding qualities can be raised 10 per cent by adding 3 cu. yds. of silt and ground plastic clay per 1000 sq. ft. (Note: there is a wide variance in the composition of soils in the same broad classification in different localities. For example, clay is clay to most people; however, southern

red clay (Kaolinite) has a great deal of sand and iron oxide (color) and is not plastic; yellow northern clay (Montmorlinite) has very little sand, is very plastic (that is, it shrinks and swells), is very hard when dry and is very greasy when wet.)

5. There is sufficient evidence to prove that soil testing is superior to existing guessing methods. The agronomist can determine percentages of materials, percolation rate, and compaction ratio and can recommend a formula of certain amendments that can be added to improve and remedy the soil structure. Some of these amendments are new and as yet haven't stood the test of time; however, present indications are favorable and exciting.

soil amendments effective in reducing compaction

Sand. Should be washed sharp mason's sand with a sieve analysis as an indication of particle size range. It is currently believed that a minimum range of particle sizes with less than 10 per cent passing through a #50 sieve is most desirable. A majority of the particles should be approximately ½ millimeter size range (pass through a #20 mesh sieve, be retained in a #35 mesh sieve) (1). (Note: Do not add too fine sand. When fine sand is mixed with silt or clay, it will become concrete-like, actually defeating the purpose and giving more compaction instead of less.)

Peat moss. Raw or cultivated reed sedge or sphagnum moss has a high moisture absorption capacity, providing a cushioning effect between soil particles, and helping to granulate the soil as it decomposes. Use 1 to 2 cubic yards per 1000 square feet. It is seldom necessary to apply at rates over 10 per cent volume. When peat and sand are added at "on-sight" mixing, the peat should be spread first with the heavier sand on top to facilitate good mixing. (Note: Do not use sedimentary peats. They usually contain high percentages of mineral and colloidal matter which causes them to compact, thereby defeating the purpose.) In the skinned area, eliminate peat and add more sand and calcined clay to the composition.

Other organic materials. Raw sewage sludge (dry), granulated seed hulls, and tannery waste material can be used, but they decompose much faster than peat moss. Sawdust (preferably redwood) decomposes quite slowly. Apply at the same rate as peat moss. Some turf men think sawdust is not desirable because it holds too much water.

Calcined clay (21). A relatively new inorganic product on the market which is being extensively used to improve soil structure and avoid compaction. Chemically Aluminum Silicate, it is baked (like pottery) and granulated. It is quite resistant to decomposition and has a tremendous water retention capacity with some claims up to 140% to 160% of its own weight of water.

The Boston Red Sox have undertaken an all out experiment, and it will be interesting to wait and observe the results. They have loaded their infield with this product—3 lbs. per sq. ft. or 1 in. depth, adding up to 1½ tons per 1000 sq. ft. This is roto-tilled to a 4 in. depth making it a 25 per cent mixture at that depth. They added a shallow tile system and 200 staggered sump drains, 10 in. in diameter and 3 ft. deep, filled ⅔ full with crushed rock (see Tiling, Secondary System). They hope to be able to discard the tarpaulin. They scarified the mound and home plate area than added equal parts of calcined clay and red stone dust for binding. To darken the color they used a fine spray of Gulf Oil Company's Sani-Soil-Set (28).

On the St. Louis Cardinals' new field, now under construction, the plan is to use a mixture as follows: sand (45 per cent), calcined clay (25 per cent), soil (10 per cent), and peat moss (20 per cent). Turf specialists comment on this mixture: "Sounds like a golf green." "Not enough binding soil." "Too much peat moss." It will be interesting to follow the results of this soil mixture.

Some companies recommend three to five 50 lb. bags of calcined clay (21) per 1000 sq. ft. Apply evenly with a spreader and roto-till thoroughly. When used on grassed areas, golf greens, football fields, or turfed infield, aerify from several directions, spread calcined clay evenly, and drag with a steel mat.

Because of its moisture-absorbing ability, calcined clay is often used for hurried emergency drying of wet spots before a game. A few bags carefully spread can bring satisfying results.

Calcined clay is available from different companies under the following trade names: Diamond Grit, Lusoil, Prep, Terra Green, and Turface (21). Calcined Clay now comes in various sized granules for specific jobs: sand-like granules for the skinned area and coarser granules for turf.

Chemical soil conditioners. These are also new to the market. Non-ionic wetting agents when sprayed on will attach to the soil particles; they help to prevent compaction and "grease" the soil particles, so to speak, by lowering surface tension for greater percolation of water. The effectiveness is not permanent. After an early spring application of 8 oz. per 1000 sq. ft., periodic applications of 5 oz. per 1000 sq. ft. seem to be most effective. Incidentally, the blades of grass sprayed with this product at the rate of 2 to 3 oz. per 1000 sq. ft. will have a lower surface tension so that dew will not stay on the blade itself. An application could be effective from 3 to 6 days under favorable weather conditions. The trade names for these products are: Aqua-Gro. All-Wet, Dialoam and Turf-Tonic (25). The chemical Calcium Chloride has been used to hold moisture and prevent blowage. Its value is debatable because a rain will destroy its effectiveness, and it is destructive to the grass and leather of baseball shoes.

All amendments must be thoroughly and uniformly mixed in the soil to the required depth. Roto-till or roto-plow and disc several times. Check periodically as to uniformity of the mix. The fertilizers (pellets with slow availability), lime, and insecticide (DDT or chlordane), as prescribed by formula from the soil analysis, should be added and mixed into the soil at the same time as the amendments above. If the soil and amendments are prepared off the site and hauled in, they are usually run through a royer for mixing, shredding, and screening out of foreign material. This is expensive because of the hand labor involved. A rule of thumb to follow for the amount of top soil needed is 3 to 3½ cubic yards for each inch of depth per 1000 sq. ft. This is approximately 20 cubic yards for 6 in. depth per 1000 sq. ft. and a bit more may need to be allowed for settling. Be sure to stockpile some of the mixture to fill and top dress low spots, pockets, and lines that will settle over tile.

After thoroughly mixing the soil, grade to elevation stakes with "York rake" (33), and rerun the grade lines with a surveyor's transit. Be sure there are no pockets or soft spots; then firm the soil with the roller.

Make an application of organic starter fertilizer (Milorganite 6-4.2-0) and work it into soil with light tilling to the depth of ½ to 1 in. Hand rake the area to grade (wood tined rakes recommended).

chemical sterilization of the soil

It is desirable to establish a firm, dense turf of selected grasses with as little competition as possible from noxious weeds, other grasses, diseases, and turf pests. It is very likely that the top soil mixture, in the area intended for seeding, could be loaded with weed seeds that are not visible to the naked eye. Or reconstruction may be necessary because the turf in the established area is very poor and has been taken over by weeds, unwanted grasses, and disease. The solution now is the "scorched earth treatment" (6)—kill everything and start from scratch.

The following methods have been used:

1. Dowfume O: a method whereby gas is blown under a plastic covered area. This method is thorough, but it is expensive and dangerous to handle. It has one advantage, however, in that the poisonous fumes will dissipate quite readily when uncovered, and the area can be reseeded in three to five days.

2. Aerocyanamide: a granular method. The granules are put on with a spreader and require a great deal of moisture to take effect deep into the soil. It will require at least two weeks before seeding can be done.

3. Vapam is a liquid spray method. This chemical is mixed with water and sprayed on the area. Three weeks will be required before the chemical dissipates sufficiently to start planting.

4. Sodium Arsenite is also a liquid spray method. Use 12 oz. actual

sodium arsenite mixed with five gallons of water per 1000 sq. ft. Reseeding can be started in 7 to 10 days, preferably the latter, to be sure. It must be remembered that these chemicals kill all vegetation, not only weed seeds. Spraying should be done on a calm day to control vapor drift. Do not spray too close to an area or the line of grass to be saved. An assistant using a large movable cardboard barricade can be of help in preventing this drift. We have used the Sodium Arsenite treatment effectively in the limestone aggregate paths to home plate area, in establishing foul lines, the outfield, and at the base of the backstop and fences. If there are some tough, stubborn weeds on the outfield warning track, this treatment could help.

mounds

Coaches and managers will claim that pitching is from 70 per cent to 90 per cent of the defense. If pitching is given that much importance, then definitely more attention should be given to the standardization of mounds. Existing inconsistencies should be guarded against. Many mounds are built like shallow cones, that is, up to a peak. There is no flatness at the top and the slope is too abrupt. When a pitcher is not accustomed to that particular mound, he is at a distinct disadvantage in holding his balance.

Measure exactly 60 ft. 6 in. from the apex of home plate and drive a stake. From the top of home plate run a grade elevation of 15 in. and mark it on the stake. The mound area should be built on a nine ft. radius starting from a point 18 in. in front of the rubber. The circumference of the circle will be 18 ft. with 10½ ft. in front and 7½ ft. behind the front of the rubber.

The top portion of the mound should be a flat alley 5 ft. wide, that is, 30 in. on each side of the stake, 24 in. in front of the stake and 18 in. behind the stake. Fill in heavier clay loam soil, packing and tamping as you progress up to the grade elevation on the stake. From the flat alley, contour evenly and gradually to the perimeter of the mound circle. George Toma (15) suggested an extension of the flat portion behind the rubber an extra foot so the pitcher doesn't have to stand like a "mountain goat" through 120 pitches per game. He also suggests starting the slight contour from in front of the rubber because some pitchers catch their spikes on the flat alley. It would also be practical to pack the mound soil up to ½ inch below the front edge of the rubber instead of flush with the top. Pitchers need that front edge to push off, and if the mound soil is flush they will inadvertently dig it out with their spikes.

Mound soils should be such that the pitcher's spikes will hold firm and then come out clean. The soil in front of the rubber and where the stride foot lands is subjected to extreme wear. This requires a clay loam which is approximately 40 per cent clay, 20 per cent silt and 40 per cent sand. In the upper Midwest, yellow clay is too plastic. It gets very hard when dry and greasy when wet. Remedy regular soil by adding unbaked brick clay (which should be kept slightly damp) and tamp it in the heavy wear spots of the mound, batter's box, and catcher's box. Charlie Mahar at Western Michigan keeps blue clay (heavy, tough, plastic clay) moist in 2 ft. $\times$ 2 ft. frames so that he can dig out and replace worn out spots in front of the rubber and where the stride foot lands. Tom Swayse at Mississippi University uses a non-plastic gray clay, which, after leveling, tamping and watering, he covers with burlap to hold the moisture. If the mound clay is too hard and compacted, cut in some calcined clay, burnt moulders sand, or limestone screenings the size of sharp sand. This will flocculate—form granules that will prevent overcompaction or excessive hardness. Do not add fine sand; this will only make your problem worse.

The pitcher's rubber should be put in place by using a carpenter's square to get it at an exact right angle to the home plate. Jack Baer of Oklahoma University suggests the following method of anchoring the pitcher's rubber on a wooden form. Nail a 2 in. $\times$ 6 in. board on the back edge of a two ft. length of 2 in. $\times$ 12 in. board, then drill holes through the two pieces of plank to coincide with the spikes on the rubber. After the rubber is in place, nail the edges to the 2 in. $\times$ 6 in. board with grooved nails of shingle nail size. An added advantage is to nail a worn out rubber on the 2 in. $\times$ 12 in. immediately in front of the 2 in. $\times$ 6 in. The toe plate is solidly anchored and the hole in front will never get overly deep (see Figure 88).

Clark Whited of the State University of New York anchors the pitcher's toe plate and home plate in concrete. He fills a form (built to dimensions) just below ground level, with concrete, and before it sets, pushes the spikes of the toe plate or home plate into exact place. He then removes the plate while the concrete sets up. Before replacing the plate he greases its spikes, making it easy to put in and take out. We have never used this, but it has its good points.

The bull pen mounds should be constructed the same way as suggested above and, if possible, should be oriented in the same direction.

A bare soil mound area with an elevation of 9 in. in a 9 ft. radius gives an 8 per cent grade and is bound to show erosion. Stockpile extra mound soil to replenish what is worn away. (See section on *Maintenance* for daily reconditioning of mounds.)

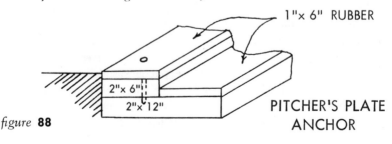

1"x 6" RUBBER

2"x 6"

2"x 12"

PITCHER'S PLATE
ANCHOR

figure **88**

turf grasses

A well-grassed turf adds immeasurably to a first class field. It is a pleasure to play on, adds attractiveness to the area, and will absorb a tremendous amount of excess moisture. A good turf that has density and deep-seated roots has a firm but springy, cushioned feel that will insure good footing without tearing out easily. This kind of turf requires a proper drainage system, good soil structure, pre-seeding soil preparation, necessary fertilizer nutriments, proper irrigation, appropriately selected grasses, and continuous maintenance and management.

There are quite a number of agronomy experimental departments in many sections of the country. The agronomists are in accord that no one grass variety is perfect because all of them have certain features that are good, mediocre, or bad. However, strains are constantly being developed or improved to the point that there are some excellent grasses adapted to fit nearly all local conditions fairly well.

Grasses should be selected from strains that have proved successful in the local geographical area. They should be vigorous, aggressive grasses that have a high tolerance for drought, compaction, disease, and local temperature variations (winter and summer). They should also have resistance to heavy wear and traffic and have a rapid and complete recovery from injury.

We can divide the country by a rough line running east and west from Baltimore, through Cincinnati, St. Louis, Kansas City, and Denver to San Francisco. North of this line is a cool temperature area in which certain grasses are more suitable. South of this line is high temperature country, reaching from the humid southeast through the arid southwest, where other specific strains are recommended. There is a certain overlap along the line itself where Soysia grass is highly recommended, and strains of both cool and high temperature grasses are sometimes satisfactory.

Cool temperature grasses. Blue grasses have been long tested favorites in cool temperature areas. There are a number of developed strains, such as Kentucky, Merion, Newport, Windsor Prato, Park, and Delta. Turf men are optimistic about new and improved kinds of the varieties mentioned. The three used most often are Kentucky (Common), Merion, and Newport. Merion is fast becoming a favorite. It is more expensive, but is less densely seeded—only 2 to 2½ pounds per 1000 sq. ft. compared to 4 pounds of Kentucky Blue. These strains are sometimes seeded straight, and in some areas certain blends are suggested for disease tolerance, vigor, and adaptation. In the upper Midwest, 3 to 7 per cent Red Top has been added successfully when a fast ground cover was wanted ahead of the slower germinating blue grass. Another satisfactory mixture has been 25 to 30 per cent of fine creeping Red Fescur (Pennlawn strain) blended with Merion, Kentucky, or both. The blue grasses will soon take over in both of these mixtures. The agronomists at Penn State report good luck mixing Kentucky

31 Fescue with blue grass strains. Recently, however, many turf men have been discouraging this practice because of the tendency of turf to become ragged and clumpy.

Kentucky or common blue grass is susceptible to leaf spot called Helminthosporium during prolonged hot, humid weather. The chemical Zineb has been quite effective for control (3 oz. per 1000 sq. ft. as a preventive, 5 oz. as cure). Merion is slightly susceptible to rust, but usually is immune if this strain is fed extra nitrogen.

Tall Fescues were introduced from Europe many years ago. Through experimentation, strains were improved and adapted in this country. Kentucky 31 is a coarse bladed grass that will provide a very dense turf if seeded very heavily. Upper Midwest regions have had best results by seeding it alone using 15 pounds of seed per 1000 sq. ft. This grass has great resistance to disease and wear, and exceptional tolerance for drought and compacted soil. This variety would make a fine turf for football or the outfield in the humid temperature zone. It cannot be recommended for use in the infield because of its low tolerance for close clipping. A fine combination might be K31 Fescue in the outfield and in foul territory with Merion bluegrass on the infield.

West of the Rockies the Alta Fescue, which was developed in Oregon, has been highly satisfactory, especially in the Pacific Northwest area of Washington, Oregon, and northern California.

In many parts of California and in the arid southwest, the Tall Fescues are the only cool season grasses that will persist, according to Dr. V. B. Younger. A variety known as Goar's Fescue was introduced and adapted for heat tolerance of the Southwest. They report favorable results by mixing Goar's (60 per cent) with Pensacola strain of Bahia grass (40 per cent) at a seeding rate of 8 pounds per 1000 sq. ft.

The Fescues will require less nitrogen and less water than most other grasses. An application of iron sulphate (2-3 oz. per 1000 sq. ft.) or one of the iron chelates will give a deeper green color.

Rapid cover grass. There are several common varieties that are quick starting, fast growing, and provide a temporary rapid cover.

Annual Rye grass (Italian) and Red Top germinate very rapidly (four to six days) and provide a holding cover while the slower germinating permanent grasses are getting started. Where Bermuda grasses and Zoysia are used, they are often overseeded with Rye grass to provide green color early in spring and late in fall.

The Minnesota Twins' stadium is also the home of the pro football team, the Vikings. They have the problem of providing a grass cover on the skinned portion of the infield in late fall for football games. Their groundskeeper, Dick Ericson, sows the area with a fast germinating Annual Rye grass and covers it with plastic to draw and hold moisture and heat for extra rapid growth.

Perennial Rye grass is a slower starter, and a tougher, longer lasting grass. There will be objectionable ragged clumps when it is mixed with other grasses. It is best used for special purposes and should be seeded heavily and alone (6 to 8 pounds per 1000 sq. ft.).

Common Bermuda is an aggressive fast germinating grass that can provide a thick turf cover in six to eight weeks. This is strictly a temporary cover because it is an annual grass, killed by winter; consequently, it needs reseeding every year. Seed is available for this Bermuda, and it is not necessary to plant it vegetatively like the improved varieties. It works best when planted alone at the rate of 1½ pounds of hulled seed per 1000 sq. ft. The growth requirements, particularly the need for close clipping and frequent cultivation, are not compatible with blue grasses and others.

Mid-continent grasses. Along the east-west line from Baltimore to San Francisco there is a narrow overlap area where certain strains of both cool temperature (Blues and Tall Fescues), and high temperature (Improved Bermudas) grasses may be satisfactory.

A strain of grasses know as Zoysia (6) has been adapted and improved for this region. The grass was originally imported from Korea many years ago. Two of the finer leaved earlier types (Emerald and Matrella) were adapted in the southeast area of Georgia and South Carolina. They had their limitations because of winter kill. A strain known as Meyer Zoysia was developed in the late 1940's. It was winter hardy and thereby practical in a much wider area. Very recently an improved, vigorous, faster spreading strain called Midwest Zoysia was developed and is now available (6).

The newer strains of Zoysia grasses are vigorous, aggressive, disease and wear resistant, and with a high tolerance for high temperature, drought, compacted soil, and close clipping. It is, however, a grass that is slow to establish, has a high initial cost of planting, has a slow (yet complete) healing recovery from injury, and like Bermuda, loses its color in the fall and is late to green in the spring.

Zoysia grasses are planted vegetatively as plugs, sprigs, or sod. Plugs, 2½ in. in size, are planted at one foot intervals. If sprigs are used, it is recommended on 6 in. centers. Sod should be from nursery stock. It is expensive and difficult to obtain. This grass spreads by stems or runners and leaves grow upright from the nodes.

Maintenance requires heavy summertime fertilization, adequate irrigation, close cutting, periodic aerification, and occasional verticutting to reduce thatch build-up.

It is suggested that for baseball and football fields Midwest Zoysia be mixed with blue grass to improve turf density, color, and wear tolerance.

High temperature grasses. A number of improved strains of Bermuda grasses have been successfully adapted to athletic fields in high temperature areas. They all have a number of good points in common. They are deep rooted, vigorous, and aggressive, with tolerance for high temperature, disease, drought, compacted soil, and close clipping. They establish rapidly, have high wear resistance, and if injured, recover rapidly and completely.

The most notable of these improved strains are Tiflawn and Tifgreen, developed by Dr. G. W. Burton of Tifton, Georgia; Tifway, or U3, developed by D. Lester Hall of Savannah, Georgia; and Texas 47 developed by Texas A & M. University. The U3 and the Texas 47 seem to have more adaptability for the more arid regions of the southwest, and U3 also is supposed to have more resistance to low winter temperatures and can be used further north.

All of these strains have no seed available and must be planted vegetatively by sprigs, stolons, or nursery sod. Rate of establishment, however, is quite good. They all thrive on generous feeding of nutrients, infrequent but deep soaking irrigation, close mowing, periodic aerification, and occasional verticutting to minimize the heavy thatch. Bermuda grasses brown early in fall and get their color late in spring. Spraying with a vegetable color is one way to alleviate this objection. In most places, however, Bermuda is overseeded with fast growing ground cover (annual Italian Rye or Red Top) to give green color early in spring and late in fall. The University of Mississippi overseeds with clover for the same purpose.

St. Augustine grass is a prolific, coarse, shallow-rooting grass with low resistance to wear, disease, drought, and compacted soil. For these reasons it is undesirable and not recommended.

Bahia grass, usually found along the gulf coast, is a coarse, deep-rooted, tough variety that can thrive fairly well on poorly compacted soil with a minimum amount of irrigation and maintenance. The Pensacola strain is recommended over the Paraguay type. Seed is available. Some success has been noted by mixing Bahia (40 per cent) with Goar's Fescue (60 per cent) (8).

Kikuyu grass, or "Elephant grass," is imported from Australia and has been used in the arid southwest and Southern California (8). It is a coarse, aggressive, deep-rooted grass that is wear resistant, drought tolerant and requires little watering. It does, however, require frequent close mowing, aerifying and verticutting. Bent grasses may make fine golf greens, but because of tenderness, susceptibility to diseases, and the need for constant maintenance, are not recommended for baseball fields.

seeding

If seed is available for the specific grasses that are appropriately selected for the geographical area, make sure they are the best. Insurance for the best is seed that is certified. There is no bargain in cheap quality seed. Good certified seed will guarantee a maximum purity from inert matter, chaff, and seeds from other grasses or weeds. It will also give assurance of maximum percentage of germination and full weight (Kentucky Blue grass will weigh 24 lbs. per bushel). Rye, Red Top, and Fescues are lighter seed. Amounts should be weighed, not measured.

The amount of seed will naturally vary with the grass selected. Examples: Kentucky Blue grass is usually seeded 4 pounds per 1000 sq. ft.; Merion Blue grass 2-2½ pounds, and Tall Fescues up to 15 pounds per 1000 sq. ft. when seeded alone. If a quick germinating cover grass is mixed with the seed, do not use more than 5 per cent Red Top or more than 15 per cent Annual Rye.

In the upper Midwest, there are three best times to plant seed: the first is early in spring; the second, late summer—usually not later than Labor Day; and the third, late in fall (dormant seeding). Dormant seeding is gaining favor. The seed is planted late enough in fall so that germination will not start at once. Instead, the seed lies dormant, getting a good jump early the next spring.

Seed is usually sown on the surface (broadcast method) with a Brillion or Vicking grass seeder. Calibrate your seeder to throw out the correct amount. Divide the quality of seed and broadcast one-half of it in one direction and the other half at right angles to the first spreading. On your infield, where sharp base lines are needed between the grass and skinned portions, have an assistant hold a large piece of cardboard or plywood along the edge of the grass lines when seed is being spread. A firm but bendable piece of roofing paper makes a good barricade at the arcs inside the bases and curves around home plate, on-deck, or fungo circles.

After the seed is spread, rake the entire area, and use a light roller to firm seed to soil. One turf specialist (2) welded expanded metal, or diamond mesh, around an old cultipacker to roll over a newly seeded plot. This serves three purposes: (1) It crumbles existing soil particles; (2) It firms soil and covers seed sufficiently for proper germination; and (3) it creates a pattern on the soil which minimizes erosion and tends to hold moisture.

Erosion control while seed is germinating and getting established can be accomplished by mulching. Straw or hay (three bales per 1000 sq. ft.) can be spread and held down by twine and sixteen penny nails or sprayed with an asphalt emulsion to form a mat (2). If you have a choice, try oat straw that has not been threshed too thoroughly. The oats will germinate quickly thereby increasing the soil holding capacity, and they can be eliminated by mowing with very little competition to the permanent grasses (2).

After mulching, the soil must be wetted down (preferably by a fine spray) and kept with moisture constantly available so that germination continues without interruption.

Seed may be pre-germinated to give grass the fastest possible start. Ordinarily blue grass will require from 21 to 24 days for natural germination. Seed that has been pre-germinated will take hold in from 5 to 7 days instead of the usual three weeks or more. If you are fighting time, this may become advantageous and desirable. Coordination of work schedules on soil preparation and pre-germination is necessary.

Seed may be pre-germinated by following these directions. Mix the seed with an expanded mica such as vermiculite (concrete aggregate grade) at the rate of 2 parts of mica to 1 part seed. Moisten the mica slightly and mix in the seed. Then add water until the mixture is thoroughly wet. Cover with a plastic tarp and keep the mixture moist (not wet) for 7 to 9 days with the temperature held at 70 degrees F. The mixture should be turned frequently during this time, and moistened if needed. Usually the seed will start to germinate in about six days, depending, of course, upon the temperature. When most of the seed has started to sprout, mix with a processed sewage sludge fertilizer (Milorganite) until dry enough to enable the mixture to pass readily through the spreader. Calibrate the spreader for the proper rate and sow promptly. Lightly roll the area, water immediately and keep moist so that germination continues without interruption (6).

Another method of pre-germination may be handy, especially for smaller amounts. Place the seed in a plastic bag and add water at the rate of one pint per pound of seed. Place this mixture in the refrigerator and leave for approximately seven to eight days or until seed begins to burst. With this method, it will be necessary to allow the seed to dry slightly before sowing. Mix with Milorganite as described above and sow promptly.

It is amazing how quickly grass will take hold after pre-germination. This writer had the experience of using this method of infield starting late in August. The grass got off to a good start in favorable weather. This diamond was used the following April. Now, we do not mean to imply that this turf was really well-established; however, it was playable and adequate.

sodding

Sodding may be necessary to establish a turf in short time. It is the most expensive method of providing turf, as the cost of the sod and laying it correctly both contribute to the expense. Most authorities on turf prefer seeding to sodding not only because of the cost, but also because seeding gives a smoother and more even surface. One comment was, "It takes two years time to get the wrinkles out of the sod." If sodding is to be done, have the soil prepared as was suggested for seeding. Be sure there are no depressions, pockets, or soft spots.

Select sod, preferably from nursery stock, that is weed free and does not have manure or fertilizer burn. Recent experimentation has shown that the sod should be cut as thin as possible and yet so that it will handle well. One authority (5) says, "The maximum root and soil thickness should be from ½ to ¾ inches below the base of the blade." Thin cut sod will weigh less, is easier to handle, lies smoother, and will root quicker. Strips should be cut 12 to 16 in. wide and the rolls from 5 to 6 ft. long for convenient handling.

Before laying the sod, mark out the infield grass line, firm the soil, and wet down with a fine spray. Lay the first row of sod to the marked out grass lines and always work away from these lines. The second and subsequent rows should be laid smooth, firmly abutted, and so the joints of the sod do not overlap. Care must be taken to do a thorough job. The sod should be tamped lightly to insure good contact. Cracks between joints should be top dressed with soil and overseeded. A recommended mixture for top dressing is sterilized soil, sphagnum peatmoss, and sand. A light roller can be used, but do not allow the sod to creep ahead of the roller. Water thoroughly with a fine spray and keep moist for at least ten days. Later on, increase the amount of moisture and decrease the frequency of application. After the sod has rooted, a heavier roller can be used to firm the contact and smooth out the sod.

turf maintenance and management

Proper and constant care is a necessity. This quotation from Dr. V. B. Younger, turf specialist at U.C.L.A., emphasizes this: "Management practice, which is ordinarily considered to be beneficial to any turf, becomes of critical importance when a field is subjected to the heavy use of athletic fields. Persons responsible for the maintenance of these areas must not neglect, even for a short time, the necessary requirements of good turf management" (8).

Irrigation. All turf will need water for establishment, growth, and repair. If nature doesn't provide rain in sufficient amount, man must provide water. The turf specialists are all in accord in saying: "Water infrequently but thoroughly; water seldom but well; water when necessary but soak deeply." Then they add, "Do not water lightly or sprinkle frequently so only the top inch or two is wet."

One group of specialists (5) has stated that soil can hold up to 1000 gallons of available water per 1000 sq. ft. to a 6 in. depth. They add further that under severe drought conditions the turf will lose a quarter to a third of an inch of water per day. Most specialists agree that when grass starts to show wilt, the area should be soaked to a depth of 6-8 or 10 in. This may be at regular intervals of 7 to 10 days under moderate temperature (with rainfall less than one inch), or every 4 to 5 days in hot temperature (with drought conditions prevailing). Play should then be restricted until the top soil is dry. The roots will continue to absorb moisture from below. Deep watering encourages desirable deep root growth.

Frequent light sprinkling encourages shallow surface roots, compaction, crab grass and other weeds.

Too much water can leave the turf waterlogged and spongy. This not only affords poor footing, but also leeches out the soil nutrients (especially potash), limits oxygen supply to the roots, and makes your turf prone to disease.

Turf men use a soil probe to check on depth and rapidity of moisture penetration. If the penetration is very slow and there is a wasteful excess of run-off water, it probably is due to soil compaction. Frequent use of the aerifying equipment will help to keep soil open and provide needed porosity.

Mowing. Mowing should be done whenever the grass grows ½ to 1 in. above the desired length. The frequency of mowing is generally governed by the rate of growth at that time. The height of cutting should be adjusted to the type of grass in the field. Blue grass and Merion should not be cut below 1¼ to 1½ in. Tall Fescue grasses (K31-Alta) thrive better on a 2 in. cut. Zoysia grasses and Bermuda grasses are close cropped to ½ to ¾ in. If your fields are not being used for a period of time, a higher cutting may be advisable. The longer leaf will allow for greater photosynthesis, thereby developing stronger healthier grass. When you again want to lower the cutting, do it gradually over several mowings.

Some turf men prefer reel type mowers, others the rotary type. The latter seems to have preference on grasses like Zoysia and Bermuda that grow from intertwined runners, whereas the reel type is more desirable for straight bladed Blue grasses and Fescues. It is desirable with all types to have sharp blades which cut cleanly. Dull blades bruise the grass and leave a yellowish appearance after cutting. Do not move the mower faster than it can do a good job. If you have disease problems and the clippings are long, it is advisable to catch clippings or pick them up with a lawn sweeper.

Fertilizers. Turf must have nutriments of nitrogen, phosphorous, potassium, and lime for establishment and continued good growth. The formula for correct amounts and the chemical ingredients should be determined by soil analysis of specific areas and with consideration to kinds of grasses involved. Local Agricultural Experiment Stations can make this analysis and give the necessary specific information.

Turf specialists are in accord that all athletic turf should have an application of complete balanced fertilizer at least once per year, and that this should be supplemented by several additional applications of nitrogen during the growing seasons.

The balanced formula may be 10-10-10, 10-5-5, 8-6-4, depending on local soil conditions. Most turf men agree that Bermuda and Zoysia grasses thrive best when the complete fertilizer is applied early in spring. They also agree that cool weather grasses (Blue and Fescue) get more benefits from fall applications. Some prefer two lighter applications—one in the spring and one in the fall.

Turf needs and thrives upon nitrogen. Additional supplementary applications are necessary during the growing season. Nitrogen is supplied in either organic or inorganic form. The organic type is available in sewage sludge, tankage, cottonseed meal and ureaform. The inorganic is available as sulphate of ammonium, urea, or ammonium nitrate. Most agronomists and greenskeepers are in favor of the organic type because its action is slowly available—it is released more gradually, is prolonged over a longer period of time, and has a residual effect. This produces a more uniform and steady grass growth. Furthermore, the organic type will not burn or injure the grass. The inorganic type nitrogen is quickly available but the grass should be dragged to get the soluble fertilizer off the grass leaves; also it must be watered in to avoid burning. Depending on the type of grass, growing season, and soil condition, turf will need from two to six pounds (actual) nitrogen per 1000 sq. ft. per year. Two of the more common organic fertilizers are Milorganite (6-4.2-0) (treated sewage sludge) and Uramite (38-0-0). If for instance, Blue grasses require 2 to 4 pounds actual nitrogen per year and the formula for Milorganite is 6-4-0, you would need 25 to 35 pounds (actual) per 1000 sq. ft. per year. If you should use Uramite with a formula of 38-0-0, you would need only 5 to 6 pounds (actual) per 1000 sq. ft. per year. A general rule of thumb is to provide ½ to ¾ of a pound of nitrogen (actual) per 1000 sq. ft. per each month of the growing season. Turf men believe it is better to feed lighter and more frequently. They prefer a constant supply of nitrogen for steady, vigorous growth and recovery from injury and wear. Too heavy feedings during the playing season will create a tender, succulent, even slippery turf that has a lowered tolerance for wear. With Blue and Merion strains you can omit feeding during the pseudo-dormant stage of July and August. Merion Blue grass requires more Nitrogen than the Kentucky strain. Bermuda and Zoysia grasses should be fed regularly during the long summer growing season.

Generally the soils in the cool temperature areas have a sufficiency of phosphorous; however, the important chemical potassium leeches out, and an application of Muriate of Potash (0-0-60) may be added once per year at rate of 2 pounds per 1000 sq. ft. One turf man (14) in the upper midwest does not use a complete fertilizer because the soil has a sufficiency of phosphorous. He periodically uses Milorganite (6-4.2-0) which has a small amount of phosphorous and then gives it a light application of potash (0-0-60) in the spring and again in the fall.

On occasion the soil has a deficiency of iron. An application of iron sulphate or a chelate of iron will result in a deeper green color and a firmer grass with extra vigor.

For the application of fertilizers, turf men favor a spreader of the broadcast type. The operator should get a uniform spread and avoid streaking, skips, misses, or overlap. The application should be made on a clear dry day when the dew is off the grass. Soluble inorganic fertilizers will burn and injure wet grass. It is recommended that a drag mat be used to knock particles off the grass leaves and that the grass then be watered to minimize chances of burning—especially on cool weather grasses. It is considered good practice to aerify the area before applying fertilizers and lime.

Soil analysis can also furnish a very accurate hydrogen-ion concentration or acid-alkalinity test. A pH of 7 on the test indicates neutral. A pH of 6 has 10 times more acid than 7, and a pH of 5 has 100 times more acid than 7. Most Bluegrasses and Fescues require a pH of 6.6 to 7. Bermudas can thrive on soil that is slightly more acid. Generally when the pH drops to 6.5 or lower, remedial steps to neutralize the acid are in order. Ground limestone which is calcium carbonate (Calcite), or calcium mixed with magnesium carbonate (Dolomite) is recommended because it is the cheapest and easiest to apply. Soil analysis dictates the amount needed —probably somewhere between 500 and 1000 lbs. per acre. Lime moves slowly through the soil; consequently turf men recommend that the area be aerified before the lime is applied, and afterwards dragged and watered to insure getting the chemicals down near the roots. In most cases ground limestone will be needed only every other year. The fall of the year seems to be the favored time for application.

Aerifying. Soil that has been subjected to a lot of traffic and heavy equipment (especially when wet) can easily become compacted. This means that the soil particles get squeezed together, destroying the structure of the soil, especially its porous nature. It becomes more and more difficult to get moisture, nutriments, and air to the soil. This encourages shallow roots, weed growth, and a weak, thin, underfed turf.

This compacted condition can be remedied through aerifying the soil with a mechanical cultivator. This machine is equipped with a series of staggered elongated spoons (6 in. long and ½ to 1 in. in diameter) that leave a great number of punctured cavities and disgorge an equal number of soil plugs on the surface without damage to the turf. These soil plugs are broken up by using a steel dragmat which helps to top-dress and level the surface. It is recommended that the aerifying machine be used over the area two or three times and from different directions. Bluegrasses and Fescues should be aerified in the spring and fall. Zoysia and Bermuda grasses may be aerified as needed during the growing season, even during hot weather. However, this can be done more often if the field is hard and the water is running off rather than soaking in. Good soil aeration must be maintained.

Greater benefit can be obtained from fertilizers, insecticides, lime, and reseeding if they are applied after aerifying and before using the dragmat. Watering now will take these chemicals down into the soil where they are most needed.

Thatch control. The thatch or mat of the turf is an accummulation of organic material. The grass clippings that are only partially decomposed and the sod itself can become overly dense and crowded. Whether it is a help or a hindrance has been a controversial subject. One group felt that the decomposition of this organic material added humus and nutriments to the soil. The present trend of belief is that the heavy thatch doesn't permit oxygen, water, and nutriments to reach the soil and at the same time provides a medium in which diseases can flourish.

Periodic thinning of this matted thatch with a verticut machine, followed by raking or use of a lawn sweeper, is now recommended as a beneficial procedure. It has been suggested that cool temperature Bluegrasses be thinned by vertical cutting in spring and fall, and that Zoysia or Bermuda grasses could be beneficially thinned periodically during the long summer growing season.

Chemical control of weeds, worms, and disease. We must protect our turf from too much competition from weeds, worms, and diseases. There are many good herbicides, pesticides, and fungicides available today, with new and more specific ones being developed constantly. The recommended chemicals have all been tested; however, certain ones seem to be more effective in different sections of the country. It would be advisable to check with your local Turf Experiment Station.

Before using any of these chemicals, read and understand the manufacturer's labels regarding directions and recommendations as to amounts, rates, frequency of use, method and appropriate time of application. Many of these chemicals are volatile and poisonous. Follow the directions for care of handling explicitly—play safe. Manufacturer's recommended safety procedures are: Mix in the open; be up-wind from mixing container; use special containers used only for chemicals; clean all equipment thoroughly with ammonia, activated charcoal, and detergents; wear rubber gloves, long sleeved shirts, and launder clothes before wearing them again. It might be advisable to use a face respirator that covers the eyes. Burn empty chemical containers. Empty excess chemicals in an isolated place and cover with dirt. Finally, wash carefully using plenty of soap.

The chemicals are applied with a low pressure sprayer using flat spray nozzles which are calibrated to spray the proper amount. The operator should be careful. Stop spraying in high wind to prevent chemical drift that may do damage to other areas.

For broad leafed weeds such as dandelion, ground ivy, plantain, buckhorn, purslane, use 2, 4-D (Amine) in mid-spring or in fall. Do not use during hot weather. Use ¼ to ½ oz. per 1000 sq. ft. Add a little ordinary detergent for better coverage.

Clover, chickweed, black medic, yellow sorrel, pennywart, and ground ivys are effectively controlled with 2,4,5-T, M.C.P.P. (Mecopex), or Silvex. Knotweed is affected in growth by M.C.P.P. and Dicamba, or use Zytron in the fall.

Grassy weeds like crab grass, poa annua, and nut grass have been controlled by post-emergent application of P.M.A. (Phenyl Mercury Acetate) or D.S.M.A. (Disodium Methyl Arsenate) early in the season. Later applications of A.M.A. (Ammonium Methyl Arsenate-Amine) have been effective. Goose grass is controlled by Benfin, and Nimblewill by Zytron. Do not use Phenyl Mercury compounds on Merion Bluegrasses.

In the past couple of years pre-emergent herbicides have been used effectively for grassy weed control, especially crabgrass. Very good luck has been had with a trade preparation called Dacthal. The results have been about 95 per cent effective. Bandane, Treflan, and Zytron are other pre-emergent herbicides. The spraying is done in early spring. These herbicides are not selective to crabgrasses alone and can injure other germinating seeds. After using the above pre-emergents, grass seed should not be planted until late summer or early fall. Dupont Chemical Co. recently came out with a new pre-emergent called Tupersan that is supposed to be Bluegrass seed tolerant in from three to five days.

For control of worms—army, web, grub, cut, earthworms, and night crawlers—there are a number of different pesticides. They are D.D.T., Chlordane, Dieldrin, Aldrin, Heptachlor, and Malathion. There is a great deal of difference in the potency of these chemicals. All should be watered in immediately so that the pesticide is diffused into the worm infected soil. Earthworms and night crawlers areate and leave organic matter in the soil. Hence they are beneficial to many turf areas. However, on a baseball infield, they are a nuisance. They come to the surface at night and leave little mounds of soil. When these mounds dry out the infield can become very rough. Besides the above chemicals lead arsenate has been effective in controlling this worm.

Some of the more common fungus diseases that affect turf are helminthosporium (leaf spot), fairy ring, foot rot, melting out, and fusarium roseum. Contact a turf specialist for diagnosis of the disease and for the specific chemical treatment. The most effective fungicides for control are Zineb, Actidone, R.Z., and Kromad. Apply with a high pressure spray (90-100 psi) to adequately wet crowns and the soil.

Renovation versus reconstruction. On a deteriorated turf, the decision must be made—renovate or reconstruct? A rule of thumb set forth by one group of turf specialists (6) is as follows: "Reconstruct if your turf has more than 50 per cent weeds with a large proportion of crabgrass and knotweeds. Renovate if your field has less than 50 per cent weeds with little crabgrass and knotweed."

If reconstruction is necessary, Sodium Arsenite may be used to sterilize—"scorched earth procedure" (6). Then condition the soil with thorough aerifying for improved porosity, vertical cultivation to loosen top soil, fertilizer, lime (if necessary), reseeding, mat dragging, and good water management. If only renovation is required, aerify thoroughly, cultivate vertically, fertilize, reseed, and water adequately. Renovation may only be necessary in spots or isolated sections. The best time for either renovation or reconstruction is in the fall, that is, in the cool temperature time starting in late August or in dormant seeding time late in October or early November.

other physical features

Field lighting. Lighting was a "shot in the arm" to baseball. It has greatly extended the hours a facility could be used and has been a practical convenience for players and spectators.

The main objective in lighting a field is to provide sufficient illumination of good quality for comfortable and accurate visibility. This will enable the players to perform their visual tasks without handicaps and allow the spectators to easily follow the course of the play.

To have good quality lighting one must give consideration to: Reducing glare (direct or reflected) to the minimum; eliminating harsh shadows and blind spots by uniformly diffusing the distributed light; and aiming light beams to avoid directing the light into the eyes of players or spectators. Design engineers attempt to solve these problems by: proper beam control; proper luminaire tower location; proper aiming and direction; proper lighting units; and adequate mounting heights for lights.

The following is recommended: That all wiring be handled by underground cables; that steel poles or towers be used; that weather proof lighting units of the type G.P. (general purpose—1500 ps-52a) with incandescent filament be used; that the minimum horizontal (h) footcandles be at least 30(h) for the infield and 20(h) for the outfield (a good average coefficient is 50(h) and 30(h)); that the light units be cleaned periodically; and that a periodic check be made of mounting bolts, wire connections, corrosion, and all safety features.

A good lighting project is expensive, and it could be very easy to make costly mistakes. This is such a highly technical subject that if you are contemplating installing lights, you are urged to contact the source (4) from which the above information was taken (by permission) and to seek assistance from local lighting engineers and manufacturers of this type of lighting equipment.

Dug-outs. A baseball facility should have dug-outs to protect players from the weather and the obtuse remarks of irate fans. There are a number of construction considerations:

1. Length: Dug-outs should be long enough to accommodate players, managers, trainer, and coaches. A length of 40 ft., which will allow 28 people to sit on the bench at one time, is suggested.

2. Height: They should be high enough so that occupants can

stand up without bumping their heads. A partial roof can reduce the height.

3. Width: They should be wide enough to allow limited traffic back and forth. A fair average would be 8 ft.

4. Depth: They should be deep enough to give consideration to the spectators seated behind them. However, they should be shallow enough to enable occupants to see the game over a turtle backed infield. Coaches and players detest a "worm's eye" view from a deep-pit type dug-out. A depth of 24 in. is suggested. At that depth one can see well, and can save on dug-out width because only one 12 in. step is necessary to get out. If the depth is more than 24 in., the concrete below the bench should be built higher, and two steps will be necessary.

5. Winged Ends: To give an unobstructed view of the whole playing area, winged ends on the dug-out are a convenience. Wings hinged approximately two-thirds of the way back in order that they may be opened or closed are recommended.

6. Location: The front edge of the dug-out should be flush with the sideline, and the center should be equidistant from home plate and the base on that side. In other words a dug-out 40 ft. long would be 25 ft. up the line from both home plate. This will prevent many overthrows from going into the dug-out and out of the field of play.

7. Base Construction: The base should be solidly anchored with concrete footings. Bring in waterline and prepare outlets. Tamp 4 in. of sand firmly and cover it with a sheet of 4 mm plastic as a vapor barrier before pouring concrete. This plastic sheet could be wide enough to cover mason work up the sides to ground level. It will prevent water seepage through hydrostatic pressure and prevent frost damage. It would still be in order to waterproof the sidewall below ground level. The concrete floor should be graded to a sewer outlet at each end, and the surface should be rough troweled.

8. Wall Construction: Concrete block is recommended for ease of construction and economy. Face the block by bolting on 2 in. $\times$ 8 in. boards.

9. Interior Appointments: Cover the runway and steps with heavy roofing material or belting material glued to the surface. Benches should be 18 in. high and 16 in. deep constructed with a back rest. Box-like benches with hinged tops could be used for storage. If this type is used, the benches should set on the edge of 2 in. $\times$ 4 in. boards to allow air space underneath. Many dug-outs have a storage closet at one end which is good if it is not too large and does not obstruct the view. Put in plenty of hooks to hang jackets and screw hooks into the face of dug-out roof for the gloves of the players. Some teams have installed a 4 ft. fence immediately in front of the dug-out to protect players and to keep more balls alive in fair territory. Some players, however, object to watching the game through a fence.

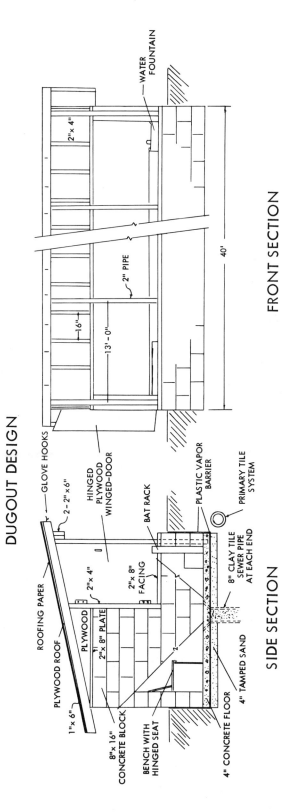

DUGOUT DESIGN

FRONT SECTION

2" x 4"

WATER FOUNTAIN

2" PIPE

16"

13' - 0"

40'

ROOFING PAPER

GLOVE HOOKS

2 – 2" x 6"

HINGED PLYWOOD WINGED–DOOR

PLYWOOD ROOF

1" x 6"

8" x 16" CONCRETE BLOCK

BENCH WITH HINGED SEAT

PLYWOOD

2" x 4"

2" x 8" PLATE

2" x 8" FACING

BAT RACK

PLASTIC VAPOR BARRIER

PRIMARY TILE SYSTEM

8" CLAY TILE SEWER PIPE AT EACH END

4" TAMPED SAND

4" CONCRETE FLOOR

SIDE SECTION

figure 89

10. Economy Shelters: Construct a shelter bench on ground level with a 4 ft. roof and winged ends. If this is too costly, at least put up a 4½ to 5 ft. roofless wall behind the players bench to give the players a little privacy (see Figure 89).

Backstop. If the facility has a roofed grandstand, installation of an "oooops" net strung on cables to the roof of the stands is recommended. Most installations, however, have an upright backstop. It should be installed 60 ft. from home plate. The center section of 42 ft. is at right angles to the plate with wings extending up the sidelines to a point where the extended lines from 1st and 3rd base intersect the sideline. The recommended height is 18 to 20 ft. Attach an extended wing 10 to 12 ft. in height as far as the dug-out. At this point install a players' gate. The anchor and corner posts should be 4 in. in diameter, made of steel, and anchored securely in concrete. The top is tied together with 1½ in. pipe welded onto the posts. Chain-link fencing (9 to 12 gauge galvanized) is most durable. It would be practical to clamp creosoted 2 in. × 10 in. planks to the inside of the posts and staple the screen to the boards to prevent curling. All fencing should be on the infield side of the posts to provide a flush surface. To make this point clear, keep posts outside of the playing field. Paint the structure with rust-oleum and give it a finish coat of dark green enamel to enhance the background. Spray the base with Sodium Arsenite to kill weeds and grass. A 3 ft. high pad at the base will protect baseballs from damage.

Fences and gates. It is recommended that the sideline and outfield fence be constructed from galvanized chain-link fence with 2 in. × 2 in. mesh and from 9 to 12 gauge wire. The sideline fence should be 4 ft. high and the outfield fence 8 ft. high. The posts should be 2 in. galvanized pipe or the newer "H" or "I" shaped supports. These should be anchored in concrete 2 ft. below the surface and 10 ft. apart. All corner posts should be 2½ in. pipe and braced from both directions.

The fence should be installed on the inside (the playing side) of the field. The posts are outside of the fence. Dig a shallow trench and set the fence slightly below ground level. Stretch the fence tight with a pulley arrangement. Fence improperly installed can curl and become a real safety hazard. It was formerly recommended that "knuckled-selvage" (curled back on itself) finish, be used, but it is being replaced by a strand of heavy gauge crinkled wire that is wired to the fence and anchored to each post. This prevents curling, especially if it is strung tight. The exposed twisted wire ends at the top of the fence are hazardous. It may be wise to use the "knuckled-selvage" method to turn back the sharp edges, and then install a rail close to the top wire with 1½ in. pipe.

A player-pedestrian gate should be installed at the home plate side of each dug-out. A double gate for vehicles and equipment should be conveniently placed on each sideline. Any other gates, including bullpens, will depend on the local layout. Gate posts should be 2½ in. for single gates, 3 in. for double gates, and should be well-braced.

The center field section of fence should be primed with rust-oleum and then painted with a dark green enamel. This is to enhance the background for hitters. If the center field background is bad, it is often advantageous to erect an artificial background. This background is made by covering a metal frame with dark canvas. The canvas should be vented by cutting 6 in. half circle arcs. These arcs are not openings, but merely slits. The frame is made of 2 in. galvanized pipe, 40 ft. long and 20 to 30 ft. high.

Snow fence is often used as temporary outfield and sideline fencing, especially where multiple purpose of area is necessary. If it is used, make sure that the metal posts are outside and driven into the ground below the top of the fence level as a safety measure. The problems of wood and sheet metal fencing are dependent on local conditions.

Sterilize the soil at the base of the fence line with an application of Sodium Arsenite. Killing the weeds and a narrow strip of grass will give sharp definition.

Stabilized areas. This refers to warning track, on-deck circle, fungo circle, coaches' box, path to home plate, and the area in front of the dugouts including a lane along the sideline fence. The materials used in these areas are aggregates that are mechanically stabilized to stand excessive wear and tear of constant traffic. The purpose of the warning track is obvious. It is a safety factor to warn players of their proximity to the outfield fence.

Recommended installation procedure is to use 3 to 4 in. of coarse fill, such as crushed rock, cinders, etc., and then top with 2 to 3 in. of a finer aggregate. The aggregate materials are many: limestone of a "dirty" ⅜ in. grade, crushed brick, clay mixed with coarse sand, crushed red stone and clay, mine slag and steel mill slag. Sometimes these aggregates are sprayed with a light coating of asphalt for binding purposes.

The Minnesota Twins use a trade name product called "Tartan" (30) for their on-deck circle, fungo circle, path to the plate, and a border around the edge of coaches' box. It is a tough material that seems to be impervious to any abuse, and is very attractive—and expensive. Kansas City has imported an aggregate called "Red Dog Cinders" (27) from Strawn, Texas.

It is suggested that the border of the coaches' box and the path to the plate be outlined with 2 in. × 4 in. boards set on edge and flush with the ground. Paint these borders with white outside oil paint to sharply define these areas. A painted strip of "Tartan" (30) around the coaches' box, on deck and fungo circles adds attractiveness.

Scoreboard. An electric scoreboard is an attractive appointment to a field and will enhance interest in the game. It should have the names of the teams, score by innings, and the number of balls (green), strikes (red),

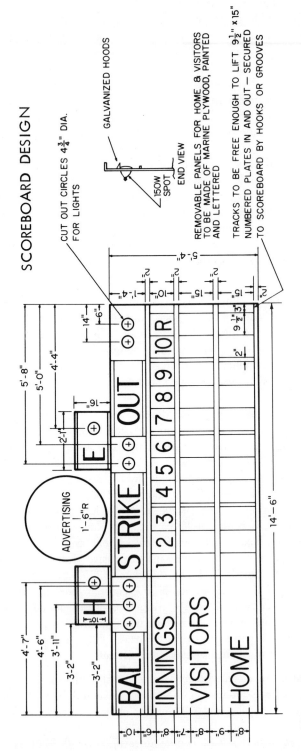

SCOREBOARD DESIGN

CUT OUT CIRCLES 4¾" DIA.
FOR LIGHTS

GALVANIZED HOODS

150W
SPOT

END VIEW

REMOVABLE PANELS FOR HOME & VISITORS
TO BE MADE OF MARINE PLYWOOD, PAINTED
AND LETTERED

TRACKS TO BE FREE ENOUGH TO LIFT 9½" x 15"
NUMBERED PLATES IN AND OUT — SECURED
TO SCOREBOARD BY HOOKS OR GROOVES

ADVERTISING
1'-6"R

BALL STRIKE OUT

E

H

INNINGS 1 2 3 4 5 6 7 8 9 10 R

VISITORS

HOME

figure 90

outs, (white or yellow), and hits or errors. Marty Karow at Ohio State used discarded traffic lights to build a scoreboard. Sealed beam spot lights are now available in colors. To control the board from the press box, a remote control unit hooked up to an underground cable is needed. Some have used hand switches on the scoreboard with the attendant keeping in communication with a "walkie-talkie." Do not place the scoreboard in dead center field as it may interfere with the hitter's background. If the location is such that the sun shines directly towards it, shield your lights to make them more visible. (See Figure 90. This scoreboard was designed by Danny Litwhiler for Florida State University.)

Batting cage. A tunnel type batting cage is convenient and practical. Nylon or cotton netting (24) that is weather proofed with vinyl and made to measure is available. Hang a piece of canvas for background. Some have padded the back portion of the cage and have secured a 5 ft. strip of canvas at the top to protect the balls (see Figure 91).

Barricades. Barricades are a valuable and practical piece of equipment for the protection of players during daily and pre-game practice. Make the frames out of aluminum pipe with the base pipe at right angles to

MINNESOTA TWIN'S BATTING CAGE

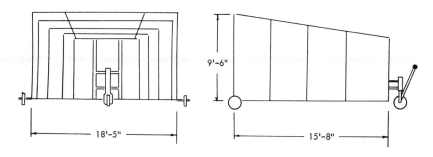

I. S. U. BATTING CAGE

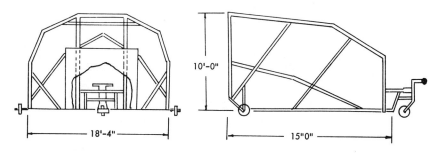

figure **91**

the frame for stability. Cover the frame by lacing on a vinyl-coated nylon net. Make the pitcher's barricade 42 in. high and 5 ft. wide. To protect the first baseman and the ball rustler in back of second base make the frame 8 ft. × 8 ft.

Bat racks. It is recommended that a compartmented box 30 in. high be placed on the dug-out step and fastened to one of the supporting pipes. Another suggestion is to attach a compartmented box to the home plate end of the dug-out. At the top of the backboard fasten a piece of plastic which can be rolled up and secured and unrolled in a hurry to cover bats during a rain shower.

Flag pole. Anchor the pole in concrete, and locate it in straightaway center field. The flag pole should be painted green—never white or a bright color.

Foul line poles. These poles should be distinct. Major league parks are using 75 ft. steel towers with 18 in. detection screens. Most installations could use and afford a 20 ft. steel pipe 3 in. in diameter securely anchored in concrete. Foul poles should be painted white or with a luminous paint to make them stand out. Fly an 18 in. pennant from the top of the pole as a wind indicator for the players.

Distance markers. Players and fans like to know how far balls are hit. Large distance markers will supply this information. They should be vivid and readable from the stands. Firmly cleat together 3 pieces of 1 in. × 8 in. board 4 ft. long. Paint the marker with an undercoat followed with a coat of black enamel. Seven different markers will be needed. Secure them to the top of the fence, one down each line, one in center field, and two each in right and left center field.

Base anchors. The "Hollywood" type bases are an asset to the game. They are tough, durable, convenient to handle, and permanently located. Measure carefully to locate the bases and set chalk lines. The outside edge of first and third base will touch the outer edge of the foul line, the back edge (outfield side) will intersect the line exactly 90 ft. from the apex of home plate. The base is anchored with a metal receptacle placed in concrete. Dig a hole 1 ft. sq. and 1 ft. deep and fill it with 6 to 7 in. of concrete. With a carpenter's square find the base center by measuring 7½ in. from each side of the base line and press the receptacle into the fresh concrete so that the top is within 2 in. of ground level (be sure that the receptacle is plumb and square with the foul line). The *center* of second base is 127 ft. 3⅜ in. from home plate and the outfield sides of the base another 7½ in. Set the chalk lines at the back edge of the base and dig a hole, pour concrete, and plumb and square the receptacle with the base lines from first and third and the center of the base at the 127 ft. 3⅜ in. mark. Let the concrete set up before replacing the dirt.

Auxiliary area. It is suggested that a special area be developed outside the sideline fence for additional practice activities. Michigan State laid out a skinned portion area equivalent to the regular diamond area around second base and first base and cut a six foot baseline extending from first base to the second base-shortstop area. They use this facility for extra infield work especially double play practice, run-downs, pitcher covering first, pitcher holding runners on base, pick-off plays, and base stealing starts.

Considerably more batting practice can be had by hanging batting cages of weather-proofed netting (vinyl-coated) of the compartmented type (24C) patented by Danny Litwhiler, or the regular full length enclosed type (24). The netting can be hung on a frame made of pipe or hung on cables (equipped with turn buckles) which are attached to eye-bolts that are drilled through supporting telephone poles of 8 to 10 in. diameter. As many as five batters can hit at the same time.

Heater. In the northern states, the colleges play on some mighty cold days in the early spring. A dug-out heater operated with propane gas can give a little comfort to your pitcher's arm and the batters' hands. Danny Litwhiler at Michigan State has heated dug-outs. They have adapted a 50,000 BTU kerosene blower type heater to blow hot air through the dug-out. This hot air passes through a 4 in. galvanized pipe and blows out through ¾ in. holes which are pointing up and in toward the seat. These holes are bored every 2 ft. The only objection is a slight kerosene odor which is easier to take than the cold weather.

Bleachers. Determine where bleachers are to be placed and pour permanent concrete footings. Secure 10-12-15 tier bleachers and as many sections as the situation demands. Have guard rails at each end and across the top. After erecting bleachers, have them inspected by a qualified person. Get a signed receipt of inspection as your protection against a liability suit.

Grand stand. A grand stand is a permanent structure and preferably should be covered. Give consideration to locker rooms for home team, visitors, and umpires. These rooms should be equipped with lockers, showers, toilets, and training facilities. Install public toilets and a concession stand. Include storage rooms for baseball equipment and maintenance tools and equipment. The press box should be covered and equipped with tables, chairs, public address system, scoreboard control box, and a record turntable with an amplifier.

Landscaping. Carefully selected bushes and shrubs outside of the fence lines can enhance the attractiveness of the area, add a good background, and provide a windbreak.

maintenance of baseball fields

Adequate and constant maintenance is vital to a good field. A dressed-up field that is neat and well-manicured is beautiful. Everyone concerned with the game takes pride in an attractive, well groomed field. This requires a groundskeeper who is an interested, dependable, and dedicated man. If you have a good groundskeeper, recognize and respect him: he is a very important man to the program. It is necessary to get the field in top shape and keep it there with a minimum of care, equipment, and labor.

1. *Tools and Equipment*

Drags	Rakes
Line Marker	Brooms
Line Trough	Shovels
Spiker	Wheelbarrow
Chalk Line	Sprinkling Can
Edge Cutter	Tamper
Tarpaulins	Small Sprayer
Watering Equipment	Batters' Box Marker
Mound Mat	Base Receptacle Covers

If you do not own, arrange for access to:

Mowers	Roller
Tractor (small)	Verticutter
Spreader	York Rake
Aerifier	Sprayer with boom
Roto-tiller	Flame thrower (portable)

2. *Materials*

Line marking (ground calcium carbonate—Ca CO_3)
Line paint (Water-latex-oil)
Fertilizers and lime
Herbicides, pesticides, fungicides
Chemical conditioners: "Aqua-Gro," "All-Wet," "Turf Tonic" (25)
Calcinated clay: granulated
"Diamond Dust" (ground calcinated clay) for drying wet baseballs
Stock pile of soils for fill and top dressing
Stock pile of heavy unburnt brick clay to repair mound, catcher's and batter's box
Gasoline: to dry out limited area. Use with extreme caution.

3. *Other Equipment*

Tunnel batting cage	Stretcher
Barricades	Litter barrels
Bat racks	

daily routine of maintenance before practice

Remove tarps from pitcher's box and home plate
Wet down skinned portion and baselines
Put out the bases
Erect barricades for pitcher, first base, second base
Spot batting cage

daily routine after practice

Cover the base anchor receptacles
Drag the skinned portion and base lines
Recondition the mound, batters' box, catcher's box
Cover the mound and home plate area with tarp
Recondition the bull pen
Replace and tamp any loose divots

day of game check list

Remove tarp
Mow the grass
Scarify skinned area with spiker
Drag smooth
Water the diamond
Set chalk lines and mark officially
Place batting practice pitcher's mat on mound
Place barricades: pitcher, first base, second base
Put batting cage in place
Paint or wash bases, pitcher's rubber, home plate
Paint or mark fungo and on deck circle, coaches' box
Ready the bull pen
Hang flags on the foul line poles and flagpole
Clean dug-outs and pick up litter
Check scoreboard
Check all lights
Check press box and public address system
Prepare locker rooms

after batting and infield practice prior to game

Redrag skinned area
Remove barricades, batting cage, mound mat
Prepare the pitcher's mound
Rake, tamp, and mark batter's and catcher's box
Throw out resin bag

fall renovation

Fall is the best time to prepare a field for the next year. A thorough job at this time will leave a minimum of work for the spring when, because of soft ground, it is difficult to do heavy repair. Aerify the turf from several directions. Apply fertilizer (and lime if necessary), then drag area with a steel mat and apply water. Any reseeding or sodding can be done now.

Measure carefully and set the chalk lines to recut edges of all grass lines, arcs, boxes, and circles. Thin and sweep out blowage soil that may have collected along the edges. Verticut your infield grass to thin the heavy thatch and remove the clippings.

The skinned area and base lines may need a few loads of fill dirt. It may be necessary to amend the soil with some sand or calcined clay. Roto-till and mix the soil plus amendments thoroughly. (Even though amendments and roto-tilling are unnecessary, aerify the skinned portion for winter action.) Winter freezing and thawing will make the loosened soil more friable and workable. Break up any clumps by dragging a board float, working from the edge of the outfield grass to the edge of the infield grass. Finish by smoothing with a steel mat drag. Rebuild the mound, home plate area, and bullpens by spading and blending in some heavy clay loam.

When the field is idle for a period of time, rain and/or frost will work the granular material of sand and calcined clay to the surface. After the field dries, these materials are subjected to blowage and drifting. In an attempt to control this, the Michigan State University groundskeeper places boards in the low spots and at the edges of the skinned portion, on the leeward of the diamond. At the University of Colorado they stake down bleacher boards (on edge) at right angles to the prevailing wind to control soil drift.

Make all necessary general repairs to fences, dug-outs, barricades, etc. Turn off water and "bleed" the pipe lines to prevent freeze damage. Remove wheels, nets, and canvas from batting cage. Store all field and maintenance equipment where it has the protection from winter weather.

early spring

Assuming the fall work was done as suggested when dry enough to prevent damage, scarify lightly to hasten surface drying. Roll the whole area, outfield and infield, to smooth out roughness that is caused by "winter heave"—periodic thawing and freezing. Give the skinned area an application of "Aqua-Gro" (25): 8 oz. per 1000 sq. ft. Then spray the turf with Dacthol, a pre-emergent herbicide to control crab grass.

additional suggestions for maintenance

Marking the field. Do not be careless or slipshod when putting in the official white lines. Straight, sharp lines dress up the field and gives it good definition. Get a good chalk line of 200 to 300 ft. and, to prevent having a periodic "birds nest," wind it on a board 3 in. wide and 15 in. long with a notch cut in each end.

Ground white calcium carbonate ($CaCo_3$) is now recommended instead of lime. It comes from rock quarries and from Mississippi River shells, and is inexpensive. Some of the trade names are "Dri-Mark," "Safe Mark," "White Line," and "Athletic Line." It works best on infield base lines, and the batter's and catcher's boxes. After marking the line, sprinkle on a little water to set it and prevent blowage.

Good commercial line markers for both calcium carbonate and water paint are on the market. A paint striper (26) that has interchangeable 2, 3, and 4 in. rollers has given satisfactory service.

Many groundsmen are now using a homemade slanted line trough for several purposes. It is constructed with two pieces of 1 in. × 6 in. boards 12 ft. long for the slanted sides, and has a wedge at each end (6 in. across the top, and 3 in. or 4 in. at the bottom). A cleat across the center will act as a handle. After setting the chalk line, place the 12 ft. trough over the line. The line is marked by tapping the sides of a trough with a discarded plastic detergent bottle (that has holes punched in the bottom) filled with line marking material.

Establish an attractive, long-lasting foul line on the outfield grass with the following procedure: Carefully set a chalk line all the way to the foul pole. Place the line trough on the chalk line and sterilize the 3 or 4 in. strip with Sodium Arsenite. Choose a calm day and keep the spray nozzle deep in the trough. After a few days, remove the dead grass from the line. Reset the chalk line, place the trough in position and paint with a cheap outside white paint. One can also use the trough and Sodium Arsenite treatment at the base of the backstop and fences. These spots often look ragged and make it difficult to see baseballs.

Batter's box markers. Build a frame within a frame, 4 ft. × 6 ft. in size, with 1 in. × 2 in. boards cleated 2 in. apart all the way around. Cover the 2 in. bottom representing the width of the line with copper screen 2 in. wide and staple it in position. Across the top at exact center, nail on a 2 in. board long enough to protrude 6 in. beyond the edge. This 6 in. extension is to give the exact measure of distance from the plate

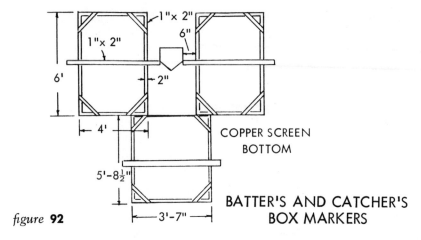

figure **92**

BATTER'S AND CATCHER'S BOX MARKERS

at the angle of the break at the side of home plate. Put this frame in readiness ahead of time by placing a thin layer of line marking material on the copper screen. Just before the game, after the home plate area has been reworked, carry the batter's box to that area. Line up the handle extension with the plate—make sure the frame is squared off, then gently set it in place. Lift one end one inch off the ground and let it drop. Do the same for the other end. Then move the frame to the other side of the plate and go through the same procedure. The lines will be sharp and accurate (see Figure 92).

Catcher's box marker. This is a three-sided frame within a frame, made the same as above with the unscreened side toward home plate. The dimensions of this box are 5 ft. 8½ in. deep and 43 in. wide. Put the frame in place by squaring it behind both batters boxes. Lift each side one inch and drop (see Figure 92).

Bases. Wash the rubberized plastic base covers with a detergent solution and a scrub brush. Paint with a paste made with line marking material ($CaCo_3$) mixed with water. This paste can also be used on the pitcher's rubber and home plate.

Coaches' box. For sharp definition, outline your coaches' box with paint or chalk and include the edges of on deck circle, fungo circle, and paths to the home plate area.

Base anchor receptacle cover. One groundskeeper (15) had this idea that works well for the "Hollywood" type bases. Drill a hole in the center of a 3 in. diameter cover for an electrical junction box. Place a screw through the center of the cover into a square piece of wood 1½ in. × 1½ in. and 3 in. long and attach a 6 in. length of white shoe lace. Place this plug into the base receptacle after taking out the base. When dragging over the area the cover will prevent the receptacle from being filled up with loose dirt and the shoe lace will help locate the base anchor.

Drags. Many different types of drags are used on baseball infields: steel mats, sections of carpet or rug, cocoa mats, sections of chain link fence, wood floats with overlapping boards, wide brushes with long heavy fiber, and even old bed springs. A hand pulled, narrow steel mat, 7 ft. wide and 18 in. deep, was prepared by one groundskeeper (15). The mat is cut so that it will not roll up (this is opposite the usual way of cutting). On the long edge anchor a 7 ft. length of 2 in. $\times$ 4 in. board. Screw eye bolts into the board and attach a pulling rope. The rope should be long enough so that the mat stays flat on the ground while it is being pulled. To the top of the board nail a piece of carpet 7 ft. wide and 3 ft. deep that will extend behind the steel mat by 18 in. This helps to hold down dust and smooths the ground well. Four men, each with a drag, can cover the skinned portion with one trip over and back. Use a smaller 4 ft. $\times$ 18 in. mat, made the same way, to drag the baselines and home plate area. When dragging, never overlap the edges of the grass. This will prevent building a ridge. Do not drag always from first to third or vice versa. Occasionally drag from the edge of the outfield grass by pulling loose dirt up to the edge of the infield grass. Always pick up the drag and carry it rather than drag it off the diamond. If loose soil gets into the edge of the grass from dragging or blowage, sweep the edges with a stiff fibered broom, using an underhand push stroke against the narrow edge of the fibers.

Rakes. A board rake will be handy for moving and smoothing dirt around the mound, home plate area, and base paths. Make one by using an old mop handle that has forked metal prongs. Spread these prongs and bolt them to a piece of ½ in. $\times$ 4 in. board that is 24 to 30 in. long (see Figure 93). Another way is to attach the handle to a piece of 2 in. $\times$ 2 in. board that is 20 in. long, and bolt this to a 2 ft. length of masonite that is 4 in. wide. Wire leaf rakes can be of help to dry out wet soil. This can be accomplished by scarifying the surface to get air into the soil.

Tamper. A rectangular piece of iron 6 in. $\times$ 8 in. $\times$ 1½ in. welded to a 4 ft. length of 1½ in. pipe will be more satisfactory than the usual round tamper. Cover the bottom with a piece of burlap and tie it around the handle to prevent picking up damp soil. A small burlap bag used to ship bolts to hardware dealers fits nicely over the tamper.

Edge cutter. Use a straight-edged ice scraper, a sharp narrow straight-bladed shovel, or a serrated wheel-type edge cutter. Put the chalk line in place and spike it down every 15 ft. This will make a taut line and assure straight lines.

Spiker. Scarify or loosen the top soil periodically, especially when the surface dries out after

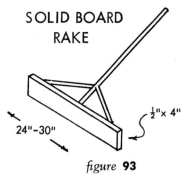

SOLID BOARD RAKE

24"-30"

½"x 4"

figure **93**

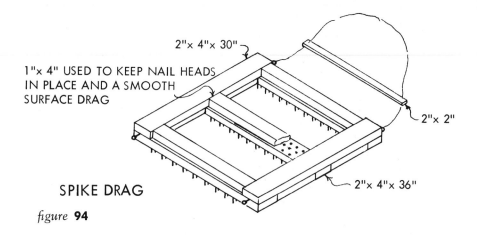

2"x 4"x 30"

1"x 4" USED TO KEEP NAIL HEADS
IN PLACE AND A SMOOTH
SURFACE DRAG

2"x 2"

2"x 4"x 36"

SPIKE DRAG

figure **94**

a rain. A well known groundskeeper (15) uses a practical homemade spike. It is a 3 ft. × 3 ft. frame made from five 3 ft. lengths of 2 in. × 4 in. boards. The corners and the ends of the center board are dovetailed to make the frame lie flat. He drills staggered holes (slightly smaller than spikes) through the boards about an inch apart. Through these drilled holes he drives his big spikes. He then faces the frame by nailing on a 1 in. × 4 in. board to cover the nail heads and keep them from coming out. The rope is attached to two eye bolts screwed into the 2 in. × 4 in. Incidentally, he screws two eye bolts into the other end so that he can pull from that direction when the spikes start to bend backwards. A larger frame can be made with a platform top, in order to weight the spiker with cement blocks when it is necessary to scarify soil that is more solidly compacted (see Figure 94).

tarpaulins

Every baseball installation should have a ground cover for the mound and home plate area. In the event of rain these vital areas should be kept in playable condition. It is dangerous for a pitcher to throw from a slippery mound. A heavy plastic cover of 6 mm. weight or a nylon cover will do a good job. It can be held in position with discarded tires, boards, or staked down through grommets put through a doubled edge. Plastic or nylon is more satisfactory than canvas, because it is lighter to handle and will not mildew or mold. If canvas is used, it will be necessary to dry it out before folding and storing.

Of course, it would be nice if everyone could afford a nylon or neoprene (24) coated cover for the entire infield area. These covers are now available in one piece (160 ft. square) that can be rolled or unrolled from a long 12 in. aluminum drum with a power take-off machine.

In hot humid weather, it is easy to scald or even kill the grass by smothering. Do not leave tarpaulins on over 12 to 24 hours—depending upon the weather conditions.

wet grounds

Calcinated Clay, for example "Diamond Grit," can do wonders in drying out the soil. Claims are made that it is capable of absorbing up to 120 times its weight in moisture. Wire rakes help to get drying air to the top soil. Wet spots can be burned with gasoline or a portable flame thrower which is now available mounted on bicycle wheels for maneuverability. Gasoline, however, can be dangerous to use and has been known to kill grass areas it contacted and take the life out of the dirt. A length of rope or hose dragged across grass areas of the infield and the outfield will knock rain drops off the grass blades thereby allowing the grass surface to dry faster. "Diamond Dust," a powdered calcinated clay, is handy to have around to dry out baseballs. Diamond Dust and Diamond Grit have been in use by Major and Minor league clubs, colleges and recreation departments since 1956.

repair of mound, batter's box, catcher's box, and bullpens

Recondition your mound daily by sweeping loose particles out of the worn spots. Sprinkle in a small amount of water, add moist unburnt brick clay, sprinkle a little more water, brush dry, loose dirt over the top to grade level; tamp well and wet down. Recondition the batter's box, catcher's box, and bullpens the same way.

mound mat

Help keep your mound in better condition by using a mat for batting practice pitchers to throw from during pre-game batting practice. One suggestion is to use a piece of discarded carpet (5 ft. × 10 ft.) that is spiked in place through doubled-over corners. Some groundkeepers use a rubberized plastic mat, and others have used a belting material that naturally lasts longer than carpet. It is advisable to restrict warm-up drills and pepper games to the areas in front of the dug-outs and around the backstop to prevent excess wear and tear.

We would like to thank the following specialists for bulletins and pamphlets on their major fields and for permission to reprint some of the source material.

1. Cook, L. G., "Turf Management on Athletic Fields," Extension Service, Rutgers University, New Brunswick, N. J.
2. Cummings, G. W., "Grounds Maintenance." Landscape Architect, Iowa State University, Ames, Iowa.
3. Daniel, W. H., "Turf Bulletins." Midwest Regional Turf Foundation, Purdue University, Lafayette, Indiana.
4. Illuminating Engineering Society, "Sports Lighting—Current Recommendations and Practices." Prepared by the Committee on Sports and Recreational Areas. Illuminating Engineering Society, 345 E. 47th St., New York 17, N. Y.
5. Musser, H. B., Duich, J. M., Harper, J. C., "Athletic Fields—Design, Specifications, Construction and Maintenance." Extension Service, Pennsylvania State University, University Park, Pa.
6. Roberts, E. C., Taylor, B. S., Cott, A. E., "Play Safe—Football and Athletic Fields Should Be Turfed." Extension Service pamphlet #314, Iowa State University, Ames, Iowa.
7. West Point Products Corporation, "Improving Athletic Field Turf Grass." West Point Products Corporation, West Point, Pa.
8. Younger, V. B., "Turf Bulletins." U.C.L.A. Extension Service, University of California, Los Angeles, California.

Individuals to whom we wish to express our gratitude for specific information and suggestions.

11. Cummings, G. W., Campus Landscape Architect, Iowa State University, Ames, Iowa.
12. Firkins, B. J., (deceased), Agronomist, Iowa State University, Ames, Iowa.
13. Moburg, R. H., Architecture Student, Iowa State University, Ames, Iowa.
14. Taylor, B. S., Turf Specialist and Groundskeeper, Iowa State University, Ames, Iowa.
15. Toma, George, Groundskeeper, Kansas City Athletics, Kansas City, Missouri.

To provide information that may be useful, trade names of some products and the names of manufacturers are listed below. No endorsement of name products is intended, or criticism of similar products not mentioned.

20. Aerifier—West Point Products Corporation, West Point, Pa.

21. Calcined Clay:
    Dialoam—Eagle-Picher Industries, Cincinnati, Ohio
    Diamond Dust—Danny Litwhiler—East Lansing, Michigan
    Diamond Grit—Danny Litwhiler—East Lansing, Michigan
    LuSoil—Minerals & Chemicals—Philips Corporation, Menlo Park,
      New Jersey
    Prep—Floridin Company—Pittsburgh, Pennsylvania
    Terra-Green—Oil-Dri Corporation of America—Chicago, Illinois
    Turface—Wyandotte Chemicals Corp., J. B. Ford Division,
      Wyandotte, Michigan
22. Fiberglass mesh—Johns Manville Corp.
23. Mat Drag—Turf Supply Co., Des Moines, Iowa
              —West Point Products Corp., West Point, Pa.
24. Netting—Carron Net Co., Inc., Two Rivers, Wis.
             —Davis Mills Inc., Lake City, Tennessee
             —Menonomie Fish, Net and Twine Co. (Victory Nets), Me-
    nonomie, Mich.
25. Non-Ionic Wetting Agent:
    Aqua Gro—Aquatrols Corp. of America, Camden, N. J.
    Cleary All Wet—W. A. Cleary Corp., Skokie, Ill.
    Turf Tonic—National Chemsearch Co., St. Louis, Mo.
26. Paint Striper (Dearborn)—R. E. Munsey, Inc., Birmingham, Mich.
27. Red Dog Cinders—H. L. Van Der Veer, Strawn, Texas
28. Sani-Soil Set—Gulf Oil Company
29. Tarpaulins: Nylon, Vinyl, Neoprene
               —Hoosier Tarpaulin and Canvas Goods Co., Indianapolis,
               Ind.
               —Revere Plastic Co., Little Ferry, N. J.
30. Tartan—Minnesota Mining Co., Minneapolis, Minn.
31. Transite—Johns Manville Corp.
32. Verticutter—West Point Products Co., West Point, Pa.
33. York Rake—York Modern Corp., Unadilla, N. J.

index

Dug-out,
    physical features of, 303–304
    reasons for, 4, 303
Dumb-bells, 249

E

Epidermiphytosis, 259
Equipment,
    care of, 235–236
    cleanliness of, 235
    inventory of, 235
    price of, 235
    purchasing, 235
    quality of, 235
    service of, 235–236
Error,
    base hit or, 198
    direct, kills earned run, 221
    not erased by assist, 209–210
    or run-batted-in, 198
    scoring, 211–212
Ether, 262
Eyeglasses, 266
Exercises,
    pitcher's, 250
    pre-seasonal, 247–249
    running, 248
    stretching, 248
    weight-work, 249

F

Fadeaway ball, 8–9
Fair ball, 200
Fast ball, 4
Fence,
    breaking away from, 96
    climbing by outfielder, 95–96
    playing ball from, 96–97
    rebound plays from, 96
Fence crashing, avoidance of, 94–95
Field,
    conditions of, 37
    development of, 275–320
    dimensions of, 271–272

Field (*Cont.*)
    drainage facilities of, 276
    factors for consideration in construction of, 268–270
    grading of, 276–278
    irrigation system of, 280–281
    renovation of, 314
    safety precautions in developing, 274–275
    tiling system, 281
Field, maintenance,
    check list, 313
    daily routine, 313
    materials for, 312
    tools and equipment for, 312
Field maintenance equipment,
    drags, 317
    edge cutters, 317
    rakes, 317
    spiker, 317–318
    tamper, 317
Field, marking the,
    base anchor receptacle cover, 316
    bases, 316
    batter's box, 315–316
    catcher's box, 316
    coach's box, 316
    line markers, 315
Field, physical extras for,
    back stop, 306
    barricade, 309
    base anchors, 310–311
    bat racks, 310
    batting cage, 309
    bleachers, 311
    coach's box, 307
    distance markers, 310
    dug-outs, 303–304
    fences, 305–306
    flag pole, 310
    foul line poles, 310
    gates, 305–306
    grandstand, 311
    heaters, 311
    lighting, 303
    on-deck circle, 307
    scoreboard, 307–308
    warning track, 307

L

Late hitter, 113
Leather goods, 235
Leg, broken, 263
Lineup card, 145
Liniments, use of, 266
Lockjaw, 258
Lysol, 259

M

Manager, student, 232–233
Mask, catcher's, 33
Massage, 265
Merit system, selective, 232–233
Mid-week games, 237
Minor injuries, treatment of, 265–266
Misplay, relation of runs to, 223–226
Mitt, 233
Moist heat, 261
Mound, 289
    mat, 319
Muff, erases stolen base, 217
Muscle,
    bruises, 261
    development of, 261
    protection of arm and shoulder, 265
    treatment of, 261

N

Nail injuries, 265

O

Offensive strategy, 107–145
Official scoring, 179–228
Ointments, 259–260
On-base average, 179
Order, batting, 141–143

Organic materials, use of, 286
Outfield,
    fly ball to, 89–90, 91–94
    practice, 91–93
Outfielder,
    defense plays of, 88–93
    ground balls to, 92–94
    playing, 88–97
    quiz on, 97–98
    requirements for, 87
    stance of, 90
    sunglasses for, 93
    throwing to infield, 41
Oversliding bases, 202

P

Pads,
    heel, 261
    hip, 243
    knee-joint, 242–243
Pants, adjustment of, 242
Passed ball,
    definition of, 218
    error instead of, 215
    stolen base on, 216
Peat moss, use of, 286
Pepper games, 250
Percentage records, determining, 194–195
"Perfect support," 222–223
Physician, 256–263
Pick-off plays,
    count system, 78
    daylight system, 78
Pinch hitters, box score lines for, 187–188
Pitch outs, 15–16
Pitcher,
    arm movement of, 3
    ball grasp of, 3–4
    change of, 226–228
    control, 10–11
    covering first base, 203
    curve ball pitching, 7
    delivery of, 4–6
    earned run off, 220